Contents

Acknowledgements

When I began this project I had a strong sense of purpose but knew very little about how to proceed. I am very grateful to have had the encouragement, the benefit of probing questions and the professional knowledge of my editor, Kent Kreuter. When the writing is especially clear we can thank him.

John Harper of Schott Publishers, London, has long been a friend of Orff-Schulwerk in America. I thank him for his support of this project. Though we have worked together at a great distance, I have appreciated the good humor and expertise of Simon Mathews, Schott Production Manager for this book.

This book reflects my experiences at The Blake School and I am indebted to H. John Stander, former Head and now Tyler Tingley, Head of School, Beth Passi, Lower School Director, and my colleagues for their encouragement and understanding. A sabbatical leave gave me the opportunity to begin this project. I am particularly grateful for the children who teach me each day as we make music together.

My love for music and teaching was given early direction by the inspired pedagogy of Jos Wuytack. Hours of lively discussion with Eunice Boardman broadened my interest in curriculum and teaching sequence. In recent years Richard Gill has stimulated me with new, creative Orff approaches to music learning and music literature.

I am indebted to the music teachers with whom I have been privileged to work: Nancy Miller, who combines teaching, movement and music with joy; Judy Bond, who assures us of a wonderful musical adventure with 'It will all work out'; Mary Goetze, who nourishes the artistry of the child's voice with clear sequences and beautiful music; and Cindy Hall, who makes the most simple music come alive with drama and playfulness. Two colleagues have been particularly helpful by reading and commenting on the material at several stages of this book's development. I am thankful for the insights and criticism of John Woodward and Jay Broeker.

Finally, I acknowledge my greatest debt to Jane Frazee. She is a master Orff teacher, and ardent, effective champion of artistic teaching, my mentor and friend who continues to challenge and amaze me by demonstrating how much more I can learn about the art of teaching and the art of making music.

ARVIDA
STEEN

EXPLORING
ORFF

A
Teacher's
Guide

SCHOTT

Mainz · London · Madrid · New York · Paris · Tokyo · Toronto

This book is dedicated to
Philip Steen,
Cynthia, Carla and Marjorie

ISBN 0 930448 76 6

Designed by Geoffrey Wadsley
Typeset by August Filmsetting
Music set by Barnes Music Engraving
Printed in U.S.A.

Preface

This book has two ancestors. Lowell Mason, who established vocal music in the curriculum of the Boston Public Schools in 1838, believed that children ought to be taught to sing as they were taught to read. In other words, Mason viewed music literacy as the foundation of school music teaching and the key to broader understanding of the art.

A little more than one hundred years later Carl Orff developed a different approach to pedagogy, one in which the student was presented with musical problems and expected to improvise independent solutions. Music insight and independence were the result of this experimentation with all elements of music.

It is the special contribution of this book to forge a fresh approach to music teaching and learning from these two very different sources. This well-crafted synthesis offers the busy teacher help in organization and evaluation, as well as an abundance of ideas for classroom improvisation and musical experimentation.

Finally, every page of this book is full of the conviction of a caring, able, experienced teacher. Arvida Steen's exemplary work demonstrates that young children can master musical material in a typical school situation – and that exploration is the means to mastery. Many children's lives have already been affected by her teaching; this book ensures that many more will benefit from what she has learned.

Jane Frazee
Director, Institute for Contemporary Music Education
University of St Thomas

Introduction

There is no question that Orff-Schulwerk has become established in the practices of many American general music teachers. Summer workshops can be found in nearly every corner of the United States and Canada. The American Orff-Schulwerk Association and Music for Children—Canada continue to develop chapters, hold national conferences and attract increasing numbers of members. Listings for music positions in elementary, middle-school and college-level institutions will often request Orff certification. Since its introduction to North America in the late 1950s Orff-Schulwerk has taken root and flourished in music classrooms everywhere.

Surely the reason for this success lies in the fact that Orff-Schulwerk is a teaching approach which promises that we and our students will interact as partners in making music. Playing instruments, singing and moving are treated as ensemble experiences, requiring mutual awareness in order to create successful musical expression. Students are not passively involved in their education. Rather, the room is full of their purposeful activity. We teachers are the guides who introduce the focus of the lesson, and then encourage the students to develop it until they take over, making music on their own. The responsibility for music belongs to all of us, teachers and students.

This cooperative approach to music making has been facilitated by Carl Orff's view that music can grow, organically, from small motives to phrases and sections, from simple to evolving complexities. Since these initial ideas are small ones, they can be provided by the children as well as by the teacher. Hence, the development of the lesson can involve every member of the class; all ideas may be examined through individual and group effort that may lead to improvisation and perhaps ultimately, to composition. The fact that the student is an integral part of this process is, of course, powerful and exciting.

Consequently, if improvisation based on the musical ideas of students is to be an integral part of music making, the structure of the lesson will need to be flexible, allowing for student responses, suggestions and pace of learning. This emphasis on improvisation also means that instruction is not given for its own sake, which students take or leave. Rather, instruction through improvisation invites the interaction of students with the music, each other and the instructor. Music taught with this in mind promises to be flexible and adaptive to student's abilities and motivations.

For Orff-Schulwerk teachers, a principal aim of this interaction is the development of the musically self-sufficient student. To achieve such independence students must be able to remember music, as well as read and write their own musical ideas and those of others. Reading, writing and remembering become important to students when their ideas are encouraged and when they realize they have many musical possibilities from which to choose. For instance, my students want to remember, read and write when they realize that they can then compare and select from an ever wider body of musical materials. They are also motivated to master these skills when they realize they will be able to preserve what they and their class create. It is this linkage of skill with motivation that is one of the great strengths of Orff-Schulwerk. When students are involved in the processes of creation they will want to acquire the tools needed to make them, ultimately, musically independent.

The same interplay between motivation and skill acquisition is involved in performance. Children quite naturally speak, sing, move and play instruments. Yet their contributions are obviously limited by their skill level. There is no better way to create the desire to raise that level than to include their contributions in the musical output of the class. The level of skill our students use when performing, as well as when reading and writing, is an acknowledgement of their independence and understanding of music. As their awareness of their musical control and expressiveness is enhanced they will perform with increasing independence from our instruction.

Musical growth for students in an Orff-Schulwerk program is assured because participation with others is central to instruction. We share with our students the responsibility for modeling musical behaviors. They share with us the responsibility for expanding the themes of each lesson. The enhanced responsibilities of student to student as well as student to teacher leads virtually without exception to increased student motivation and to student growth.

In an Orff-Schulwerk classroom our growth as music teachers is also assured. To guide and open up instruction to embrace our students' ideas require quick analysis. We must be able to make musical decisions based on knowledge of rhythm, melody, form, timbre, range and technique. In order to encourage our children to contribute their ideas we must be able to recognize, remember and perform them as we hear them. The tools of orchestration enable us to adapt and adjust settings during the lesson to match the comfort level of individuals and classes. These skills are important when we plan each lesson and when we respond to unanticipated problems presented by each class. If we are open to learning about music with our students we model the behaviors we value in our students. A classroom where everyone is learning is an exciting place to be. With so many reasons to recommend the approach, we are sometimes unprepared for its difficulties.

When we begin to use Orff-Schulwerk in our teaching we are often confronted with unexpected problems. Instruction that in theory appeared to be so much fun and free of encumbrances may be, in practice, full of pitfalls; a structure to hold a series of lessons together isn't always clear. Nor did Carl Orff provide much in the way of a solution. Instead, he was determined to avoid the old practices of his day that stressed learning through lectures rather than learning through participation. Hence, when we look to *Music for Children* for method and structure — as distinct from materials — we find little that is relevant for American elementary school children. Since most of us are under the stress of teaching many large classes in quick succession, the lack of method and structure can lead to confusion.

A second problem is that the Orff approach abounds in choices. Published lessons and settings encourage the use of movement, speech, song and instruments. In the flurry of introducing many activities we run the risk of losing the focus on learning and knowing music. Instead, we end up concentrating on the activities rather than the musical concepts present in each performance. The proliferation of materials published and presented at workshops and courses encourages activity-centered teaching and requires us to be skillful in selecting materials and planning lessons for specific learning tasks.

But if an abundance of activities can pose problems so can too great an emphasis on structure. When we sense an absence of structure we strive to provide it, sometimes to the detriment of our underlying Orff philosophy. Lessons beautifully taught that remain at the imitation stage of development are not lessons that acknowledge a philosophy of group interaction and improvisation.

Orff's challenge to us is not to see how closely we can imitate his classroom practices. Instead, he challenges those of us attracted to his philosophy to adapt his pedagogical examples and his musical ideas to the new situations in which we find ourselves. He did not guide the development of curriculum or materials. He left it up to each generation of teachers to reinterpret his ideas for themselves. There is no promise of a safe method here. There is rather the basic idea that is open to each of us to interpret for ourselves. The goal of this book is to help each of us develop a curriculum and lessons that address our children's needs with our best thinking and planning.

The possibilities and problems sketched above lead inevitably to three questions facing every music teacher.

- How can I form a curriculum that addresses my students' needs?
- How can I choose the best materials for my lessons from the abundance of materials available?
- How can I plan lessons that have a clear focus, and are also open to frequent student contributions?

Exploring Orff addresses these critical questions in the chapters that follow. A curriculum outline is presented, but it will be viewed as a flexible tool which will help us respond to the changing characteristics of our classrooms and schools. Suggestions for several arrangements of goals within a grade level, and from grade to grade, are given. The outline may also be used as a reference to connect it and the materials that follow with a curriculum you are already using. The link between curriculum goals and student progress – lesson planning – is addressed in a chapter which discusses the elements of a good plan. In Part II a flexible curriculum is outlined. Lesson suggestions for each objective are given, illustrating various ways to encourage individual and group participation. Following the lessons references are made to materials from other Orff-Schulwerk publications which may be used to address the same goal.

The pioneering work of designing a curriculum for teachers of the Orff approach was *Discovering Orff* by Jane Frazee with Kent Kreuter (New York: Schott, 1987). This invaluable book introduces the reader to Orff media, pedagogy and orchestration theory. A curriculum for grades one through five demonstrates the application of Orff's ideas to teaching elementary music in American schools. The book is a basic resource for the teacher who wishes to understand the Orff philosophy and classroom application.

I was attracted to this approach by the curiosity and passion for learning demonstrated by Orff teachers. That is the spirit in which *Exploring Orff* is written. Orff-Schulwerk is applied in a wide variety of teaching styles and environments, demonstrating that many interpretations are possible. This book seeks to support your using this approach by adding my thoughts concerning curriculum and lesson planning. A variety of materials and resources are offered to give flexibility to your program as you guide your children to explore, learn and apply their understanding of music.

This book cannot help but reflect my own experiences with my children and our shared journey toward musical independence. This book will achieve an even greater goal if it can help you and your students achieve your objectives while exploring music through Carl Orff's challenging approach to learning together.

Part One:

1 · Planning your Curriculum

If you teach, you have a curriculum, for as you teach you convey expectations for yourself and your students. As their experiences in lessons accumulate you inform students, and the community they come from, of what they know about music and how important you and they consider 'knowing' to be. Your curriculum then evolves in time from your expectations as expressed through your lessons, your students' responses to your instruction, and their own expressions of the presumptions they bring from home, their classmates and their community. A curriculum formed in this way may work, but in time it may become unwieldy and difficult to define, fun but excessively teacher-centered. It may also be difficult for you to evaluate your students' growth, and you may be ineffective in predicting the success of your teaching. You may have success and not know why, or be frustrated with the outcome of your teaching and not know how to improve it.

On the other hand, curriculum planning can be a dynamic thought process which determines and organizes our instructional goals. Our goal planning can be very pragmatic, supplying us with the steps that lead us from one day to the next. However, using the curriculum in only that way limits its usefulness to us. Because knowing music involves the interaction of many factors – not just a sequence of learning tasks – a curriculum that is most useful will reflect a thought process that considers all of them. Learning results when the teacher, student and music interact in the classroom. Each factor contributes to the quality of that outcome. The teacher and the student each bring skills and knowledge to the learning task. The task itself makes demands on both the teacher and the student. And without an accommodating environment and carefully chosen materials, learning can only be accomplished with difficulty. When we understand the total act of learning we see that the curriculum can be a tool to acknowledge and make the best use of all factors. If we view it as organizing only the learning task we risk experiencing unexpected results. But when our planning reflects all factors we can predict that learning will take place, for the teacher's skill, the task, the students' ability to perform the task, the materials and environment have all been

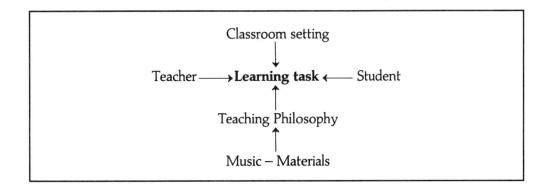

considered. When we have all the elements which influence our planning in mind we see that the best curriculum is one that reflects a specific situation.

Because each teaching situation is unique, you cannot expect other curriculum guides to fit your students' needs. Instead, these guides, including the one in this book, serve as models from which you may extract what fits your situation best. These guides also help you to envision goals beyond what may seem possible at first. Of course, you may enjoy finding that your students seem to learn at a rate that other guides outline. Yet the best curriculum is the one *you* plan and review for *your* students in *your* school.

The Students

The first and most influential factor in your curriculum planning is the focus of your instruction, your students. They come to class with some knowledge of and attitudes about music, and skills to perform it, which combine to affect their readiness to learn more. Your choice of goals for them should be influenced by what you know about them. The students' knowledge, attitudes and skills come from their homes, the community, the school and their classrooms. There are several ways you can gather information about your students that will help you choose goals appropriately. One way is to converse with classroom teachers who can inform you not only about individuals, but can also tell you about how their students work with one another, and how they structure their classrooms so that learning takes place. From these discussions you will discover the kinds of instruction that are familiar to the students, and what other teachers consider your students' social behaviors and motivations to be. You can also learn about your students' interests, motivations and background through informal chats with them at recess, in the halls or during lunch. Interacting with them in a personal way has the added benefit of creating an atmosphere of cooperation and friendly respect that enhances your instruction.

Answering the questions below will give you additional information that will help you select and then sequence goals. It will be especially helpful to consider this information when selecting materials and choosing the means of performance to accomplish learning tasks.

1 Do the students enjoy school? Do they enjoy music class?
2 How has the music program been structured in the past? Is there a record of what the students have been taught? The answer will help you understand their motivation and expectations for learning.
3 Where outside school do they hear music? Do some students participate in music activities after school hours?
4 Do some students take piano or instrumental lessons?
5 Do parents take an interest in their children's performance in music and in other school programs?
6 What ethnic and cultural characteristics do your students represent? (If their culture is kept alive in part through music, there may be ways to relate the music in your program to the music in your students' heritage. You may be able to select melodies and rhythms that will bring their music into the classroom where common music elements can be compared and performed. Group instruction is built on common musical experiences, and your students' music may be different from yours. You may

decide to learn more about their musical culture so that you can teach them with more understanding.)

It takes time and effort to know your students, especially when you see hundreds each week. Find easy ways to collect and organize information to help you with this process. You may wish to keep anecdotal notes in the margins of lesson plans or in a small notebook that you carry from class to class. In this informal way you will begin to gather useful information that helps you reflect on your instruction and analyze your students' responses. In time this understanding, along with the student performance on your evaluation instruments, will help you teach the individual rather than merely the lesson and give focus to your curriculum planning.

1   Learning Environment: School Setting

Next, let us consider your students' learning environment. There are two primary factors in that environment which influence your instruction: the importance and function of music within the school program and the physical setting. Your position was formed for you by school policies and priorities, which in turn reflect the policies and priorities for education in the community. Knowing about the philosophy of your school and how it is expressed through classroom instruction and supervision, playground activities, schedules, relationships of other subject disciplines to the school program, and other features unique to your situation, will help you know what influences your students and what they are learning.

Another way to learn about the school environment is through conversations with other teachers. Your students come to you from another classroom and a collection of other experiences. When these teachers tell you what teaching strategies they use and what they perceive to be the abilities of individuals and groups they also describe your students' primary learning environment. These discussions may help you identify some possible useful teaching practices which you may match with your own to increase teaching efficiency. Children learn with more confidence when behavioral expectations are similar as they move from classroom to classroom. The information from other teachers may cause you to change the sequence of certain goals because you realize the students will not be as ready to fulfill your objective as you thought. For instance, it may not be effective to introduce music reading until general reading has been introduced in the classroom. Introducing new meters with half or eighth notes as the beat may be taught more effectively when the students understand relative values. Your goals for music instruction are more likely to be met when they reflect your awareness of the social and learning environments of your students which are influenced by your school and the community.

How often you see the students and for how long you see them each time affects their retention of music concepts, and the frequency of practice activities influences their ability to acquire new skills. The number of classes you teach each day, and even the order in which they are scheduled, affects the time you spend to prepare your room with equipment and materials that support each lesson. Your stamina and how you use your voice become factors in schools where you may teach large classes or many groups in succession without rest. The length of each class and the frequency of instruction also affect the level to which you can direct children to explore music on their own, and the freedom and time you can give to students to improvise and create.

Our students move on to other music programs during and after their years in elementary school. They may become part of an instrumental program in the fourth or fifth grade. In middle school they may continue their music studies in choruses, bands and general music classes. Coordinating approaches to teaching reading and writing skills with others in the music faculty will affect the goals you select and the manner in which you will teach them.

There are reading tools which have been identified with specific methodologies which verbalize rhythms and pitches, providing an intermediate step between perceiving sound through performance and conceptualizing sound as a written symbol. For many children this is a necessary step in helping them generalize and categorize their understanding of musical sound. These tools also help students internalize and retain the specific musical patterns they hear. If you and other music teachers in your school community use rhythm or melody syllables you will want to acknowledge this in the way you write your curriculum objectives. Because these are tools of aural analysis which precede written symbols, and later are tied to written analysis, you will need to acknowledge their importance to your program by stating when they are to be introduced and how you intend to use them. A definitive method of using rhythm or pitch syllables has never been specified for Orff teachers. It has, however, been common practice for American Orff teachers to use solfege with moveable *do*, rather than the European system of fixed *do* or numbers for scale pitches. Teachers have used various rhythm syllable systems such as the Kodály rhythm duration syllables, the French time names, the Gordon rhythm duration syllables, or numerous duration systems which teachers have invented themselves.

When you plan your curriculum and the lessons which follow, remember that these systems are tools that help children build associations about pitch and duration. We should also remember that when a system takes longer to assimilate than a more direct approach to music symbols it is an indication that the system is not efficient or has outlived its usefulness for our students. Whatever system is chosen, it should be used consistently from grade to grade, and should enable the child to make an easy transition from elementary music to general music, choral or instrumental programs.

2   Learning Environment: Room Setting

The room you teach in is a second environmental factor which influences your program. Orff-Schulwerk teaching revolves around four activities; speaking, singing, moving and playing. Moving and dance require enough classroom space to allow students to walk, skip, gallop and run with some freedom. Many teachers remove the chairs and have students sit on the floor in order to make the space more flexible for movement, instrument playing, and small group projects. The floor then needs to be smooth, warm and easy to clean so that it is an inviting, safe surface on which to dance or sit. Your children's playing and singing will also be affected by the acoustics of the space. It is difficult to teach group improvisation at the instruments in a large, highly resonant gym or multi-purpose room. The ideal room is large enough to encourage movement while containing the light quality of children's voices and delicate instrumental colors.

The Orff approach uses barred and untuned percussion instruments. You need both performance and storage space for these instruments. I find that when untuned

14

instruments are stored on peg boards or in open baskets or bins their visibility prompts the desire to use them. Several teachers store theirs on a table where each instrument shape is outlined. Then it is easy to return each instrument to its assigned place. Otherwise, the old adage 'out of sight, out of mind' reminds us to plan more deliberately by taking time to bring out instruments for each lesson. It is also harder to tell children where to find instruments that are hidden from view. The height of chairs and tables used for instrument practice should allow your students to play with shoulders relaxed and hands at about keyboard height. Of course, the beauty of sound affects the musical results, so being able to purchase instruments of high quality becomes a factor in encouraging student participation. We can see that the physical setting, your classroom, and the school's expectations and customs of instruction combine to affect strongly your teaching and influence your selection of curriculum goals.

The Teacher

Many would say that *you* are the most important factor in determining your curriculum, for your musical and teaching abilities determine how you instruct. As you teach, your students are affected by your background, just as your instruction is influenced by their backgrounds. Your plans and designs for learning are expressions of your vision for your students and reflect your style of interaction with the music and the class. When your teaching acknowledges your strengths and your goals your motivation and that of your students will be high. Fortunately, within the philosophy of Orff there are innumerable teaching models possible because there are many ways to model musical behaviors. Some teachers may be experts in American folk music and may have strong vocal training. Others may be skilled jazz musicians who are familiar with traditions of improvised music. Still others may have extensive training in dance, and feel comfortable teaching both folk and creative dance to their students. Each of us has definable performing abilities and unique sources of musical literature from which we draw our own musical understandings. While we all share a basic music background and goals common to other teachers of Orff-Schulwerk, each of us will have a different practical curriculum for we each have a specific style of interacting with music and students and a different body of musical strengths from which to teach. Your students will benefit most if your curriculum draws upon your unique performance skills and knowledge.

Curriculum with an Orff Influence

Finally, we consider the influence of Orff's philosophy on our teaching. While music as artistic expression is greater than the sum of its parts, children understand it more clearly when a single element (rhythm, melody, harmony, texture, or expressive characteristics) is isolated from the whole. A curriculum will often present the elements of rhythm and melody as separate topics, ordered from the simplest (e.g. rhythm to internalized beat) to the more complex (e.g. rhythm as a pattern in a new meter). An Orff teacher will draw these topics from musical examples, explore them, and then place the elements back into the context of the whole, the music. Students begin learning by *imitating* the teacher who demonstrates through music examples and then guides the students to explore the music's content. This exploration can take many forms. Students may *reapply* what they know when they sing, drawing the melodic pattern in the air and then finding the same contour in notation. A child may *transfer* the knowledge of duration when she speaks a poem with repetitive patterns and then substitutes instead for specific isolated words a sound on a percussion instrument. The duration may become more clearly defined by *comparing* whether the triangle, woodblock or ratchet plays an eighth-note pattern most accurately. Variations of a single idea can be explored by doubling or otherwise *altering* its length, or changing the timbre, or shortening the durations by half. It is often difficult to distinguish precisely when students move from exploration to improvisation. Exploration and improvisation are often taught by Orff teachers as part of a process that encourages examination of a musical model. For example, the student may learn to expand a given motive into a phrase and finally into a section. Elements of both exploring the motive and improvising new music may be present. Improvisation, however, doesn't just happen, but it is expressed through the students' musical skill. Our students need performance skills, and, in addition, they need to know how to *think* about the music as they are listening to and performing it. Your curriculum needs to reflect the commitment to learn about music not only by imitating musical examples, but by exploring and improvising as well.

It is difficult to demonstrate an understanding of music without some performance skill, particularly when the philosophy is centered on learning by doing. To be able to demonstrate knowing melody through singing requires the ability to sing in tune. To be able to respond to rhythm and phrase in movement requires the ability to walk, run, skip, hop and gallop, matching the tempo, dynamics and rhythms of the examples. If the child is to respond on instruments, playing techniques are required. Rhythm performance with body percussion and on instruments requires a steady internalized beat and the dexterity to perform long and short durations using both hands. As you define the concepts you wish to cover, consider the skills needed to express an understanding of each. An accumulation of these skills then represents the children's level of musical independence.

This listing of skills must then be ordered to reflect the motor skills and learning characteristics of students at each level. Attention to a logical order of concepts focuses on knowing music, while attention to a sequence of skills to be developed focuses on understanding the innate and developing abilities of the child. Both concepts and skills must be learned before musical independence can be achieved.

Defining Broad Curriculum Goals

Begin your curriculum planning by selecting your broad curriculum goals. The statement of these goals will reflect your understanding of how your program fits within your school's philosophy and the overall goals for music in your school system. They will also acknowledge your physical setting, time for instruction, and the characteristics of the student body. Most importantly, these statements will predict the level of musicianship your students will attain before going on to middle or junior high school.

Sometimes it is helpful to place your goals for each grade in an abbreviated form on a chart, such as the one found on page 222 of *Discovering Orff*, or the chart at the end of this chapter (p. 24). This helps you see how sections of the curriculum fit together. Augment the chart of musical elements with statements concerning the skill level required in each performance mode (singing, playing and moving) and any special materials you wish to use. The paragraphs which introduce each grade level in Part Two are examples of goal setting for this stage of curriculum writing. It is helpful also to acknowledge what public performances are required at each level to prepare you to integrate that responsibility with curriculum goals. This helps you plan ahead so that these performances demonstrate what your students are learning as well as ways to entertain the audience. You may also wish to acknowledge ways you can use the curriculum of other school subjects to enhance your own. For instance, my first graders write and 'publish' books. Singing their stories with instrumental sound effects is a more exciting improvisational experience than singing the story of, say, 'The Three Bears.' Yet both materials are effective tools for teaching vocal improvisation. In the fall of the year I select folk songs and poetry in duple meter, containing half notes, that also happen to be songs about bugs for my second graders who are studying insect life cycles. Instrumental timbres and playing techniques can be reviewed while the students improvise descriptions of the characteristics of their favorite insects. The form of our music can illustrate the life cycle of the butterfly, moth or firefly. In each case, I have used my students' experiences in other situations to motivate a more meaningful musical experience.

Model Curriculum

There are a variety of models for Orff curriculums to use as a basis for designing our own. Examining these models can help us determine how a structure supports the Orff approach, which is unique in its emphasis on exploration and improvisation. The historical model can be found by studying *Musik für Kinder* (*Music for Children*) by Carl Orff and Gunild Keetman. Orff and Keetman based *Musik für Kinder* on the musical examples they used in programs broadcast on Bavarian Radio, beginning in 1948. These programs were received by elementary classrooms and were used by classroom teachers for music instruction. The first volume of *Musik für Kinder* was published in 1950 and in the following four years four additional volumes appeared, each one reflecting the progress of continuing radio teaching activity.

The volumes of *Music for Children* are arranged to move from the pentatonic scale (Vol. I) to the hexatonic scale (Vol. II), to diatonic and Ionian melodies (Vol. III). Other modes, Aeolian, Dorian and Phrygian, appear in the last two volumes. Harmonies progress from pedal tones and borduns to shifting triads, and then to functional harmony in Volume III.

One strong focus is on rhythm and speech, or the use of chant to structure rhythmic phrasing. Yet the order of presentation is determined by scales or melodies and form, beginning with four-beat echoes, followed by layered accompaniments using whole, quarter and eighth notes in drone patterns of four or more beats. Notes at the end of each volume encourage teachers to invite children to create introductions, accompaniments, codas, melodies and contrasting sections, by moving, playing, speaking and singing. According to Orff, reading and writing were tools that the students would acquire as the perceived need arose. The range of difficulty of parts as the book progresses implies that the players have a wide span of abilities and levels of musical perception. In the Introduction of the first volume of *Music for Children* (Margaret Murray edition) Walter Jellinick of London stated that 'the volumes were intended for children of all ages rather than of a specific age group.' The volumes were intended to suggest ways to teach, drawn from the materials and ideas used in the radio broadcasts of 1948 to 1952. Carl Orff stated in his autobiography that the last two volumes were written for adolescent children, which is what many of the young radio performers had become as the programs progressed. This is a program of teaching examples that was pragmatic for its time, written nearly fifty years ago for schools which were recovering from a decade of disruption. The program and its pedagogical theory were an immediate and lasting success. The materials continue to be used by Orff teachers, for they model beautiful, effective ways to perform on the instruments in pieces that have artistic merit.

Discovering Orff clearly models a curriculum sequence that addresses the goal of literacy and musical independence. Frazee's book offers a curriculum sequence that addresses the characteristics of present-day American classrooms. The sequence unfolds slowly, from simple to complex. In Frazee's sequence, rhythm skills develop from beat awareness in Level 1 to durations shorter than the beat, then to durations longer than the beat. In the intermediate grades, sixteenth notes and syncopation are taught. Binary-rhythm skills are well developed before triple meter is presented in third grade, and compound meter is presented in fifth grade. By the end of Level 5 basic rhythm concepts have been introduced to be read, written and used in performance.

The discussion of melody starts in Level 2 with students reading and writing three-note melodies, beginning with *mi–re–do* progressing to the pentatonic scale. Hexatonic, then diatonic scales, Ionian and Aeolian, are introduced step by step, from the middle of Level 3 to Level 5. Forms evolve from the motive to the phrase to sectional forms. Harmonies are introduced aurally through counterpoint devices, especially ostinato, and through accompaniments of pedal tones and borduns, and then to tonic, dominant and subdominant chords. The sequential curriculum Frazee outlines has a similar base of learning music as that of the original volumes, but adds a clear sequence of concepts and skills from simple elementary rhythm and melody structures to increasing complexities, with harmony, texture and form.

From these two examples we can conclude that the Orff approach is able to embrace more than one organizational structure while being guided by the original philosophy and process of learning. The first example is a collection of suggested teaching pieces which imply that performance is a means to teach music. It was written to instruct groups with a wide age span in a unique educational climate. The second example states that music independence is one of several central objectives. Sequenced goals evolve slowly for specific age groups and learning characteristics of American students. Each author suggests that these plans are models to be thoughtfully adapted with changes to reflect new teaching situations.

Each curriculum, however, is put into action through shared characteristics. Both curriculums use speech, song, movement and instruments in varied but integrated ways of performing music. Each places value on the process of learning or the interrelated importance of imitation, exploration and improvisation. The student as composer is equally present in the lesson with the student as the performer. Most importantly, music is viewed as a pleasurable experience shared in a community where each participant is encouraged to contribute to the final musical result.

Sequencing Objectives within Each Level

Broad goals must then be broken down into smaller steps which lead to the specific objectives for each grade level. In my curriculum these grade objectives address eight topics which parallel the structure of my school's music curriculum, kindergarten through grade 12. The topics are:

1 Elements of music (rhythm, melody, texture, timbre),
2 Reading music,
3 Music History and Style,
4 Listening to Music,
5 Performing Music,
6 Creating Music,
7 The Role of Music in Society, and
8 Valuing and Evaluating Music.

These may not be the topics your school system uses, though many elementary curriculums focus on topics 1, 2, 4, 5 and 6. Then, as I develop my list of yearly objectives, I consider how I can address these topics, for many can be integrated. For instance, I may combine learning about style with ostinato and texture. I consider the physical development and social skills of my students which determine the initial behaviors I may expect at the beginning of each year and also contribute to the ability of my students to demonstrate what they know. My expectations are again influenced by the schedule, my equipment and the classroom environment. Many model curriculums, such as state guides and textbook outlines, are based on what we know generally about successful sequences. Others, such as the Orff curriculums just discussed and the one which follows in Part II, are based on generalized teaching situations and philosophies. Yet none of them addresses the specific characteristics of individual teaching situations.

A sequence of musical concepts and skills becomes a tool to guide instruction in logical steps. These steps should be ordered so that achieving one objective predicts the next step. If the progression from one objective to another is too wide or the skills are not yet developed the children will fail to accomplish the task. If the steps are too small the children may become inattentive or may be involved only superficially. It is important to analyze each area of your curriculum carefully and select objectives that flow logically and obviously for your children.

When you formulate your curriculum objectives for each grade you will want to keep in mind how we think we learn. Learning is often described as three-dimensional. You are probably already aware of *naming*, or presenting our learning objectives (the first dimension), for it is dealing with new learning that drives our music programs. However, there are two other dimensions that determine how useful the new learning becomes. These are the *experiences* that precede and prepare conceptual learning, and the *conscious application* which follows. The presentation of the symbol for a quarter note, for instance, follows extensive preparation begun in kindergarten, where our students moved to the beat, played it, and felt it as they sang together. As they participated we used the word 'beat' to ask for their responses. Later they compared it to quarter-note durations, naming these as they chanted 'Beat, beat, beat, beat,' and then 'ta, ta, ta, ta,' with their movement and sounds. When rhythm and solfege syllables are used in the curriculum they should be introduced aurally first. When children can identify a minor third as *sol–mi* and sing or play it in dictation activities, they are ready to take the next step, which is to see it on the staff as ♩. Similarly, when the students quickly name the duration their movement and chant describes as 'ta' against the internalized beat they are ready to label it visually as | or ♩ .

Experiencing one concept can take place while another is being *named* or defined. For example, first-grade children may sing 'Hot Cross Buns,' a melody which uses *mi–re–do*, while you present the durations of it as symbols, representing the rhythm of the words. The children will identify and write the rhythm patterns while internalizing the melody.

 written by students

m r d   m r d   d d d d r r r r m r d   experienced aurally

This song may then be introduced again in the second grade, reviewing the rhythm while *naming* the pitch pattern and then making *conscious application* by identifying the melodic motive in other songs. Making a sequence of concepts that can be experienced now for presentation later will help you provide the background needed to prepare each one.

To form your curriculum, you will be preparing a sequence of objectives which guide skill development and name new musical concepts. Materials chosen for making conscious or naming the new concept must be selected carefully so that it is easy for the teacher and the child to identify what is being learned. If the child can perform then describe the new concept and give it a name, a symbol, and identify it through hearing, reading and writing, we can be quite certain the student *knows* it. Yet the formal presentation of an objective is only the middle of the process leading toward independence. But unfortunately, that's very often where instruction concerning that objective ends.

A new knowledge or skill upsets the equilibrium of what is already known. This is because each new fact and skill must have a chance to be examined and evaluated against what is already familiar. Sixteenth notes, for example, are presented as short durations but may be heard and labeled as eighth notes if the students are not sure of the underlying beat. Therefore a third dimension, *conscious application*, should follow the naming and should include applying a symbol in as many forms and media as possible. Accompaniments can be composed using increased skill consciously to apply the new concept, or improvisation opportunities can be structured to recall what is already learned. Each opportunity to practice and apply helps your students reinforce and enrich their understanding of specific concepts. Then new learning becomes integrated with what is already known and can be demonstrated confidently by your students. As you move through your sequence and plan your lessons you will think of ways to weave the new and the familiar knowledge into their music making.

Here are examples of weekly objectives which provide experiences to prepare future conscious learning, give a name and a symbol to a new concept and then consciously apply music skills and knowledge learned previously during a week's instruction in early second grade. The students are learning the definition of meter, a new concept, while practicing reading familiar rhythms found in pentatonic melodies.

Week Four

Name, give symbol	*Consciously apply*	*Experience*
1 Define 2 meter and use bar lines to demonstrate an understanding of meter	1 Perform familiar rhythms from 1st grade in song accompaniments	1 Sing/play pentatonic songs for later analysis.

This is only one possible mix of objectives. Your situation determines what should be anticipated through your lesson and what skills need practice as you guide new learning.

This example of a week's objectives may be appropriate for fourth grade.

Week Ten

Name, give symbol	*Consciously apply*	*Experience*
1 Introduce *fa* in staff notation approached in steps, in melody and countermelody	1 Play only *drmfsl* in accompaniment, patterns learned by reading score.	1 ♩. ♪ taught by rote in song.

The curriculum outlined by a grid of goals at the end of this chapter represents the model against which I measure my yearly curriculum evaluation. The first chart represents the naming and symbol-giving stage of instruction. The second chart suggests that in the semester before we name or give a symbol to a concept the teacher needs to check that adequate background experiences have been given. For example, it is important that the children know several songs with half notes before they are introduced to the symbol to read and write. They also should be able to describe in words the experiences that form the concepts you will be representing in written symbol form. The child must have the skill to perform a given task through singing, moving or playing before she or he can use it to respond correctly to the written symbol. If the child fails to respond correctly at the reading–writing level he may not have a secure motor response to demonstrate the concept accurately, or may have not connected the performance skill with the correct perception. Because we cannot express what we know about music or participate in it without skills, experiences that prepare learning become an important part of our sequence planning.

A third chart will help you keep track of those skills and understandings which will need reinforcement and conscious application. Lessons may require students to learn instrumental parts by reading to accompany a song setting, or a specific familiar rhythmic or melodic motive can be used in comparison with new material. The conscious application chart is an example of a tool to help the teacher integrate new skills and guide students toward mastery of their musical understandings.

The curriculum outlined on the first chart at the end of this chapter begins with kindergarten goals and ends with sixth-grade goals. Kindergarten goals are very important for two reasons. Since this is an age when school children's aural skills are most acute, it is our best and earliest opportunity to begin to train children to sing tunefully. During this year the children will benefit from many experiences that encourage solo singing as well as group singing. It is also a time to build accurate motor responses to beat and rhythm. Their love of movement games, storytelling, exploring sounds and their sense of discovery provide the teacher with playful ways to build a wealth of experiences and a repertoire of songs that becomes the foundation for conscious learning in the next levels.

Some elementary schools, like mine, do not include the sixth grade. Consequently this book ends with a fifth-grade curriculum sequence. In discussions with fellow teachers who teach sixth grade I discovered that many had curriculum goals that paralleled those of fifth grade. They felt that a review of basic musical concepts through more challenging material, using the concepts but demanding higher skill levels, best met the needs of their students. Opportunities to solve problems and create in small groups and through the various means of performance the Orff approach provides are especially appropriate at this level. Performances for others often provide the motivation and rewards for achieving a higher level of musical independence.

There are many topics which are typically taken up at certain grade levels. For instance, uncommon meters are presented at upper-grade levels while common meters of 2 and 3 are studied in the early levels. Compound meter and the order of presentation of melodic pitches, however, often appear at different points in curriculums, depending on the author's point of view.

Some curriculums introduce pitch notation in grade two with three pitches, *mi, re, do*. Other teachers prefer to introduce conscious recognition of pitch relationships in first grade through the chant motive, *sol–mi*, and *sol–la–mi*. This curriculum will propose beginning pitch notation with *sol–mi* near the end of first grade. However, it will show how introducing melody notation could occur at several other points in the sequence.

Our language, as expressed rhythmically through poetry, folk songs and nursery rhymes, falls easily into compound meter or small divisions of three within larger divisions of two. Many young children are familiar with scores of folk rhymes and songs which illustrate compound meter. 'Hickory Dickory Dock' is one of numerous examples of rhymes prevalent in our literature which has the natural rhythmic cadence of 6/8 meter. The chart outlining this curriculum suggests that it is possible to introduce 6/8 meter in the first grade with practice of aural recognition through movement, galloping as well as running with the underlying beat. Notation of this meter, however, is delayed and introduced in grade four.

It may seem logical to pursue all your rhythm objectives for each level before moving on to another set of goals. However, it may be the least interesting way to proceed and you may also lose opportunities to practice rhythm skills efficiently, for example, while naming new concepts on another topic. In ordering the objectives for a year, for example, consider teaching a series of rhythm lessons covering the first block of objectives, while reviewing the melody skills of the previous year. Then, as these new rhythm skills are being applied, introduce new pitch concepts, reserving the more challenging rhythm concepts for later in the year when physical dexterity is greater.

Finally, a curriculum is a tool, not a dictator of what you teach. Check your curriculum often even weekly, but no less than quarterly. I check off objectives met each week, while reminding myself what comes next. Some weeks I move right on to the next objective. Sometimes I choose to extend study of an element or skill because the interest is high, or because the children's performance skills need more practice. Your list of curriculum objectives is a tool for keeping track of what you have accomplished, and of how long it took. In this way you can reconsider the effectiveness of the selection and sequence of your objectives. At the end of the year it is important to review the whole curriculum and evaluate how it can be improved for use the next year. This will not be a lengthy project if you have taken notes frequently along the way.

Curriculum design guides you to a dynamic decision-making process. The process leads you to accept, reject and order your goals and objectives in logical, clear ways. At the end of the year when you evaluate, examine each objective you selected. Is it still appropriate for students at that level? If you shift it to another place in your order, or reject it, consider the effects, for it means postponing or removing the potential for that learning to occur. However, you are also choosing objectives which you believe to be more important and appropriate for your children's need to succeed in becoming self-sufficient musicians.

A curriculum should never be static, but instead a lively process of decision making that responds to changes in instruction and continually mirrors the highest possible music objectives for your students. Knowing your curriculum through the process of accepting some goals, rejecting others and ordering the results gives you an intimate knowledge of what you are committed to doing. It should be a well-thumbed document frequently marked with pencil and pen.

Teaching from your own sequence of objectives is guaranteed to be more rewarding for both your students and yourself, for you know your musical destination and the way to arrive there. In the process, it will be an exciting journey.

We learn by experiencing music. Then we name and label our understandings before we consciously apply what we know. The first grid which follows, however, outlines our goals to name and label concepts and understandings, for this is what drives the curriculum. The other goals for experiencing and making conscious application must reflect that order.

CURRICULUM GOALS GRID

Name and label concepts and understandings: perform, read and write

Grade	Rhythm	Melody	Texture	Harmony	Form
K	**Aural analysis only** Fast/slow Beat in $\frac{2}{4}$ & $\frac{6}{8}$ Shorter, same, longer/beat	Expressive speech/ singing High/low Contours Matching pitch Develop repertoire	Maintain beat alone Maintain beat with speech, song Perform alone and with group	Tonic ostinatos, Chord bordun drones	Same/different (call response) AB Verse/refrain
1	Beat competency ♩ 𝄽 (rhythm) $\frac{6}{8}$ (aural)	Aural analysis s m s m l s m l d m r d	Monophonic Counterpoint with ostinatos	Tonic ostinatos Simple bordun, chord, level	(motive aa) ‖: :‖ AB
2	(rhythm patterns) $\frac{2}{4}$ $\frac{2}{4}$ (rhythm patterns) $\frac{4}{4}$ $\frac{4}{4}$	Read, write s m s m l s m l d m r d d r m s l	Speech, song, with 2 parts 2-part canon Vocal ostinato Instrumental ostinato 2-part canon	Bordun, + broken Bordun, moving, 2 people	Motive to phrase, e.g. a a b a a a a b a a b c A B aaab abbc A aaab
3	(rhythm patterns) $\frac{3}{4}$ $\frac{3}{4}$ anacrusis ♪	Name lines and spaces *do* pentatonic *la* pentatonic *do* hexatonic d r mf s l d	Speech, song with 3 parts 2–3-part canon	Arpeggiate bordun Moving bordun Bass ostinato of chord roots	4-bar phrase $\frac{2}{4}$ & $\frac{3}{4}$ Rondo A B A B A A B A C A
4	tie, (rhythm patterns) (rhythm patterns) $\frac{3}{4}$ $\frac{3}{8}$ $\frac{6}{8}$ patterns	*la* hexatonic l td r m s l Diatonic: Ionian (*do*) Aeolian (*la*)	Speech, song with 3–4 parts 3–4-part canons	Chord, I I–V	Rondo Chaconne
5	$\frac{6}{8}$ patterns (rhythm patterns) $\frac{5}{8}$ $\frac{5}{4}$ meters	Diatonic: Ionian Aeolian Dorian Mixolydian	Counter-melody 4-part canons Paraphony	Half, full cadence I–V I–IV–V	Theme and variations Unequal phrase lengths

Grade	Rhythm	Melody		Texture	Harmony
6	𝄽 c ¢ ⁶₈ ⁵₈ ⁵₄	Modes: Ionian Aeolian Mixolydian Dorian Other scales: gapped, whole note, melodic minor	Up to 4-part canon at the 5th, 4th or octave 2–3–4-part singing	I–IV–V I–ii–V i–V i–iv–v	12-bar blues Sectional forms, e.g. march & trio, popular song

MAKE CONSCIOUS APPLICATION GRID

Read and write parts for song settings, instrumental pieces; improvisation; composition

Grade	Rhythm	Melody	Texture	Harmony
K	Responses to beat	Expressive singing Awareness of matching pitch	Solo and group singing with pitch awareness	Monophonic
1	Beat Rhythms, ───────── Ostinato ♩ ♫ 𝄽	Tuneful singing ───────── High–low contour	Unison sing, Solo sing with 1 accompaniment	Drone Tonic, bordun ostinato
2	♩ ♫ 𝄽 ‖: :‖ ───────── ²₄ 𝅗𝅥	Aural analysis of melodic patterns ───────── Read, write melodic patterns in F	Monophinic 1 ostinato ───────── Theme and ostinato	Instrumental parts vocal Instrumental pieces
3	𝅗𝅥 ²₄ 𝅝 ⁴₄ ───────── ³₄ 𝅗𝅥.	Read, write melodic patterns in F, G, C. in d, e and a	2-part Canons 2 instrumental parts Instrumental Pieces	All borduns Melodic ostinatos
4	anacrusis ♪♩ ♩ ♪ 𝄾 ♫♫ ♫♩ ♫♩ 𝅗𝅥. ♪♪ 𝅗𝅥.	Pentatonic song Hexatonic song in F–d, G–e, C–a Staff letter names	Melodic Ostinatos 2-, 3-, 4-part canons for voice/ instruments	All borduns Bass ostinato (Chord roots)
5	𝄾 𝄾 Common meters Syncopation Augmentation, diminution	Ionian, Aeolian melodies	2 vocal ostinatos with song Instrumental melodies and 4 parts	Canons, 2–4 parts I–V in all scales
6	Rhythms, uneven phrases Common meters Unusual meters	Modes	Part singing	Chords I–V, I–IV in all scales

EXPERIENCE GRID

Perform only, often from imitation; aural analysis

Grade	Rhythm	Melody	Harmony
K	Basic locomotor movement Beat, movement Shorter than, same as, longer than beat	Expressive speech Solo speaking singing Build song repertoire	Use accompaniments to outline phrases
1	Duple, triple meters *(rhythmic notation)* *(rhythmic notation)*	Experience *s m, s m l* Songs in pentatonic/ diatonic Experience *s m d* *m r d, l s m r d*	
2	*(whole note, whole rest notation)* ¾ *(dotted half note)*	Pentatonic patterns *s l d r m, s l m r d* *d l s* Do- and la-centered pentatonic	
3	Anacrusis *(eighth, quarter, eighth notation)* Sixteenth patterns Dotted rhythms *(dotted quarter, eighth)* 6/8 *(eighth, dotted quarter)*	Hexatonic Do- and la-centered Interval identification Diatonic	Harmonic ostinatos Movement response to harmonic changes by phrases
4	typical patterns *(rhythmic notation)* Meters 2,3,4,5	Diatonic scales (modes) Interval identification	Half and whole cadences Sing chord roots
5	Syncopations 4/4 *(rhythmic notation)*, *(rhythmic notation)*, etc. Unusual meters 5/4 5/8 7/8	Modal melodies	Chord accompaniments, I–ii, i–VII I–vi, i–III I–IV–V, i–iv–v
6	Changing meters	Gapped, unusual scales	Chord accompaniments

2 · Lesson planning

The lesson is the event that bridges the gap between what the student knows and can do and what you, the teacher, think the student should learn next. It is the point of transfer from the musical goals and objectives in the curriculum to the action by students that demonstrates their musical learning.

The lesson plan focuses your teaching activity from the beginning, when you can purposefully initiate instruction, to the end, when your students have demonstrated that the goal has been reached. At its best, a step-by-step plan provides for participation and exchange of ideas between you and your students. A plan should free you to interact with the students while giving everyone the secure feeling that a good outcome will result. This chapter will discuss lesson planning, beginning with writing the lesson objective, then choosing the material and activities, planning the body of the lesson, and bringing the lesson to a close. Sample lessons will illustrate several ways a simple four-part outline can be molded to reflect the nature of the task and the learning characteristics of the students who are participating.

Before you begin lesson planning, review some of the information you have already gathered. First, your lesson objective is drawn from and further defines your curriculum objective and has been selected because it is the next logical step for this particular group of students. In thinking about the learning task and your students, review several possible ways this lesson may be presented. Consider the abilities and motivations of your students as well as previous experiences they bring that prepare them for this new step. Will you need one or several lessons to present this concept or skill? Music lessons are often scheduled far enough apart so that children feel most successful if each lesson has a sense of completion and accomplishment. This means your stated objective must be achievable in the time you have for one lesson, and your curriculum objective may need to be broken into several steps to be addressed through the objectives of several lessons.

Stating Your Objective

Perhaps the most important step in lesson planning is stating the objective. It has been proven that when a teacher's objective is clearly written the teaching improves because students and the teacher know what is expected. When you write a clear objective it is easier for you to assess whether the students have learned as you predicted. It also helps you determine the next step, the objective for the following lesson.

The statement of your lesson objective should include three kinds of information:
1   the *focus*, or what is to be learned;
2   the *level of understanding*, or mental effort that is required; and
3   *performance*, meaning what the student will do to show mastery of the objective.

The *focus* refers to your curriculum objective, or what is to be consciously learned or named. Examples of focus may be introducing the whole-note symbol, adding low *sol* to staff notation, or the skill of performing sixteenth notes. The *level of understanding* tells you what is being demanded of the students. Words such as 'imitate,' 'discover,' 'recall,' 'explore,' 'improvise,' 'read' or 'aurally identify' define to what degree the students are expected to understand. Finally, the objective will tell you how the students are to demonstrate their level of understanding so that you can observe and evaluate. There are several typical ways in Orff classes that students may *perform*: through speech, song, body percussion, dance, movement and playing instruments. The objective will identify what skills the child will be asked to use to demonstrate each step of the lesson plan. Here are some examples of objectives that include these three factors.

Objective: The students will identify and perform rhythmic ostinatos containing half notes as accompaniments to songs, demonstrating an awareness of tempo and dynamics.
Focus: half notes in ostinatos.
Level of understanding: identify, discover, in tempo, dynamic levels of accompaniment.
Performance: sing, play on body percussion and instruments.

Objective: The students will sing, identify and label on staff *la* and *sol* below *do* in several pentatonic songs.
Focus: low *la* and *sol*.
Level of understanding: identify, label on staff.
Performance: sing, listen, read and write.

As we become proficient in writing our primary objectives, we may add a second objective that identifies skills and concepts we may ask our students to review by consciously reapplying in this new context. A third objective can remind us of what is to be experienced as preparation for future conscious learning.

Our objectives can be realized when we also recognize how music is learned and remembered. We draw on our children's abilities to remember the music as they learn in this lesson and from lesson to lesson. When we recognize the ways these memories accumulate, we can enrich learning by giving our students various experiences to address individual learning styles and several means of recalling what is learned. Music is the sound and the performance of that sound, not just the written symbol that stands for it. There are at least five ways human beings think about and remember music. First there is motor or kinesthetic learning which develops its own memory that helps us perform from 'muscle memory.' Children use this knowledge when they come into the classroom after a long absence and pick up mallets to find on an instrument a favorite melody or rhythm learned long ago. It becomes an important part of improvising when our automatic responses act simultaneously with our conscious analysis of the task. The second type of learning is cognitive, or 'this is what I know' learning. It needs one of the other types of learning to be expressed, but may not be expressed if the skill called upon is lacking. You may ask a child to demonstrate an understanding of whole-note duration by hearing it and drawing the symbol, or by choosing finger cymbals to play it, or by moving in long steps to demonstrate it. Yet another important way to show what you know is to describe it in words. Words tell what you know specifically and then become symbols for generalizations of a larger body of related information. These symbols gain richness of meaning as a result of increasing experiences. For example, rhythm syllables become symbols of specific durations, but these durations occur in an accumulating number of patterns. Another kind of learning is needed to use a music symbol system or music notation. As has been suggested, the written-symbol system is often most successfully built on experiences that are summarized in words before they become notation. Finally, and most importantly, we must remember that as we hear music expressed we give it meaning. Like knowing about music, demonstrating what we hear in the music depends on our ability to perform or use words and music notation. Our aural skills, on the other hand, determine the extent to which we can use our ability to demonstrate our understanding of music we hear, for we depend on remembering the detail of one music event which we then compare with the next. I have found that some children hear subtle pitch differences and retain long melodic phrases accurately, while other children remember the rhythm with little pitch recall. Some children hear the harmonic implications of melody years before other children. Children have different learning styles and musical strengths. Each lesson should include kinesthetic stimulation and conscious listening and cognition expressed through words and music symbols. When we include a variety of ways to interact with music we accommodate individual students so that each can learn and recall through one or more means.

When you write your objective, ask yourself 'do the students have the skills to perform the task I have set for them?' If the skill level of most of your students is lower than what is required by the task, you may choose to go back and teach that skill before returning to the objective. Or you may choose a skill area less demanding for the students to use to demonstrate their understanding. Also consider your students' energy and attention span, which will influence their ability to meet the demands of the lesson.

After considering all these issues you are ready to write the objective which states the specific focus, the level of understanding demanded, and the form of performance it will take. At first this seems to be a very complicated task, but with practice it becomes an automatic way of looking at instruction. The reward is that you will no longer think of yourself as the leader, but rather as the motivator and guide in helping students to interact with music.

Selecting your Materials

The selection of materials, such as songs, poems, instrumental pieces, or arrangements, is important to the success of the lesson. The materials should encourage involvement by appealing to the child's way of thinking. Using familiar material previously learned for another purpose may focus the learners quickly because they know and can perform the music confidently already. A higher-level thinking process may be added as a next step in the lesson by asking the children to analyze the song for a new focus. Then a new song, sharing many characteristics of the first, may be introduced to highlight the difference between the two and identify the theme of the lesson. One of the songs may become material for the exploration following the initial activity. Other materials, because of their form and length, provide models for improvisation and composing, illustrating specific concepts in their structure. Some materials, because of text, phrasing or other characteristics, can generate new ideas from students that will reinforce the focus of the lesson. You may wish to begin a collection of materials organized by usefulness for teaching skills and concepts as identified by your curriculum.

The materials we choose determine the potential for our students to respond musically. The Orff teacher's emphasis on folk literature (rhymes, poetry, stories and songs) developed from a recognition that its very survival indicates an ability to communicate. We select folk melodies because they are artfully simple and easy to sing, while offering infinite varieties of expression. Popular music and art songs which you choose for lessons should meet the same criteria as that of a good folk song. The lyrics should also be selected for the musical ideas they might inspire, their expressiveness, and what they can teach us about ourselves, another culture or another time in history.

Instrumental pieces for Orff instruments from any of the *Music for Children* editions continue to be popular because children instantly recognize the quality of the sounds the music encourages. The use of ostinato and motive-to-phrase structure helps to make these pieces accessible to your students. It also illustrates how your students might develop their own instrument pieces.

After selecting the material, you will plan the body of the lesson which orders the events that lead to the conclusion.

Introduction of the Lesson

It is important to begin your lesson with the familiar. In Orff lessons the students typically imitate the teacher. The activity may be an echo exercise which helps the students to recall similar tasks and provides them with a background from which to act. You may ask them to sing a familiar song or two that may become the basis of the development of the lesson. This activity should be quick, fun, musical and motivating. It can introduce the focus of the lesson as well as set the mood and style of the next activity. The teacher is often most prominent and important in this part of the lesson because imitating a model is an easy way to warm up the body, voice and mind.

The Body of the Lesson

The activities which follow the introduction identify the purpose of the lesson and offer several ways to reach the objective. It is this part of the lesson that can most easily be planned to meet the needs and learning styles of individual students. During the body of the lesson students can learn more about the focus by comparing, identifying the concept in a different sound source, such as a recording, or by transferring what they have just learned to another performance mode (e.g. a melodic phrase from voice to xylophone). Activities set up to question what is happening in the music will encourage students to solve problems and explore as they make new applications of what they know. Depending on the age and social skills of the class, this can happen individually or in pairs as well as in the whole group. Improvisation can be a type of problem solving. For example, when students are asked to improvise a phrase of a given length, including syncopation in measure one or two, the student is problem solving. Literacy tasks, such as completing a written phrase, or writing what is heard, can give the student a means of demonstrating understanding and independence from the teacher. As students acquire skills to play, sing, move, read and write with each step of their learning they also develop the potential to generate their own ideas through improvisation and composition. Ideally, each lesson should contain an element of this highest level of understanding of even the simplest music concept.

In teaching through the body of the lesson the teacher moves from the role of model to that of facilitator, helping students to apply what they already know and can perform to new learning and consciousness of music.

The Conclusion

The conclusion is important because it re-identifies the focus of the lesson and acknowledges the success in reaching the desired goal. The student will feel rewarded when he or she can identify what was learned. The teacher can evaluate the success of the lesson if the last activity provides an opportunity to observe individual students in actions that demonstrate understanding. At times a simple pencil and paper exercise that sums up the focus of the lesson may be used. Taping a 'final performance' and then listening to it is an evaluation exercise for both students and teacher that encourages students to discuss music using words as symbols of music concepts to describe what thay have experienced and then heard on tape. Remember to allow time for ending the lesson with a sense of accomplishment and resolution. It will be easier to begin again with the next lesson when the student can link a new task with previous successful lessons.

Overall, the steps in the lesson plan are not dramatic. In fact, they are easy, small steps that move from the known to an element of the unknown to a new level of understanding. Good lesson-planning takes time, but it saves time and energy in the classroom and boosts our self-esteem and that of our students when our goals are successfully met.

The lesson-plan format that I use most often is outlined below. It refers to the points just covered and encourages us to take brief, concise, sequential steps throughout the process. I have used this format when I taught the lesson plans which follow in this chapter. However, these plans are models or study guides. I hope you will study them and change them to maximize your teaching style and your students' learning and performance strengths.

Sometimes my lesson fails to meet the objective I set. When this happens, I re-examine each step to determine at what point difficulties appeared. I use the following questions to help me learn from the experience and to give me the information I need to plan the next step.

1   Did I pack too many activities into the time available? Was the lesson cluttered with too many things?
2   Did the students have the skills to do what was required? Did they have the knowledge or background to understand the objective as presented by the lesson?
3   Were the instructions clear in stating each task? (Sometimes I don't anticipate questions that arise and divert the focus of the lesson.)
4   Were the steps small enough to assure that at least 80% of the class could stay with the pace of instruction? Was the pace too fast, or too slow?
5   Did I dictate the lesson through imitation activities or did I share the development with students?

6 Was the objective clear to the students in the first place? How were they to know that they had achieved the goal?

7 Was it the right task on the wrong day?

Once you know what is wrong with a lesson it becomes easier to plan the next one. Sometimes it means reviewing the background in more depth before returning to the objective. You may choose another means of performing the tasks or new materials that provide better motivation. You may decide to repeat the lesson but cut out some of the activities to clarify the process. You may choose to practice giving clearer directions. You may even decide that your timing was premature and you will move to another goal while preparing more background experience. Often you can learn as much about effective teaching from the less successful lesson as you can from the tried and true ones.

A Lesson Plan Format

Objective
Grade
Materials and preparation needed

I	**Presentation**	• warm-up or familiar activity, often imitative, to activate memory for focus of lesson
II	**Exploration** (body)	• a series of events elaborating on lesson focus
		• may use transfer to several performance modes
		• may practice, re-identify, or modify familiar music, or create new music
III	**Conclusion**	• summarizes through one of the following:
		○ problem solve
		○ give evidence of literacy or independence
		○ improvise or compose
IV	**Evaluation**	• by students through performance, critique, reading or writing
		• by teacher observation, or use of written tool, or critique of tapes

Lesson Plan 1

GRADE 1, Semester 2
OBJECTIVE
The students will read patterns with ♫ ♩ 𝄾 and will improvise patterns containing the same durations.
MATERIALS AND PREPARATION
'Five Little Snowmen', *Music for Children* (American edn., Vol. 1, no. 33).
Notation of verse 1 rhythm on board.
INSTRUMENTS
BX, BM, 2 × ⊟ △ ◍

Presentation – (song learned in previous lesson)

On board

♩ ♫ ♩ ♩ 1 Invite a student to clap one of the patterns. Class echoes
♩ ♫ ♩ ♩   correct reading.
♫ ♫ ♩ ♩ 2 Continue until all patterns are read.
♫ ♫ ♩ ♩ 3 Review song, melody and verses. Compare word rhythms of
              verse 1 with notation. Rearrange patterns.

Exploration

1 Learn BX part from imitation of ♩ ♩ ♩ ♩ and sing. Student notates part. Transfer to BX.
2 Add triangle in rest of measures 2 and 4. Add to notation.
3 Perform song with accompaniment.
4 Add four more four-beat patterns to those on the board, using student ideas. Practice these.
5 Students each choose one pattern from board. Practice. Sing and play, then perform patterns as solos in sequence. Alternate with song.
6 Erase all notation.

Conclusion

1 Ask group to choose a body percussion sound for the beat to accompany the singing and new sections.
2 Invite ten children to sit on the inside edge of the circle. Place five unpitched instruments inside the circle. As verse 1 is sung the first four children each plan a four-beat pattern as a solo performed in the order they are sitting. Outside circle continues body percussion part. Verse 2, the next three players perform in order, listening to body percussion part in empty measure. Verse 3, the next two players perform, listening to two measures of body percussion. Verse 4 the last player performs, followed by three measures of body percussion. Verse 5, body percussion alone and decrescendo.

Five Little Snowmen

Five lit-tle snow-men, stand-ing by my door: out came the sun and mel-ted all but four.

Evaluation

Can the students identify any of the patterns the soloists used? Were the patterns played accurately? Did new patterns appear?

Lesson Plan 2

GRADE 3, Semester 2

OBJECTIVE

The students will identify *fa* by recognizing it in a melody, singing and playing patterns that contain it, and by reading and writing it.

MATERIALS AND PREPARATION

Song and setting with instrument parts on visuals, 'Early in the Morning,' four mystery envelopes, melody on visuals, rhythm only.

INSTRUMENTS

BX, AX, ⊟ △ SM, worksheets for 'Evaluation' (4 barred instruments).

Presentation
1 Establish focus by singing patterns containing pentatonic pitches, teacher on neutral syllable, class in syllables
2 Echo patterns, teacher using *d r m s l* and humming *fa* in each pattern.
3 Sing 'Early in the Morning' from rote.

Exploration
1 Place rhythmic notation of melody on staff. Class performs.
2 Teacher sings each phrase on neutral syllable, class echoes with solfege. (Students recognize *fa*.)
3 Ask students to add noteheads for pitch to rhythm notation. Name new pitch, observe its placement in scale and circle it as it appears in song.
4 Sing song in solfege and with words.

Expand application of concept
1 From visuals, sing accompaniment parts, using *fa*. Play and sing.
2 Ask students to supply a melodic motive, beginning on *sol* for ‖: ♩ ♩ ♩ ♩ :‖. Notate.
3 Use motive as bridge to sing between A and B sections and as an introduction.

Conclusion
1 Sing song with accompaniment for A section.
2 A 'postman' delivers four envelopes to four singers.

Contents of envelope 1

For B section the four students arrange their messages to create a melody. They lead the class in singing it.

Final form — A bridge B bridge A

Evaluation

On a sheet of paper place the following melody. Students will circle *fa* and place an 'x' in the box next to the correct title of the melody.

☐ Cumberland Gap
☐ Twinkle, Twinkle Little Star
☐ America The Beautiful

Early in the Morning

American Folk/AS

Lesson Plan 3

GRADE 5, Semester 2

OBJECTIVE
Students will identify, analyze and then perform patterns with changing accents and syncopations.

MATERIALS
'Scherzo,' *Music for Children* (American edn., Vol. 3, no. 110). Make visuals of melodic rhythm.

INSTRUMENTS
▭, △, Timpani on G and D, AX, SX, BX, SRs,

Preparation

1. Ask students to form circles in groups of 5 to 8 and walk to the beat as you perform the melody A. Listen and add a stamp and jump-turn, as indicated in the music, beats 7 and 8.
2. As Teacher performs B, students perform grapevine, left foot to center, right back, then left behind, right beside three times, then stamp and wait two beats.

Exploration

1. Teacher plays recorder, 'Scherzo,' A section. Class listens to identify pitches of measures 1, and 4 and 6.
2. Label rhythmic notation with pitch names. Students play measures 1, 4 and 6, Teacher 2, 3 and 5. Repeat step A to learn measures 2, 3 and 5.
3. Add accompaniment from body percussion model. Notate rhythms only to clarify patterns. Perform melody with accompaniment.
4. Pat eighth notes, accenting every 1st of 4, 1st of 3, 1st of 2.
5. Introduce ♩ ♫ ♩ ♫ ♩ ♫ for AX in B section. Then ♪ ⁊ ≀ then ♩ ♩ . Ask students to suggest unpitched timbres for each pattern.
6. Ask students to follow notation as Teacher performs melody.

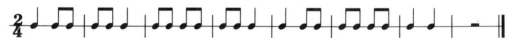

Correct notation as they pat Teacher's rhythm.
7. Perform these rhythms on untuned instruments as the B section.*

Conclusion

Perform as ABA with instruments and dance.

Evaluation

Tape the performance. Class listens to evaluate the accuracy of accents, and relationships of rhythms to each other.

> *In the next lesson transfer the rhythms of the B section to barred instruments and recorders as indicated in the score. An alto glockenspiel may be substituted for another recorder in B. Voices on 'la' may be added to melody for A.

Scherzo

References

Deans, Karen, ed., *Documentary Report of the Ann Arbor Symposium on the Applications of Psychology to the Teaching and Learning of Music: Session III. Motivation and Creativity.* Reston, VA: Music Educators National Conference, 1983

Frazee, Jane, with Kent Kreuter, *Discovering Orff; a curriculum for music teachers.* London: Schott, 1987

Orff, Carl, *Documentation, Vol. 3 – The Schulwerk.* English Edition (translated by Margaret Murray), New York: Schott, 1976

Orff, Carl, and Gunild Keetman, *Music for Children*, adapted by Margaret Murray, 5 vols. London: Schott, 1958–66

Orlich, Donald C., Robert J. Harder, Richard C. Callahan, Donald P. Kauchak, R. A. Pendergrass, Andrew J. Keogh, and Harry Gibson. *Teaching Strategies, A Guide to Better Instruction*, 3rd edn., Lexington, Ma: D. C. Heath, 1990

Roehmann, Franz and Frank R. Wilson, ed., *Music and Child Development; Proceedings of the 1987 Denver Conference.* St Louis: The Biology of Making and MMB Music, 1990

Taylor, Rebecca, ed. *Documentary Report of the Ann Arbor Symposium, National Symposium on the Applications of Psychology to the Teaching and Learning of Music.* Reston, VA: Music Educators National Conference, 1981

Warner, Brigitte. *Orff Schulwerk: Applications for the Classroom.* Englewood Cliffs, NJ: Prentice-Hall, 1991

Part Two:

3 · Kindergarten

The kindergarten student begins the year wanting to play, for his best and favorite way to learn is through 'hands on' experience. There is no dividing line in the child's world, for her play is her work, her work is play. Through the child's playful experiences in kindergarten he learns new skills, is introduced to new materials and acquires social skills. Setting limits become important, for the child learns that her personal freedom is balanced by the needs of her classmates.

Goals

Our first goal for our kindergarten students is to help them develop skills that enable them to learn through group instruction. Group instruction requires individual responses within the group. Some children respond well to specific individual instruction but become lost, even disruptive and require help in understanding their roles when instructions are given to the whole class. The direction to make a circle, for example, requires the child to choose independently a place among his classmates (a social decision) while determining the shape of an abstract figure (a concept). Forming the circle also requires cooperation with classmates, another learned behavior. Our classes constantly test these little ones on cooperative skills, for we ask them to share space while moving freely, share instruments and patiently wait for turns. We ask them to play thoughtfully and musically when their undeveloped muscles instinctively love to initiate sounds indiscriminately. We also ask them to share time in discussions, taking turns to contribute ideas, and even judge what interactions are appropriate. All these behaviors are challenging and should be practiced in an unpressured environment over the year. The children should become comfortable with these social expectations before you begin more focused music instruction.

When we consider the challenges our kindergarten children face in becoming acclimated to school we realize that we can help them by using some special skills ourselves. We can be careful to give short, one and two step directions, moving from one stage of an activity to another at a pace that gives them time to respond, but not enough time to lose focus. We can give them opportunities to respond as individuals. In movement activities, for example, each forms the letter B in her own way. Yet we can guide them to become cooperative by planning short projects such as asking partners to discover many ways to make sound out of a single piece of paper.

Lastly, it is important to constantly reinforce evidence of their growth by approving their appropriate behaviors with our body language, smiles and words. In this way they are encouraged to build habits of learning that assure progress. From our interaction they know what is appropriate because it pleases the teacher and the group. From this level of comfort nearly all children find it irresistible to participate in music activities. We can appeal to their sense of fairness as we guide them to govern themselves when performing play parties and sharing instruments. We use instructional time well when we engage them in activities that help them master constructive social behaviors, and that reinforce their enthusiasm and curiosity for music. Our recognition of their developing curiosities, cooperative behaviors, willingness to learn, and other evidences of helpful social behaviors will guide them far more than corrective measures that risk injuring their young, fragile egos. When they are at their best, exciting learning takes place.

Repertoire

We teach our children through a developing repertoire of songs, games, movement and instrument activities that will support cognitive learning later on. This repertoire builds common experiences upon which more formal group instruction is based. In kindergarten we use these experiences to help children identify and examine concepts by developing increased abilities to listen to all sounds with discernment for specific qualities and to use music terms to describe what they discover. Practice with them the accurate use of terms such a 'high'/'low,' 'fast'/'slow,' 'shorter'/'longer,' 'soft'/'loud;' they provide the basis from which musical understandings are drawn.

Kindergarten Objectives

We begin our formal study with rhythm. The children will experience beat and tempo, or the rate of beats, before they are required to identify and perform it accurately. Later in the year they will experience different durations which they will then identify as the same as the beat and sounds longer than or shorter than the beat.

Because this is an optimum time in their development to discriminate between musical sounds we will want to give the children many opportunities to explore the various qualities of sound their voices can make. You might begin by having your students identify four primary ways of using their voices; speaking, whispering, shouting and singing. The class will also quickly discover that each quality can sound higher or lower. From these experiences that give children awareness of vocal control they develop the discrimination to identify their vocal responses to specific pitch. Equally important at this level is the experience of singing many songs expressively. Expressive singing builds enthusiasm for creative performances. They should also have opportunities to sing alone and with the group while developing good breathing habits and expanding their vocal range.

Children learn holistically especially at this level. Songs, stories and poems provide the motivation to explore timbre, textures and dynamics as they use their voices, instruments and movement for interpreters. Accompaniments will evolve from their movement exploration of rhythm, while an awareness of form develops for activities that require discriminating listening to repetition and contrast.

Listening is a primary way of receiving information for youngsters. They can surprise us by making unexpected observations about the music they hear, especially when we help them acquire the vocabulary to tell us. While this book will not outline a formal listening program, hearing a few minutes of music from a variety of good recordings during each lesson will contribute to a broad base of experiences the child can draw upon later.

Below is a list of specific objectives. They may be taught in this order, for each one in each topic area follows logically. However, if time is needed to practice a given skill, you may insert several other objectives from another area. For instance, you may find that you want to spend more time developing an awareness of silent or internalized beat. Rather than moving on to more demanding rhythm skills you may practice sounded and silent beats while identifying and exploring the timbres of untuned classroom instruments.

These objectives may be broken down into easily assimilated steps for your particular children. For instance, learning to echo may be introduced successfully early in the year, but you will present echo activities with small increases of skill demands throughout the year. It is a sign that you are knowledgeable about your students' abilities when you choose to break down further some of the following goals.

Kindergarten Objectives

Skills for group instruction

1   Perform simultaneous imitation using movement, instruments, and vocal sounds.
2   Explore, then define space as self space and classroom space. Practice using these spaces interchangeably in group activities.

> Consider moving on to no. 3, imitation, or spending more time with simultaneous imitation and space management, while introducing vocal exploration ('Melody,' 1) or timbre exploration ('Timbre,' 1).

3   Perform delayed or echo imitation using the voice, body percussion, instruments, and movement.

Timbre

1   Explore the techniques of playing untuned classroom instruments, identifying each by sound and by family name (metal, wood, scraper and shaker, or drum) and by specific name (e.g. triangle, woodblock, cabasa, or hand drum). Use timbre to illustrate poems and stories.

> Consider moving to 'Rhythm,' 1 and 2. Continue with 'Timbre,' 2 in the second semester.

2   Identify orchestral instruments by family name (string, wind, brass, percussion) and by range (high/low) from the sound of recorded examples as well as from live performances.

Rhythm

1   Practice beating accurately by imitation, with body percussion, movement, speech and on instruments.
2   Respond accurately to various tempos in movement, with body percussion and on instruments. Apply the terms 'fast,' 'slow,' 'faster,' 'slower' to identify tempos and tempo changes.

> Consider introducing phrasing or introducing 'Melody,' 1, 2, before continuing with 'Rhythm,' 3.

3   Respond appropriately to meters (e.g. march or walk to 2/4, 4/4, 6/8; swing to 3/4; gallop to 6/8, etc).
4   Discover and perform the beat on body percussion, on untuned and barred instruments, or with speech, to accompany a song or chant.

> Do not delay vocal exploration ('Melody,' 1, 2) beyond this point. Consider including playing beat patterns on barred instruments ('Accompaniments,' 1, 2).

5   Identify the silent beat, or rest, and imitate patterns containing beats and rests, performing them as others chant, move or sing.
6   Demonstrate awareness of sound durations in movement, on instruments, and with vocal sounds as the same as, longer than, or shorter than the beat.
7   Demonstrate awareness of durations longer than the beat.

Melody
1   Explore vocal qualities and then label them as 'speaking,' 'shouting,' 'whispering,' and 'singing.'
2   Explore pitch, and then label pitches as 'high,' 'low,' 'higher than,' or 'lower than,' in speech, song, and on instruments.
    (*i*)   Interpret poems and stories by using high and low sounds on barred instruments.
    (*ii*) Use words, gestures, and drawings to encourage awareness of high and low pitches in his/her vocal performance.
    (*iii*) Use gestures, words, and drawings to encourage awareness of melodic contour (moving upward, downward, or repeating).
    Consider moving to the next set of melody objectives in the second semester. Preparation now may include developing a repertoire ('Repertoire,' 1), or exploring texture ('Texture,' 1, 2).
3   Sing in response to another voice and identify the pitch of the response as the same, higher, or lower than the first voice.
4   Sing, to imitate a short vocal model of one to three pitches.
5   Explore and compare melodic motives and melodic contours through chants, songs and singing games while developing a song repertoire.

Texture
1   From recorded examples and class ensembles distinguish monophonic music (one line) from polyphonic and harmonic music (more than one line).
2   Perform the beat while chanting or singing a simple theme.

Accompaniments (harmony)
1   Accompany others by playing beat patterns on the tonic note of a barred instrument.
2   Accompany others by playing beat patterns on a chord bordun.
3   Play instruments assigned to specific word cues in poems, stories and songs.

Form
1   Respond to phrasing as musical breathing.

Repertoire
1   Develop a repertoire of songs and singing games from which understanding can be drawn in the first and second grades.

Materials and teaching suggestions will be given for each objective in the above outline. Remember that not all the steps which you need to lead from one curriculum objective to the next may be present in this outline. Following the lesson suggestions is a listing of materials from other sources which will be useful to present or practice the same objective.

Skills for Group Instruction

1   Perform simultaneous imitation using movement, instruments, and vocal sounds.

Simultaneous imitation is the easiest instructional tool to introduce and use. We simply ask the students to do as we do. Most typical music classroom activities can be introduced in this way. These suggestions have helped me to keep simultaneous imitation activities pleasurable, yet focused on learning through experience:

- Know your lesson material and the process you want to use so that all your attention can be focused on the children you are leading.
- Proceed fast enough to maintain interest by changing the motion or sound but slow enough to insure everyone's success.
- Stop while everyone is still having fun.

Begin by meeting your students at the door, using hand gestures and an expectant expression to invite them to walk into the room behind you. Change your body level, the length of step, the sound of your footsteps or tempo of your walk, often enough to keep them involved. Move them into a circle or cluster formation and sit down.

Mirror movement in place is the next step and is a useful way to teach more refined responses, such as clapping by using one hand as the instrument, the other as the mallet. Patting the thighs and lightly stepping, with clapping, are gestures of body percussion that become the strokes they will use to play the instruments. Begin to sing 'Monkey See, Monkey Do', inviting them to follow your motions as you change them for each verse. Usually the children will sing with you as well, and after hearing several verses, encourage them to sing and move. Both the singing and movement are simultaneous imitation.

Monkey See, Monkey Do

1. The mon-key claps, claps, claps his hands,   The mon-key claps, claps, claps his
2. Oh, we can clap, clap, clap our hands,   Oh, we can clap, clap, clap our

hands.   Mon-key sees and mon-key do,   The mon-key does the same as you.
hands.   We can see and we can do,   Oh, we can clap the same as you.

3. Oh, we can tap our foot . . .
4. Oh, we can pat our head . . .
5. Oh, we can wink our eye . . .
6. (Verse of your choice.)

Another time the name of a student may be substituted for 'monkey' and that child can decide and lead the motion.

When you chant nursery rhymes and poems, accompany them with body percussion. At first you will use one gesture moving with the beat throughout the poem. When the children can follow you quickly, change the motions to fit the phrases and meaning of the words. Children at this stage do not distinguish between beat and rhythm, or quarter note pulse and word rhythms. You can help them become aware of these differences by carefully using the correct words in your directions 'Follow my beat as I pat my knees.' Then as you begin to pat to introduce the poem, chant softly 'beat, beat, beat' until everyone is following.

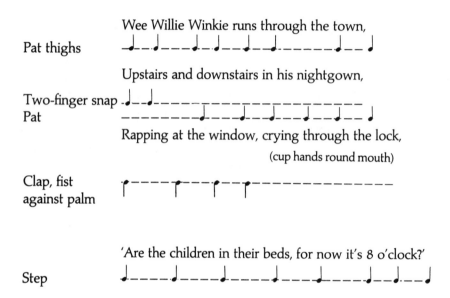

Another time, for 'Little drops of water,' you will say, 'Follow my beat. I will change the place where I feel it. Don't let me trick you!' Make your motions clear and deliberate so they can follow easily.

> Little drops of water, (*two-finger snap*)
> Little grains of sand, (*brush palms*)
> Make the mighty ocean, (*brush feet on floor*)
> And the pleasant land. (*light hand clap*)

After the children have chanted and followed the motions several times, bring out untuned instruments, a timbre for each body percussion level. I often use large, deep-sounding drums and cymbals for stepping; hand, conga and bongo drums for patting, wood timbres for clapping, and high metal sounds for the two-finger snap. Now the children become the directors as the instrument players follow their gestures for each timbre.

Up until now you have chosen the movement responses to the underlying beat rather than to the rhythm of the texts. Next, look for poems and songs which you and your students can interpret together through simultaneous action. With the children, determine the sequence of motions to interpret this old nursery rhyme. This is what my children decided to add:

> The grand old Duke of York, (*walk in place*)
> He had ten thousand men. (*count fingers*)
> He marched them up to the top of the hill (*hands clap beats, moving up*)
> And marched them down again. (*clap, moving down*)

Additional resources
Fowke *Sally Go Round the Sun*
  'Ordinary Clapsies' (p. 76)
  'Head and Shoulders' (p. 46)
Frazee with Kreuter *Discovering Orff* p. 55
  A good discussion of simultaneous
  imitation
Johnson *The Magic Forest*
  'Charlie over the Water' (p. 9)
Wirth et al. *Musical Games*
  'Oh Say, Have You Heard about Harry?'
  (p. 156)

2   Explore, then define space as self space and classroom space. Practice using these spaces interchangeably in group activities.

Each kindergartner in my class is given an imaginary space bubble at the beginning of the year. It may be the child's arms' span wide and long, and as high as he can reach. It may be the size of her body in a space suit. If the space bubble touches anyone or anything it disappears! Invite your children to see how close they can get to a partner without actually touching, or to a chair or the wall. Then try taking a walk to the beat of your drum, staying in their bubbles. If they touch they are frozen in position, while others move around them. When they understand what is meant by moving one's personal space in the classroom space, try this activity.

Chant this counting rhyme while bouncing at the knees.

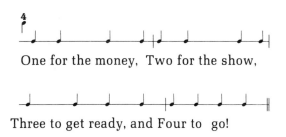

One for the money, Two for the show,

Three to get ready, and Four to go!

Ask the students to cluster near you while keeping their personal spaces. Bounce at the knees to the beat as you chant the poem together. On the word 'go' you will continue to sound the beat on a drum while they move away into space. When the drum stops they no longer move. Chant the poem again, bouncing the beat in their personal spaces scattered around the room. On the drum beat, they return to cluster around you again. Varying the tempo and dynamics helps create suspense and interest as they practice moving in personal and class spaces.

> Consider moving on to no. 3, imitation, or spending more time with simultaneous imitation and space management, while introducing vocal exploration ('Melody,' 1) or timbre exploration ('Timbre,' 1).

3   Perform delayed or echo imitation using the voice, body percussion, instruments, and movement.

One of our most effective teaching tools is having the class imitate us. Echo activity or remembered response is a good example. It requires the child to listen first. It then requires timing, for the child is expected to respond immediately on the next beat. Unlike simultaneous imitation, when we repeat the pattern until the children are following correctly, we expect an accurate response after we have finished. This requires the child to observe, remember, and then act thoughtfully. Begin by pointing to yourself to indicate 'my turn,' and then when you have recited a phrase, nod to the class to invite them to respond.

The Squirrel
Whisky, frisky, hippety hop,
Up he goes to the tree top!
Whirly, twirly, round and round.
Down he scampers to the ground.

I like to begin imitation activities using large muscle responses. Ask the children to guess what animal your motions describe. Without saying the words of 'The Squirrel' aloud, swing your arms across your body and back, and then jump twice. They then imitate your motions. Move your hands in a climbing motion for four beats, or 'Up he goes to the tree top.' Then whirl and twirl in a small circle, and follow with scampering hand motions down to the ground. The students imitate each movement. Go through the sequence several times, and then add the words to help the children solve the puzzle of the mystery animal. This can be followed by a section of motions that describe squirrel activities led through simultaneous imitation from ideas of one or more children. From this short poem you and your students may develop a story about the squirrel, alternating the poem and its movement (A) with the children's movements (B).

There are four levels of body percussion: stepping, patting thighs, clapping and snapping. Kindergartners have difficulty snapping their fingers to make a sound, but tapping one finger against the other while raising their hands can be used. Begin with one body level of four beats to be echoed by the class. Repeat it, but with new dynamics. When their response is accurate move to another level. Watch and draw attention to appropriate musical echoes and correct other responses by repeating the example. When the children feel and identify a musical response, in contrast to a noisy, inaccurate response, they will want to make musical contributions.

Ask the children to echo this pattern:

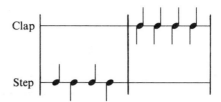

Invite them to repeat this pattern while you chant the poem. How did their pattern fit these words?

> 1 2 3 4, Marching to the schoolhouse door,
> 5 6 7 8, Hear the bell, now don't be late.

Now you can perform the beat pattern while they chant the poem. Then challenge them to put the poem together with the motion. Often the children will begin to clap the rhythm of the words, rather than the underlying beat. When this happens, help them hear and see the difference by patting the word rhythms. This is clear when half the class steps and claps the pattern while the other half stands to chant and pat the word rhythms. Choose one timbre, perhaps a hand drum, to follow the stamps and another, perhaps a woodblock, to follow the claps. Then ask them to trade parts.

Additional resources
Frazee with Kreuter *Discovering Orff*, pp. 27, 62.
    Discussion regarding echo activities.
Orff and Keetman *Music for Children*, ed. Hall
    and Walter, Vol. 1, p. 80.
Orff and Keetman *Music for Children*, adpt.
    Murray, Vol. 1, p. 53

> Here you will find examples of rhythmic patterns to be used by the teacher to practice building a rhythmic vocabulary for use in echo exercises. Perform these with a friend, or chant them and then perform them with various kinds of body percussion. You will find that echo exercises with the children will be more interesting – and you will be able to observe and interact with their responses – when you can create four-beat rhythm patterns spontaneously, based on your practice.

Timbre

1   Explore the techniques of playing untuned classroom instruments, identifying each by sound and by family name (metal, wood, scraper and shaker, or drum) and by specific name (e.g. triangle, woodblock, cabasa, or hand drum). Use timbre to illustrate poems and stories.

I like to introduce one family of instruments at a time throughout the year, beginning with the drum family. Give the children an opportunity to explore many ways to make sounds on the drums: on the rim with a pencil, with the grooved handle of a mallet, on the head with a brush, mallet, one finger, or with the finger tips. Compare the sounds between sizes of drums and types of mallets. If you don't have many drums, invent them, from the empty waste basket to an empty oatmeal box. Help the children discover good playing techniques that produce the best sounds.

The children's explorations of timbre are more meaningful and enjoyable when they can use them to record their own experiences. Ask your students to gather the memories of their next field trip as a collection of interesting sounds. In the next class make a list of these events and experiment with their voices first and then with drums (and other instruments) to express each one. Then draw a line on the board to represent the time line of the trip. Arrange picture symbols for each sound in the order of the actual sequence of events (with a little musical editing to add interest) on the time line and assign the parts to the students. As you draw a pointer along the line the students play and make their vocal sounds. Ask them to evaluate their choices of timbre, use of the voice and playing techniques, especially drawing attention to the successful sound choices.

Ikon of Field Trip

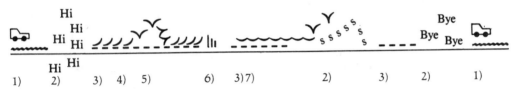

1)
2)
3) 4) 5)
6)
3) 7)
2)
3)
2)
1)

1) Motor sounds, cabasa, woodblock

2) Voices

3) − Hand drum pat

4) ⌐ Hand drum scrape

5) Y Glockenspiel

6) triangle

7) xylophone glissandos

Take time for timbre exploration at this level for kindergartners may not yet have the skill for group rhythmic response. The following poems can be accompanied with a sound carpet that introduces, accompanies and then ends the setting. Practice varying the dynamics so that the instruments add to the expressiveness of words. Use silence to highlight special effects.

Timbre Poems

For untuned metal instruments

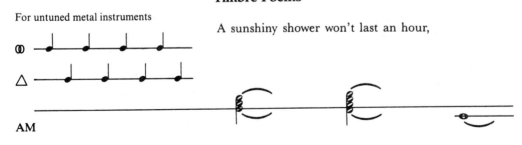

A sunshiny shower won't last an hour,

AM

For scrapers and shakers

March winds and April showers, bring forth May flowers.

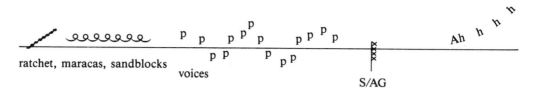

ratchet, maracas, sandblocks

voices

S/AG

For drums and metals

If bees stay at home, the rain will soon come.

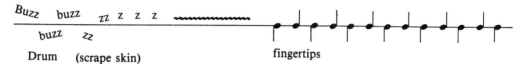

Drum   (scrape skin)

fingertips

If bees fly away, It'll be a fine day.

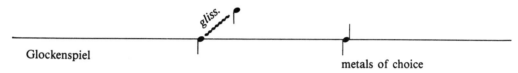

Glockenspiel

metals of choice

For untuned woods

Yankee   Doodle   came to   town,   riding   on a   pony,

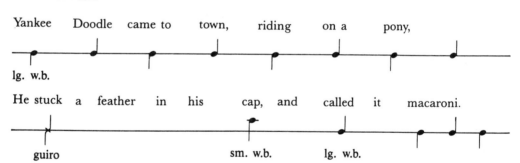

lg. w.b.

He stuck   a   feather   in   his   cap,   and   called   it   macaroni.

guiro   sm. w.b.   lg. w.b.

There are many stories which can be told through sounds as well. For example, consider building a series of sounds, one for each animal who followed Chicken Little to the King because the sky was falling down.

Additional resources
Johnson *The Magic Forest*
    'Great Big Stars' (p. 19)
    'Spooks and Spirits' (p. 37)
    'Apples, Apples' (p. 39)
Steen *Orff Activities: Kindergarten* p. 13

Consider moving to 'Rhythm,' 1 and 2. Continue with 'Timbre,' 2 in the second semester.

2   Identify orchestral instruments by family name (string, wind, brass, percussion) and by range (high/low) from the sound of recorded examples as well as from live performances.

Because young children hear timbre very acutely it is important to expose them to many different vocal and instrumental performances. Each music textbook series includes pictures and recordings to demonstrate various timbres. The Bomar Music Library recordings include one volume which addresses timbre and is supplemented with excellent photographs. Perhaps other students, parents or teachers will enjoy demonstrating their instruments for your students. Take advantage of opportunities throughout the year to introduce various performance mediums to your children.

Rhythm

1   Practice beating accurately by imitation, with body percussion, movement, speech, and instruments.

Beat competency is a major goal for this year, since being able to compare durations is the basis for all our future studies of rhythm. While you will spend several lessons at this point helping your students to feel the beat, identify the beat and practice sounding it in various ways, you will need to make the children aware of beat competency throughout the year.

It is easiest to help the children identify the beat when the chant has one syllable on each beat. Invite the children to sing this little chant with you as the class walks as directed.

Watch My Feet

Add other verses and actions, such as 'Watch my feet, they're hopping, hopping,' or 'Watch my knees, they're knocking, knocking.' The children will have many ideas which will continue the little game. They understand what they are feeling when you lightly tap your chest and sing 'Hear the beat go thumping, thumping.' During another lesson repeat the game, but each time a verse is repeated perform the motion but sing the words internally.

There are numerous movement games that you can invent to practice responding to the beat. Improvise or play a familiar song while the children move around the room. Tell the children that when you stop they must stop but they must be touching the floor on three points. Repeat the game, but change the tempo. Watch for those who can adjust, and for those the changed tempo has confused. Each time they stop, you direct them to touch with a different number of points on the floor. If improvising for this activity is a challenge for you, chant or play the words rhythms of familiar nursery rhymes. Your students will probably join in!

52

Additional resources
Frazee *Orff Handbook for World of Music – K*
    'Juba' (p. 12)
    'Lost My Gold Ring' (p. 23)
Johnson *The Magic Forest*
    'Barber, Barber, Shave a Pig (p. 45)
    'Pizza, Pizza, Mighty Moe (p. 58)
    'Spooks and Spirits' (p. 37)

2   Respond accurately to various tempos in movement, with body percussion, and on instruments. Apply the terms 'fast,' 'slow,' 'faster,' 'slower' to identify tempos and tempo changes.

Ask your students to listen for movement ideas to fit your chant, which at this point you will speak at one tempo.

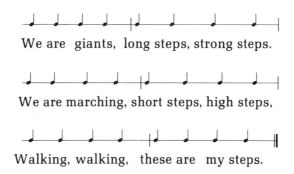

We are giants, long steps, strong steps.

We are marching, short steps, high steps,

Walking, walking, these are my steps.

Then guide them to tap their knees and interpret each phrase by changing the tempo. Help the children respond within the group to develop various movement interpretations of tempo. Now assign each line of the poem to pairs of students. Give them a minute to practice their interpretation together before they share it with the class.

> 'Once upon a time there was a boy named Davey. He lived in a city and he went to school in the city. In the morning he got up slowly (*children mirror your slow stretches*). He ate his breakfast almost as slowly (*again, mirror movements*). He looked at the clock. It was time to walk to school (*pat a moderate beat on the knees*). On the way he saw a woman, on her way to work, walking very fast.'

Then ask other children to continue the story, until Davey runs into school, just before the bell. Review the story's sequence of tempos and identify these changes as faster or slower or beats at different tempos.

Additional resources
Frazee *Orff Handbook for World of Music – K*
    'The Witch Ride' (p. 17)
Johnson *The Magic Forest*
    'Great Big Stars' (p. 19)
    'To Market, to Market' (Day 2: p. 51)

> Consider introducing phrasing or introducing 'Melody,' 1, 2, before continuing with 'Rhythm,' 3.

3 Respond appropriately to meters, (e.g. march or walk to 2/4, 4/4, 6/8; swing to 3/4; gallop to 6/8, etc.).

At this level it is not desirable to identify meter by numbers, but it is important that the children have many opportunities to hear, sing, move, and play to common meters. The following songs from Music for Children, American edn. Vol. 1 are the beginning of a collection you may gather to give the students practice in each of these meters.

2/4 'Johnny Works with One Hammer' (no. 20, p. 11)[1]
     'Mary Wore a Red Dress' (no. 30, p. 16)

Johnny Works with One Hammer

4/4 'Five Little Snowmen' (no. 33, p. 17)
     'Ducks in the Millpond' (no. 48, p. 25)

Mary Wore a Red Dress

Five Little Snowmen

1   From Lucy Sprague Mitchell (eds.) *Another Here and Now Story Book* New York: E. P. Dutton, 1937.

Ducks in the Millpond

1. Ducks in the mill-pond, geese in the clo-ver, fell in the mill-pond, got wet all o-ver.
2. Ducks in the mill-pond, geese in the clo-ver, Jumped in the bed and the bed turned o-ver.

Rise, child-ren, gon-na rise, gon-na rise, Rise, child-ren gon-na rise, gon-na rise.

6/8 'Row, Row, Row Your Boat' (no. 45, p. 25)
'Hickory Dickory Dock' (no. 51, p. 27)
'The Grand Old Duke of York' (*Discovering Orff*, p. 193)

Row Your Boat

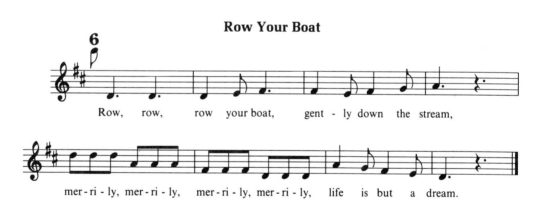

Row, row, row your boat, gent - ly down the stream,

mer - ri - ly, mer - ri - ly, mer - ri - ly, mer - ri - ly, life is but a dream.

Hickory Dickory Dock

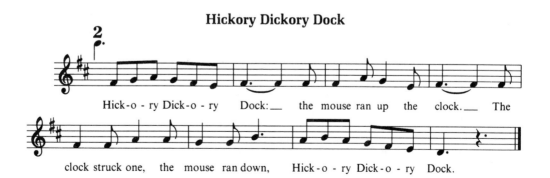

Hick-o - ry Dick-o - ry Dock:__ the mouse ran up the clock.__ The

clock struck one, the mouse ran down, Hick-o - ry Dick-o - ry Dock.

The Grand Old Duke of York

The grand old Duke of York,— he had ten thou-sand
when they were up they were up,— and when they were down they were
men,— He marched them up to the top of the hill, and
down,— and when they were on - ly half - way up, they were
marched them down a - gain.— And Hunt-ing we must go, a - hunt-ing we must
nei - ther up nor down.— A -
go. We'll catch a fox and put him in a box and then we'll let it go.

3/4 'It Rained a Mist' (no. 84, p. 47)

It Rained a Mist

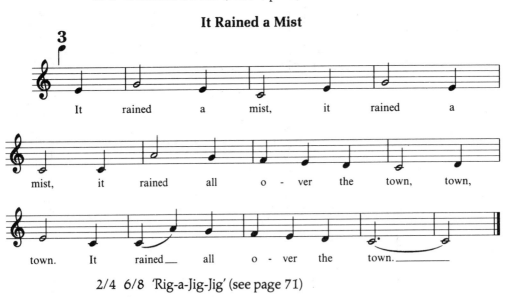

It rained a mist, it rained a
mist, it rained all o - ver the town, town,
town. It rained— all o - ver the town.—

2/4 6/8 'Rig-a-Jig-Jig' (see page 71)

4 *Discover and perform the beat on body percussion, on untuned and barred instruments, or with speech, to accompany a song or chant.*

Kindergartners will keep a more accurate beat when both arms and hands move together. There are many singing games which give us the opportunity to respond accurately to the beat. This *la*-pentatonic version of 'Go Round the Mountain' is particularly good because it provides our students with an opportunity to explore ways to move accurately in a swift-moving game.

It is important to prepare the children for the movement improvisation required in the game. While the class is seated, ask them to play the mirror game with you. You keep a beat motion, then call a child's name. As soon as he begins a new motion all follow until he calls another name. When this goes smoothly, ask the class to stand and lead in-place movement. When they are seated again, ask them to mirror your movement (change body percussion each verse) and listen for the number of verses as you sing 'Go Round the Mountain.'

Begin the singing game by motioning the children to follow you as they sing, forming a circle. You then step inside the circle and motion them to step around the circle, clapping the beat as you watch and think of a motion. Introduce the second verse by motioning them to stop as you improvise a simple motion. For the third verse choose a partner from the ring who continues your motion with you. At the end of the verse, leave the center and begin the game again with a new leader.

Go Round the Mountain

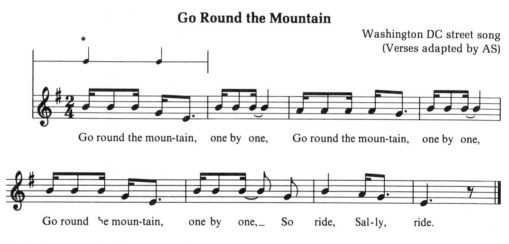

Washington DC street song
(Verses adapted by AS)

Go round the moun-tain, one by one, Go round the moun-tain, one by one,

Go round he moun-tain, one by one,_ So ride, Sal-ly, ride.

* Handclap throughout

2. Make a little motion in that ring.
3. Get yourself a partner in that ring.

Once most of the children can respond to the beat accurately using their large muscle responses, they are ready to use the more refined responses required when they play the instruments. This is the moment when all their experience using body percussion pays off, combining their skill with their awareness of ways to make beautiful sounds.

Invite several children to play drums with soft mallets for verse 1, several others to play sticks for verse 2, and pass the instruments to new players on the third verse.

Chant this rhyme while clapping and patting the beat. Then invite some children to chant the words as others chant the beat pattern. When the poem and beat pattern are well established, the children may add instruments, one timbre for high, another for low. Ask the children to choose a surprise sound for the ending.

Old Man Daisy

Old man Dai-sy, He went cra-zy, Up the lad-der, down the lad-der, O-ver my head. Bye!

Up, Up, Up, Up (wave)

down, down, down,

For this little game, which also practices maintaining the beat, place several unpitched instruments in the center of the circle, perhaps a triangle, a woodblock, a drum, and a guiro. Practice the motions needed to play each of these instruments as you chant,

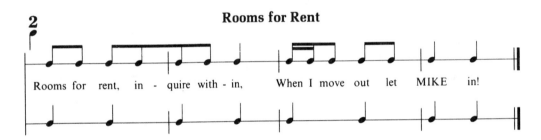

Rooms for Rent

Rooms for rent, in - quire with - in, When I move out let MIKE in!

Invite a child to sit behind each instrument. End the chant with the name of a child in the center. As the rhyme is repeated that child plays her instrument, filling in the name of another person in the center. Repeat until each child has played. As each child leaves following her turn you may signal another child to replace her.

Additional resources
Johnson *The Magic Forest*
'The Beehive' (p. 28).
This is an enrichment activity to discover
the beat in a song and setting.

> Do not delay vocal exploration ('Melody,' 1, 2) beyond this point. Consider including
> playing beat patterns on barred instruments ('Accompaniments,' 1, 2).

5   *Identify the silent beat, or rest, and imitate patterns containing beats and rests,
performing them as others chant, move, or sing.*

These last two rhythm goals are preparation for the presentation of symbols in the first grade; the quarter note, rest and eighth note. Do not proceed to these steps until the previous four objectives are successfully met by nearly all your students. Teaching these objectives may be delayed until early in the first grade.

This jump-rope rhyme is a clear example of beat and silent beat, for there is only one syllable with each. Pat the beat with them and chant the rhyme until all join in.

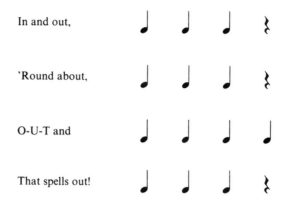

Then ask them to make small steps in place as you chant. Did they step only when you spoke? Ask them to step in place and speak, listening for the beat with no vocal sound. Then chant but jump only on the silent beat or rest. The children can practice what they hear in a variety of ways. Try walking with the rhyme, but make arm gestures only on the rests, or stand in place and step only on the rests. Perhaps half the class can move on the sounded beats while the others move the rests. Label these motions as sounded beats and rests. Using the syllable 'ta' for sounded beats and 'rest' for silent beats, ask small groups of children to make up new patterns of four beats, as in the poem, which they then chant and move in sequence. They may move their feet on 'ta' and other in-place silent motions on 'rest.'

Example:

Group 1	'ta'	rest	'ta'	rest
Group 2	rest	rest	rest	rest
Group 3	'ta'	'ta'	rest	rest
Group 4	'ta'	rest	rest	'ta'

Ask them to repeat the activity but say 'rest' internally.

The Cobbler Song

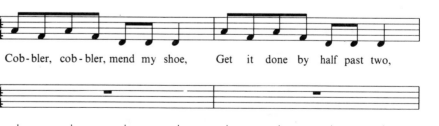

59

Tour - a, lour - a, lour - a - lu. Stitch it up and stitch it down,

While I'm go - ing round the town, Tour - a, lour - a, lour - a - lu.

Introduce 'The Cobbler Song' by asking the children to listen for clues for movement. As you sing chose a student to lead the class in mirroring motions of the cobbler. After they have heard the song several times, ask if anyone can sing the nonsense words. You will sing the words of the song as they make the motions, adding the nonsense refrain. By this time, the children will need little help in singing the whole song with you.

Next sing the song with the motions transferred to an accompaniment. Then ask the children to sing the nonsense refrain in their minds. They will discover they feel the beat and it continues to sound on the instrument. A more challenging task is to play the accompaniment, shared by two players, one who accompanies the words and another the nonsense words.

Another time place symbols for the beat on the board.

T T T T   T T T T   T T T T

Sing as you point to each hammer. Then cover one set of 4 hammers which signals them to sing and play in their minds, until they reach the next uncovered measure.

Then sing 'There's a Little Wheel a-Turning' for your students. Ask them to pat the beat as you sing but lightly tap their upper chests when they feel the silent beat.

Little Wheel

There's a lit-tle wheel a-turn-ing in my heart, There's a lit-tle wheel a-turn-ing in my

heart. In my heart,___ in my heart,_ There's a lit-tle wheel a-turn-ing in my heart.

6 *Demonstrate awareness of sound durations in movement, on instruments, and with vocal sounds as the same as, longer than, or shorter than the beat.*

One of the variations in the movement games of quick reaction to timbre is to play different durations for each instrument. You may play half notes on a triangle or small gong, quarter notes on drums, and eighth notes on woodblocks. The children simultaneously move easily to these contrasting durations. They can also name these as 'slow,' 'walk' and 'running' to describe their reactions.

When the children respond accurately to these kinds of activities and identify the beat in body percussion with little teacher preparation as they sing and speak, they are ready to become aware of other lengths of sound in comparison to the beat.

Sing 'Wee Willie Winkie' again while a child 'walks through the town.' Ask another child to play a simple bordun to match the walk (score (a)). Then invite a third child to 'run through the town.' This can be imitated on an alto xylophone on octave ds (score (b)).

(a)   (b)

Wee Willie Winkie

Wee Wil-lie Win - kie runs throught the town, Up-stairs and down-stairs

in his night-gown. Rap-ping at the win - dow, Cry-ing through the lock,

'Are the child - ren in their beds? For now it's 8 o' clock.'

The children can now hear as well as see the relationship of 'walk' to 'running.' If you are using Gordon syllables, French time names or Kodály rhythm syllables, this activity provides an opportunity to name these durations.

In the next lesson, as the children walk the beat you establish, play 'Peter, Peter, Pumpkin Eater' on the black keys of the piano. They enjoy your surprise, and you can lead them to discover that the poem is all eighth notes, or shorter durations than the beat.

Peter, Peter, pumpkin eater,

Had a wife and couldn't keep her.

Put her in a pumpkin shell,

And there he kept her very well.

Guide the children to act out the poem, using durations as short as the words and as long as the underlying beat.

Another way to experience shorter and longer durations is by chanting the names of the children. Ask the children to sit in a circle and 'pass the beat.' Each child will pat his knees once in turn. On the second round ask them to chant their names. Some will have to fit one syllable to the beat, others will have two, some will have more. Guide the children to arrange themselves into a chant of shorter eighth-note durations and quarter-note durations.

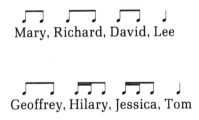

Mary, Richard, David, Lee

Geoffrey, Hilary, Jessica, Tom

Though you won't label 'Hillary' and 'Jessica's' rhythms, the children will recognize several of these names as shorter than beat durations. Days of the week, months of the year and numbers provide other opportunities to identify shorter, beat-length, or longer durations.

Sing 'Scotland's Burning' and identify the beat and shorter durations. Sing it again, using time names or 'running, running, running, running,' 'beat, beat, beat, beat,' and so on.

Scotland's Burning

Scot-land's burn-ing, Scot-land's burn-ing, Look out, look out!

Fire, fire! Fire, fire! Pour on wa-ter, pour on wa-ter.

7 *Demonstrate awareness of durations longer than the beat.*

Put triangles, finger cymbals, and drums in front of the children. Ask them to describe the sounds they expect to hear before they actually play them. Then, as they listen to 'Twinkle, Twinkle, Little Star,' they will identify the durations in the song that each instrument can play. Practice patting quarter notes and clapping the half notes, spreading the hands out to show the extended sound. Play the song with drums imitating the pats and triangles and finger cymbals the claps. Can the instruments play the rhythm of the song without help from the singers?

Twinkle, Twinkle, Little Star

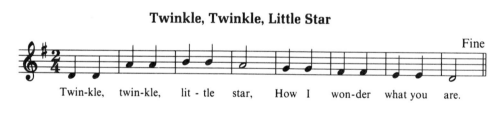

Twin-kle, twin-kle, lit-tle star, How I won-der what you are.

Up a-bove the world so high, like a dia-mond in the sky.

In another lesson ask the students to listen for long sounds. They will be able to hear them, for you can prepare them to listen by asking them to pull long, imaginary peals from the chime as you play the tick-tock of a clock. Sing 'All Night, All Day' without words as they continue their motion. Then ask them to 'play the chime' only when they hear long sounds in the song. After you have taught the song accompany it first with triangle chimes (half notes), and then with wood blocks (quarter notes). The most challenging accompaniment alternates the two parts, outlining the phrases. Your children may be able to identify your bass metallophone ostinato as 'beat-beat-long.'

All Night, All Day

Additional resource
Johnson *The Magic Forest*
    'Yangtze Boatmen's Chantey' (p. 59)
    Preparation for half note or longer
    durations.

Melody

1   Explore vocal qualities and then label them as 'speaking,' 'shouting,' 'whispering' and 'singing'.

Kindergartners enjoy exploring ways to use their voices, and it amazes them to hear you use these four voices as well. By identifying each vocal quality and producing it on command, they discover that they have control over timbre and quality. Your model can also encourage them to explore their range from high to low in each voice, helping more reluctant singers to connect the expressive potential of their shouting, whispering, and speaking voices to their singing voices.

Many nursery rhymes lend themselves to the following game. Sing one of these familiar rhymes and then ask the children what kind of voice you used. Repeat the poem in a whisper and label that quality. When you shout and then speak the poem, invite a child to imitate you. Then ask them to name your four voices, reciting the poem dramatically in each one.

Puppets can be used to identify these qualities. A bird in front of you can represent singing, while appearing perched near your ear indicating a whispered response. A dog may represent shouting when it is at arm's length, but speaking when closer to your face. Now ask the children to echo the puppets as you experiment with different ways of interpreting these familiar rhymes. Soon the puppets can direct the children to chat with them, making quick changes to highlight phrases.

> Jack and Jill went up the hill (*speak*)
> To fetch a pail of water. (*sing*)
> Jack fell down and broke his crown (*shout*)
> And Jill came tumbling after. (*whisper*)

> There was an old woman (*sing on* sol mi)
> Lived under a hill (*sing on* sol mi)
> And if she's not gone (*sing on* sol mi)
> She lives there still. (*whisper*)

Repeat this experiment in story telling for it encourages children to join in with anticipated responses. Vary the activity by signaling for solos and small groups as well as class responses.

Additional resource
Johnson *The Magic Forest*
  'Charley Over the Water' (Days 2 and 3: p. 10)

2   Explore pitch, then label pitches as 'high', 'low,' 'higher than,' or 'lower than,' in speech, song, and on instruments.
  (i)   Interpret poems and stories by using high and low sounds on barred instruments.

One of the most enjoyable, even magical, ways to explore high and low sounds is through poetry and stories. Most children find a story line irresistible and as they interpret it they use their voices in new ranges and qualities. It is a good way to continue their vocal exploration while beginning to define the relationships of pitches.

Place an alto and soprano metallophone and a soprano glockenspiel before the students. Introduce this poem by asking the children to answer your riddle. You might recite it in your most uninteresting voice, and then ask them to help you interpret the poem as they echo you.

> I have a little sister named Peep, Peep, Peep,
> She wades in the water, deep, deep, deep.
> She climbs above the mountains, high, high, high,
> Poor little creature, she has but one eye.

> (Answer: a star)

The children can help you listen to decide what words should be said by the group and what words may be spoken by soloists or small groups as they compare the range and qualities of their voices.

Ask the children to arrange the instruments from lowest to highest. Evaluate their conclusions by playing them in order. Next discover which end of each instrument is lowest, and prop the instruments up like upside-down cones. With the children develop a setting for this poem, using tremolos and word cues. One possible result is scored to guide you.

I Have a Little Sister

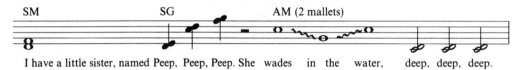

I have a little sister, named Peep, Peep, Peep. She wades in the water, deep, deep, deep.

She climbs the moun-tains, high, high, high. Poor little creature, she has but one eye.

Additional resources
Frazee *Orff Handbook for World of Music – K*
   'Jack and Jill' (pp. 4, 11)
Orff *Music for Children*, American edn., Vol. 1
   'Up and Down' (p. 10)
Orff *Music for Children*, American edn., Vol. 2
   'Eency Weency Spider (p. 69)
   This is a yearly hit with my students!
Orff and Keetman *Music for Children*, ed. Hall
   and Walter, Vol. 1
   'A Star' (p. 17)
   The teacher may play the AX or a student
   may play on Cs only.
   My children enjoy singing these words:
      Underneath the ocean, underneath the
         sea,
      Oh, whatever can it be? A whale!
   Of course, they will want to create a new
   setting, using the lowest timbres in the
   classroom.
Steen *Orff Activities*, Grade K
   'Ring a Ring a Rosie' (p. 7)

(ii)   Use gestures, words and drawings to encourage awareness of high and low pitches in his/her vocal performance.

One of the ways we can explain relative distances between pitches is to draw the relationships with gestures in movement as well as on paper. Words can then describe these visual as well as aural understandings of melodic movement, leading eventually to melodic notation.

Ask the children to answer only in the appropriate range of their speaking or singing voices or you will be mysteriously unable to hear them. What things are high on the walls of their classroom? In their closet at home? What will they find on the floor in the gym? On the playground?

To continue this exploration, arrange eight or more children of different heights in a row. As you walk slowly behind them, the students indicate the changing heights with their hands and 'oo's', sung on indefinite pitch. A student may rearrange them to make a new melodic contour as the class continues to explore their singing range.

Draw a tree on a chart or on the board. Cut out the form of a bird and place sticky tape on the back of it. As you place the bird on the ground, sing the word 'low' in that range, then 'higher' as you place the bird on the first limb. Experiment until the bird 'flies.' Of course, other children will enjoy moving the bird. Cut out a squirrel and assign half the class to follow it and half to follow the bird as they play around the tree.

(iii)   Use gestures, words, and drawings to illustrate an awareness of melodic contour (moving upward, downward, or repeating pitches).

The pantomime of using playground equipment helps children experiment with sounds that move up or down or stay at one level. The class can provide the sound effects as they mirror moving down the slide, climbing up the steps, swinging down and then up again. When you sit in a circle, join hands and move your hands up as your voices slide up, and slide down as your hands swing down. Surprise the children by freezing their hands in mid air, indicating sustaining the pitch at one level. Holding hands and moving together helps all children share the kinesthetic experience of contour.

The Fly by Bela Bartók, (RCA Adventures in Listening, Vol. 1, Record 2) describes the flight of a fly, ending with an unceremonious swat. Ask the children to mirror your fly at the end of your finger as they listen. When your fly lands on another person's fingertip, she becomes the leader. You will want to move the fly frequently as they listen. When the recording is finished draw a similar flight pattern on the board, ending with a swat. 'Read' the story by following the line with appropriate vocal sounds.

When these less definite contour exercises are successful for the children, introduce them to applying the same listening skills to their favorite songs. Draw the contour of each phrase in the air and then on the board. Sometimes it helps to use scarves or hand drums to trace the melodies boldly. Encourage thinking about melody by asking the children to sing a familiar song in their minds with eyes closed, tracing its contour with their hands.

These songs work especially well because the melodic contours are obvious to the children.

Sweetheart Out A-hunting

Sweet-heart out a-hunt-ing on a long sum-mer day. long sum-mer day.

With soft mallet

Higglety Pigglety Pop!

Hig-gle-ty, pig-gle-ty pop! The dog has eat-en the mop; The

pig's in a hur-ry, the cat's in a flur-ry, Hig-gle-ty, pig-gle-ty pop!

The Farmer in the Dell

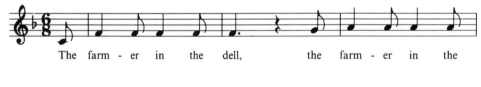

The farm-er in the dell, the farm-er in the

dell. Hi ho, the dai-ry oh, the farm-er in the dell.____

Consider moving to the next set of melody objectives in the second semester. Preparation now may include developing a repertoire ('Repertoire,' 1), or exploring texture ('Texture,' 1, 2).

3 Sing in response to another voice and identify the pitch of the response as the same, higher, or lower than the first voice.

Now that the children have become conscious of high and low sounds and can trace melodic contours they may be ready to refine their responses to identify specific pitches.

When you sing a conversation with your students, ask them if you sang higher or lower, or on the same note as they sang. Your puppets, the dog and bird, can carry on a singing conversation while the children tell you when they sing on the same pitches or higher or lower ones.

You may find a third puppet useful. The bird sings higher, the dog lower, but the third, perhaps a child puppet, sings on the same pitches as the person who sings to him. Ask the class to sing a familiar chant, such as 'It's raining, it's pouring.' Offer the bird to a child who responds in its range, the dog to a child who responds in a lower range, while the student who holds the child puppet echoes the class at the same level. Play this game for a few minutes in each lesson over a period of a month.

When a song becomes familiar, particularly if it is a chant or a small-range song, ask a group of three or four to lead it followed by another group on the next phrase. The children will respond with less tension if you direct the groups in random order, rather than from left to right. Those listening can indicate that the pitch is higher by pointing up, lower by pointing down, and matching by clasping hands.

Additional resources
Frazee *Orff Handbook for World of Music – K*
    'The Echo' (p. 6)
    The song and setting are quite
    sophisticated harmonically, but the echoes
    are easy to sing.
Johnson *The Magic Forest*
    'Yoo Hoo' (p. 8)
    Another lovely example of an echo game.

4   *Sing, to imitate a short vocal model of one to three pitches.*

Children sing most accurately when they sing alone in response to another voice. It is important to create many opportunities during the year for them to hear their own voices in relationship to yours and others. One of the easiest ways is to play roll-call games. Greet a few children each lesson by singing

[musical notation: S M "Hello, Joey"]

and hear his response. [musical notation: "Hello, Mister Smith"] To dismiss children try a variation of 'Pop Up,' a game in Volume 1 of *Music for Children* (American edition, p. 8). You sing one child's name [musical notation: "Jennifer, goodbye!"] . As she leaves she sings another classmate's name, and the chain continues until all have left. After you have played the game so the children know the process, ask them to use their ears for a more challenging task. They are to sing the next name on the same pitches as the one before. When differences occur, you may intervene by echoing the first caller. If the pitch doesn't match, ask the responder, 'Are you lower, higher, or the same?' Then you sing in the responder's range, hopefully receiving a closer answer, and the game moves on. We don't want to belabor the game or embarrass the child, but only help the child identify the difference.

Another activity that encourages improvisatory responses is the little song, 'We're Going on a Field Trip.' After four or five children have responded, sing the song again to maintain the tonal center. It helps to keep the momentum when I accompany on a bass xylophone, but I switch to a tremolo on the tonic if the children seem restricted by the metric structure.

We're Going on a Field Trip

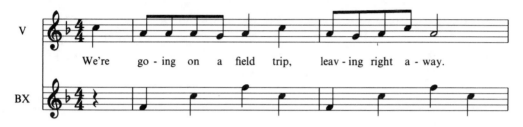

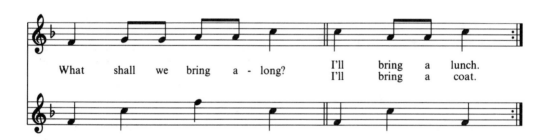

Many songs provide opportunities for solo singing. In 'Wee Willie Winkie,' Willie can act out the song as the children sing, but Willie sings the last phrase alone. The child he taps at the end can become the next 'Willie.'

There are several things you can do to help create an atmosphere for good singing. One way is to model and encourage good, supportive breathing. Children feel singing is important when they are sitting with chests high and breathing together. Another way to encourage good singing is to SING FOR THEM, but then LISTEN TO THEM. As you walk among them with an attitude of interested and careful listening they will be more aware of their own singing. And encourage them to think of singing silently or with inner hearing. We can only help children sing in tune by making them aware of good singing and how it is achieved. These are singing games which help children practice singing in a higher range.

5   *Explore and compare melodic motives and melodic contours through chants, songs, and singing games while developing a song repertoire.*

Rig-a-jig-jig

The children sit on the floor throughout the room. One child walks among them as the class sings the first section. On 'chanced to meet,' the child chooses the student closest to him. They join hands and skip. At the end of the song the first child sits and the second walks. (Sometimes games are fairest when girls choose boys and boys choose girls.) When you review the song, help the children discover the repeated pitches at the beginning, the downward melodic motives and the high ending.

Old King Glory

For 'Old King Glory,' the children stand in a circle. The 'King' walks around the circle, tapping classmates on the shoulder when each number is sung. The third child tapped leaves the circle and becomes 'king' and the first child follows with one hand on the new leader's shoulder. Continue the game until only one student remains. She may be the first king when the game is played again. My classes have two ways of assuring each student of a turn. One is to form several smaller circles, each with a king. Another is to have the first, second, and third children leave the circle, with the third child becoming the new leader.

Playing singing games is a particularly good activity for Kindergarten children because the songs and motion practice phrasing and moving with the beat. The repetitive verses give opportunities to practice singing simple melodies. Draw attention to the phrases and the changes in motion. The melodies can be highlighted by playing recorder as they sing.

When you review 'Old King Glory' call the children's attention to the wide leaps, the long sweeps down the mountain at the beginning, and the place where we seem undecided as to which way to move.

Bluebird

Blue-bird, blue-bird, go through my win-dow, Blue-bird, blue-bird, go through my win-dow,

Blue-bird, blue-bird, go through my win-dow, and buy mo-las - ses can - dy.

The traditional game for 'Bluebird' involves catching the 'bird' inside the circle. The children stand in a circle, hands raised to form 'windows.' The child or bird runs in and out of the circle. On 'buy' the children lower their arms and attempt to trap the bird.

One of my classes has developed another game. The children stand in a circle with space between each one. The child, or bird, runs in and out of the spaces or windows. On 'buy molasses' the students squat down and the 'bird' stands in front of the child closest to him at that time. When the song repeats, both children run in and out, and then stand before two people. Four are now running in and out. Continue until all are chosen.

'Bluebird' is also excellent preparation for *sol–mi* and *sol–la–sol–mi* melodic patterns to be sung in syllables in first grade and notated in second. Ask the children to sing only 'go through my window' while you sing the remaining measures. They will be able to observe that these measures sound alike. Divide the class into two groups. Ask one group to sing the first measure, you sing the second and the other group sing the third measure. It takes careful listening to discover that the third measure is just a little lower than the first measure.

Use these three songs as a beginning of a collection of singing games that are easy for your children to sing well.

Texture

1   From recorded examples and class ensembles, distinguish monophonic music (one line) from polyphonic and harmonic music (more than one line).

Set out three instruments – a xylophone, metallophone and a glockenspiel – arranged in C pentatonic. Invite one child to play 'walking music,' using two mallets, playing until you signal a stop. Add a second, and then a third child. Choose new players but ask a child to follow each player, walking in place when she hears her leader, stopping when the instrument stops. Repeat the activity again. This time the children close their eyes. You will direct the players and the children will show you how many instruments are playing by raising one, two, or three fingers. The children may enjoy discovering what timbres sound nearly alike and what ones, by contrast, are easy to hear even in a larger ensemble.

Promenade, which introduces Ravel's orchestration of *Pictures at an Exhibition* by Modest Mussorgsky, begins with a solo trumpet which is soon joined by other brasses. After you have explained to the children that this music describes a walk through an art gallery, play the *Promenade* for them. Could they hear when one person was walking and when there were more? Use their suggestions to plan movement to fit the music.

The younger children enjoy hearing the music of their older schoolmates. Play a recording of a fourth- or fifth-grade class singing a canon, drawing their attention to unison singing followed by several entrances.

2   Perform the beat while chanting or singing a simple theme.

It is an accomplishment for anyone to do two things at once. Our goal is to encourage children to move and sing, sing and play, and speak and play with equal accuracy. Children this age perform best when the hands move together, although some will be able to keep a steady beat moving bilaterally. It can be difficult to play patterns on untuned instruments, such as large cabasas, claves, vibra slaps, guiros, and even triangles. Some teachers have young children play hand drums with soft mallets to achieve an accurate, pleasant sound.

Prepare 'Two Little Sausages' by asking the children to sit in several lines, front to back. Each one pats the shoulders of the one in front using both hands. The first person plays the drum. When the large drum plays at the end they 'fall out of the pan' by rolling to the side. The first person moves to the back and the poem begins again. Feeling the beat helps many children identify what we mean by 'keeping the beat.'

Two Little Sausages

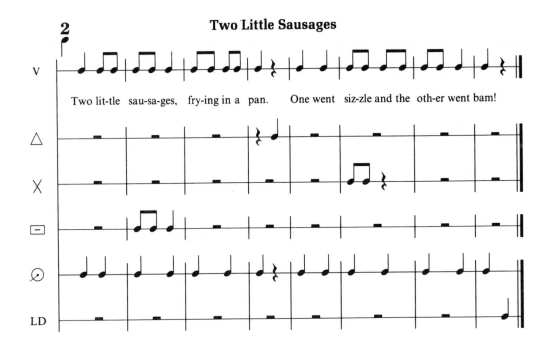

Chanting is one of the best ways to practice. Ask the children to chant the accompaniment as you speak the words of the song 'This Old Man.' Reverse roles before dividing the class into two parts, one to sing and one to pat, while whispering the words of the accompaniment. Let the children take turns playing this part on a drum or temple blocks.

This Old Man

Additional resources

Accompaniments (harmony)

Very simple settings of poems and songs are most successful for kindergarten. Use one instrument which sounds the beat, only adding other timbres on word cues or to signal the beginnings of phrases. Simplicity not only assures an accurate performance, but the accompaniments will balance the children's light voices, making a musically expressive performance possible. These settings provide children with an opportunity to play the beat in ways that add to the expression of the song.

1   Accompany others by playing beat patterns on the tonic bar.

In this setting, the bass xylophone and glockenspiels share the responsibility for the beat. Teach these parts at the same time. A child will find it easier to alternate hands on the large bass bars than the more difficult small glockenspiel bars. If playing right–left is difficult, the child can play these octave bars together. The finger cymbal plays on 'where' and 'come.' The bass xylophone alternates with the bass metallophone. If the tremolo is difficult, play the pitch once and let it ring.

Cotton-eyed Joe

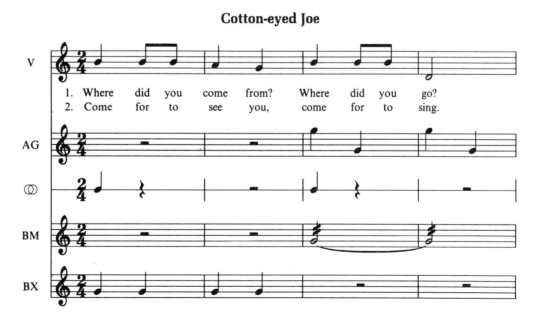

Where did you come from my Cot - ton - eyed___ Joe?
Come for to show you my di - a - mond___ ring.

2 *Accompany others by playing beat patterns on a chord bordun.*

The steady drone is one of the most characteristic sounds in Orff settings. In 'Santa Maloney' prepare the bordun by patting both thighs at once as they learn the song. A new sound is added to the beginning of each phrase and the woodblock imitates the word rhythms.

Santa Maloney

England

Here we dance San-ta Ma - lo - ney, Here we dance San-ta Ma - lo - ney,

Here we dance San - ta Ma - lo - ney   As   we   go 'round a - bout.

For 'Walk in the Parlor,' place the metallophones side by side so the children can watch the beat pass from one player to the other. Place several untuned instruments, such as finger cymbals, log drum, or woodblocks, near the children. Each time the song is sung, the player of the untuned instrument may continue two extra measures. This bridge will give you time to choose another child to pick another instrument to play during the next verse.

Walk in the Parlor

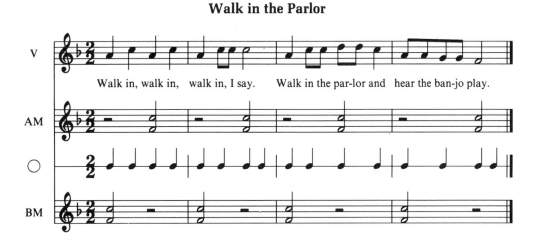

Walk in, walk in, walk in, I say.   Walk in the par-lor and hear the ban-jo play.

Form

1 *Respond to phrasing as musical breathing.*

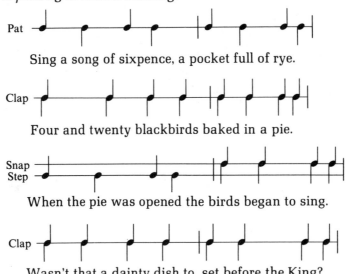

Pat

Sing a song of sixpence, a pocket full of rye.

Clap

Four and twenty blackbirds baked in a pie.

Snap
Step

When the pie was opened the birds began to sing.

Clap

Wasn't that a dainty dish to set before the King?

As you chant the rhyme, ask the children to wink each time a new idea begins. Next, ask them to follow your beat which you will change alternating between two body percussion levels for each phrase. Then ask the children to follow your motions and chant. This rhyme is fun to act out. The class will walk the beat 'around the pie' (in a large circle) for the first phrase. They will slowly move to a crouch for the second phrase, placing arms on the floor, facing center. On phrase three, they pop up their heads, one by one. Then they rise slowly, clapping on the last three beats.

A favorite instrumental piece for third and fourth grades is a march in Volume I of *Music for Children* (ed. Hall and Walter, nos. 38 and 49; adpt. Murray, no. 3, p. 95; American edn., no. 7, p. 15). Have your children listen to a recording of this piece. Use the introduction to get warmed up and ready, bouncing the beat in place. Then lead the students to explore several ways of walking which fit and breathe with the music. From their ideas choose one walk for the first phrase, changing direction for the second phrase. Choose another interpretation for the second section.

Another way to enjoy a song quietly is to indicate phrases in place. Give each child a ribbon or colored string at least a yard long. Hold it in one hand. As they sing, pull the ribbon out to reach full length by the end of the phrase. Drop one end of the ribbon and draw it out again, once for each phrase.

As they listen they can experience the breathing that phrasing implies. Pretend there is a candle in front of you by holding your finger about a foot from your mouth. Breathe in as the phrase begins and blow against your finger as the phrase is played. Breathe with the music. Encourage taking in a deep, soundless breath.

Additional resource
Frazee *Orff Handbook for World of Music – K*
'Bluebird, Bluebird' (p. 14)
The accompaniment can be played by four
pairs, one for each phrase.

Repertoire

1   Develop a repertoire of songs and singing games from which understanding may be drawn in the first and second grade.

There are types of songs that are particularly well liked by younger children because the form brings a familiar refrain back again. These songs build memory skills, prepare rhythmic responses, and contribute to a body of songs which they can sing with others. These are found in many children's folk song collections, and hopefully, you sang many of them yourself as you were growing up. Use this list to start a file of your favorites.

Call and response
>   Oh, John the Rabbit
>   Frog Went A-Courtin'

Verse and Refrain
>   Rig-a-Jig-Jig
>   Mr. Rabbit, Mr. Rabbit
>   Skip To My Lou
>   Who Built the Ark?
>   Yankee Doodle

Songs that add motives
>   I Know an Old Lady who Swallowed a Fly
>   Old MacDonald Had a Farm
>   Bought Me a Cat

Songs that tell a story
>   I Know an Old Woman All Skin and Bones
>   Fox Went Out on a Chilly Night

Counting Songs
>   Over in the Meadow
>   Barnacle Bill
>   Going Over the Sea

For many of these songs there are books with lovely illustrations. Check with your school librarian as well as your public library for the most recent publication.

You have come to the end of your students' first year of school music. If you have seen your kindergarten only once a week you will not cover all of these objectives. These will be reconsidered as possible goals for the next year. Others, such as an introduction to instruments of the orchestra, may be put aside for several years.

However, several objectives should be evaluated carefully for re-introduction and practice before reading and writing begins in the first grade. Singing with awareness of melody contour, responding accurately to tempo and rhythm, and finding the beat in speech, movement and body percussion should precede more formal music study.

Most important is keeping alive the children's curiosity and enjoyment of music making. There are indications that large numbers of children may be turned away from learning in school by early first grade. This should cause us deep concern that we provide experiences that tap the children's interest in music as one of the ways they can be expressive and alive. Music is learned by performing it, and hopefully, that is what is memorable about kindergarten year for you and, especially, for your students.

4 · First Grade

First graders begin the year with great anticipation and we want to build on their enthusiasm. Many will be adjusting to the new experience of a full, structured day of instruction. Children expect to read as a sign of their growth, and they are curious and eager to learn about their world. Classroom activities can present both rewards and frustrations, for these young learners are becoming aware of others. Fairness is a big issue for first graders, and little problems are just as serious to them as large ones. Increasingly they look to peers as well as to the teacher as sources from which to learn new skills and gain new information. Because they measure their successes by comparing the outcomes of their efforts with those of others, mistakes are threatening. They need help in viewing mistakes as opportunities for learning, and they need constructive praise and correction in order to evaluate themselves fairly.

Goals

Our first goal, after the classroom environment has been established, is to provide the children with basic rhythmic training, with beat and tempo, and then rhythmic durations. This may be accomplished best through movement activities, for first graders learn through manipulation of materials and action. Their ability to internalize what they know about rhythm is dependent on their ability to experience it in a variety of ways. They want to walk, run, gallop, walk slowly, hop and skip, all locomotor skills which are basic to rhythmic learning. Some children will accurately perform beat and beat–rest ostinatos early in the year, but others will respond best in only one or two media, and perhaps a few will require practice throughout the year before these basic skills are attained. Word rhythms as well as movement experiences will expose them to the relative durations of musical sound. The characteristic of music to move in longer and shorter sounds must be separated from the function of beat and tempo. Increased memory skills and ability to think music internally will allow them to perform music with more independence in the classroom.

Developing accurate singing skills is our second goal because this is an important period when they are learning especially by listening rather than by reading. If your time with them was limited in kindergarten, you will probably want to make this area of your curriculum a high priority, beginning with a review of kindergarten melodic objectives. The physical act of expressive singing, requiring breath support, good posture and listening, can be taught through a broad repertoire of songs that also prepares your students for music reading later on.

Children can be guided in using their ideas in creating and improvising music that reflects their own imagination and knowledge. This is our goal. First graders love to experiment, to chant, sing and play instruments. Traditional chants and stories can be told and retold in many ways, using their suggestions. They play the barred instruments with more control, providing another sound source through which they can demonstrate their abilities to hear high and low, melodic contours and pitch ranges. While engaged in these activities it is important that they also explore, using their newly acquired music skills to express their ideas. In this way the essence of the Orff approach permeates their learning.

Our fourth goal is to teach children to use the language of music before they are taught written symbols. Words are symbols which represent experiences that can be generalized into a single term. Some of these words, such as high and low, loud and soft, fast and slow, short and long, were introduced in kindergarten. They should be reviewed now. New terms will be the syllables of solfege which identify the specific relationships of pitches, and rhythm syllables which identify specific relationships of durations. These terms help many children analyze what they hear and, later, link sound with sight. If you choose to use rhythm and pitch syllables, the children should be proficient in using each one of them before the parallel written symbol is introduced. The children should also have been encouraged to demonstrate what they know about music through drawings or ikons. Conventional written symbols will be introduced only in the rhythm sequence for grade one, while notating pitch will be limited to high/low and *sol/mi* relationships in ikon representations.

First Grade Objectives

The broad goals for first grade are now broken down into objectives which follow in the same order as was used in kindergarten. First, procedures which facilitate group instruction are presented, followed by objectives organized under elements of music. Your lessons will include all elements, for music is rhythm, melody, timbre, texture and expression. However, conscious learning is clarified by lessons which focus on only one or two elements and skills. Having objectives for each element also helps you keep track of what has been covered, either through imitation or subconscious exploration, and what has been experienced as preparation before being brought to conscious awareness. The objectives under one element are meant to be followed in the sequence given. However, half the rhythm objectives may be followed by the first group of melody and timbre objectives before returning to finish the rhythm sequence. In fact, you will want to decide whether finishing all the objectives under each element is practical. If your kindergarten program was limited in what it could cover, you may choose to expand the time you spend on the non-notation, experiential objectives of grade one. Some notation objectives can be deferred until next year in favor of providing more experiences which prepare for reading and writing in second grade. There is no great hurry to learn to read music, for when the students are ready, and find it useful, they will learn quite easily. It is most important that the children experience many ways of making music and that they feel success in purposeful, playful involvement.

First Grade Objectives

Skill in group instruction
1   Review and assess class performance skills through simultaneous imitation games and activities.

2   Explore and practice using the child's own space and then class space in group activities.
3   Practice delayed or echo imitation through movement, speech, song, body percussion, and/or instruments.

Expression

1   Use dynamics — loud compared with soft, becoming louder then softer — to illustrate poetry, stories, chants, songs, movements, and playing.
2   Use articulation, smooth, detached, accented, short, to illustrate poetry, stories, chants, songs, movement, and playing.
3   Encourage artistry through the use of the child's ideas as spontaneous responses to musical stimuli. Extend and change music performances to explore and reinforce what is being taught.

Rhythm

1   Perform durations equivalent to the length of the beat in speech and movement, on body percussion and instruments.
2   Respond accurately to various tempos in movement, speech, song, and body percussion. Apply the terms 'fast,', 'slow,' 'faster,' and 'slower' to identify tempos and tempo changes.
3   Discover and then identify, through speech and song, the quarter note (♩) and rest or silent beat (𝄽).

> Consider beginning your sequence of melodic objectives here ('Melody,' 1 and 2). Then continue with 'Rhythm,' 4.

4   Identify a repeated pattern as an ostinato ‖: :‖
5   Perform, read, and write patterns containing quarter notes and rests.

> Consider exploring rhythm patterns while introducing texture ('Texture,' 1–3).

6   Explore speech materials for inflection, rhythm, and timbre.
7   Use speech as a means to transfer words to rhythm and to distinguish beat from rhythm.
8   Perform, clap and play patterns using ♩ ♫ ♩ 𝄽 .

> You may wish to delay this final goal until late in the year as a preparation for the evaluation of rhythmic skills.

9   Write four-beat patterns from dictation, using ♩ , ♫ ♩ , and 𝄽 .

Melody

1   Extend the awareness of pitch by exploring expressive speech.
2   Identify melodic contours as moving upwards, downwards, or repeating pitches.

> Consider finishing the melodic sequence while applying and practicing the remainder of the 'Rhythm' sequence (3–9).

3 Identify two pitches in chants as higher and lower, then *sol* and *mi*, with gestures, vocally, and on instruments.

4 Identify three pitches in chants as *sol*, *mi*, and *la*, with gestures, vocally, and on instruments.

5 Sing chants and pentatonic songs with simple ostinato accompaniments.

Texture

1 Perform patterns over the beat using a body-percussion sound or an instrument, while speaking or singing.

2 Perform accompaniments on barred instruments using the tonic note and chord, level and broken borduns.

> These goals may be integrated with rhythm and melody goals, as you apply rhythmic reading skills while accompanying songs and chants.

3 Learn these accompaniments by preparing using body percussion, speech and reading notation.

4 Perform a rhythmic ostinato as accompaniment to a theme.

Timbre

> Place this objective early in the year, perhaps after 'Skill in Group Instruction,' 3.

1 Learn the names of classroom instruments and the technique of playing each.

2 Identify aurally the orchestral instruments according to family, range, and name.

Form

1 Identify repeated rhythmic and melodic motives and phrases in speech and song.

2 Identify sections as same or different (i.e. AA or AB).

Skill in Group Instruction

1 Review and assess class performance skills through simultaneous imitation games and activities.

Simultaneous imitation games are valuable ways you can catch and hold children's attention, giving you time to prepare their responses to move, interpret, and play. Begin the lesson with the children seated around you. Sing the melody of 'Clap, Clap, Clap Your Hands' on a neutral syllable, such as 'loo,' moving your hand up and down to illustrate its contour. Invite the children to follow your motion, singing with you as they become ready. Then sing and clap your hands lightly, gesturing to them to join you in adding words to the melody.

Clap, Clap, Clap Your Hands

Extend the form by continuing to clap, guiding the children to follow the movements of your hands through the air in circles and loops. Return to the song, creating new verses such as 'Tap, tap, tap your foot,' or 'Pat, pat, pat your knees,' or 'Bounce, bounce, bounce with me.' Follow each verse with mirror movement, beginning with the body part just used. The next time you sing the song, continue to explore movement by imitating the sound of an instrument. Use a drum to lead the clapping following the song, a triangle to continue the tapping, or a guiro to lead shoulder motions. Then play just the instruments and challenge the children to respond with the motions each represented. Changing the dynamic levels between softer and louder, and the motions between large gestures and small, will add to the expressiveness and surprise of the activity.

As you lead your children, observe their responses. Who follows, no matter what the tempo or dynamic level? Who sings, but moves only in contrasting sections? Who has difficulty following tempo changes? Who sings enthusiastically, and who moves throughout but does not sing? These observations will help you pace your instruction and plan challenges for the range of abilities in the class.

Simultaneous imitation is a very useful way to prepare students to play instruments. For instance, the children are prepared to play the bass xylophone bordun for 'Clap, Clap, Clap Your Hands' as they sing with you and pat their knees on the metric accents. Prepare the children for the wood block part by telling them to clap on the word 'clap.' Some children at this age will find it much easier to hold the wood block with one hand and play with the other. Others may prefer alternating mallets on a wood block or the temple block.

Oliver Twist

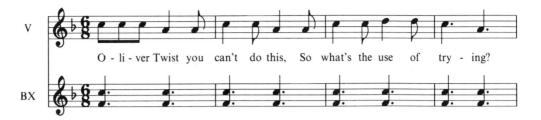

*Play an instrument for each body part, timbres chosen by the students.

There are many singing games which invite students to follow a leader. 'Oliver Twist' is one of my children's favorites because it moves quickly, with a new task for each phrase. A game may be created from ideas the song's lyrics suggest to the children. The children may be standing randomly in the room. You may be first leader, stepping, shrugging, or clapping in place to the beat, inviting the class to imitate you for the first phrase. Follow the directions of the song for the second phrase. On 'away you go!' walk to another person and tap him to be the new leader. Another time you may choose to introduce a more traditional circle game which begins with the leader in the center. As the first phrase is sung by those in the circle the leader improvises solo movement. All the participants follow the directions of the second phrase, turning in place on 'away you go!' At the same time the leader selects another player, taking his/her hand to trade places on 'away you go!' Notice that the accompaniment outlines each phrase. It can be prepared in the following way:

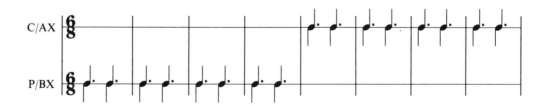

Using simultaneous imitation skillfully will help your students to enter into music activities quickly and successfully. You can train the students by having one or two of them play instrumental parts while the others imitate the rhythms with body percussion.

Taking turns several times so many children can play is possible when they have all prepared. Other timbres may be added responding to word cues on 'knees,' 'toes,' and 'hands.'

Additional resource
Frazee with Kreuter *Discovering Orff* pp. 55–6

2   *Explore and practice using the child's own space and then class space in group activities.*

My children enjoy this little 'In and Out' game. Ask your students to space themselves so that the room appears to be filled, each in his/her personal space. Encourage them to suggest ways to accomplish this by moving from one place to another without invading another child's space. To the sound of a drum or a recorder have them draw as close to you as possible without touching. Then play again, giving them a short time to move out, filling the space, still without touching others. When they can move between personal space and class space successfully, teach them this little song.

Now You Walk

adapted by AS

As they sing they walk to a new position in class space. On 'Stop!' they signal the beat, by moving their knees, hands, head, or any other body part except their feet, exploring the width and height of their own places. The accompaniment may be added, prepared by singing and patting, then walking the rhythm of each. The challenge becomes even

86

more precise when you call a number less than ten on the beat following 'Stop.' The children then count internally, and move in their own spaces. After the last beat they call 'Hey!' and walk and sing the song again.

Now you walk, and you walk, and you walk and you STOP! T. 2

C. (One, two) Hey! Now you walk,   etc.

3   Practice delayed or echo imitation through movement, speech, song, body percussion, and/or instruments.

If we can teach our children to listen carefully, we will have done them a great service. Fortunately, there are many ways to do this, and echo imitation is one of the best. We know that if the children can be encouraged to hear accurately, they will probably be able to respond accurately. In echo activities, we can correct, evaluate, and enjoy the responses if we listen and observe carefully as well. When this happens, everyone involved enjoys a musical communication.

Echo imitation is a teaching technique through which we can practice rhythm and melody skills in much the same way that we build a speaking vocabulary. Purposeful echo exercises – using body percussion levels for rhythm or a neutral syllable or solfege for melody – for just a minute of each lesson can not only warm up the children's muscles and thinking processes, but also plant responses to be made conscious later. I like to begin with very easy patterns, moving progressively to those from the lesson ahead to one or two that may challenge even the best student, then returning to end with patterns relevant to the lesson.

It is easiest to imitate the leader in the same performance medium. If you are seeking an accurate singing response you will want to sing to the child. Playing techniques are more easily imitated when we demonstrate on the instrument. Most children want to perform correctly, so we must use this teaching tool carefully, modelling from our own best musical skills in order to help the children respond to their highest potential.

When we perform the patterns in one medium, but the children echo through another medium, we are asking them to interpret our model. This jump-rope rhyme can be used to demonstrate several kinds of imitation.

> Old man Daisy,
> He went crazy,
> Up the ladder, down the ladder,
> Over my head!

Begin by reciting the poem once to the class. Ask a volunteer to recite the poem back to you. Often one child can! Then recite the first two lines. The class echoes, and continues to lines three and four. Recite the poem once more, the class echoing it entirely. They can now follow your body percussion as you chant. As you chant, pat your knees for lines 1 and 2, clapping up, then down, then above your head for lines 3 and 4. The movement is a simultaneous response. Then ask pairs of children to move to the poem as the words suggest. Now the children are imitating the words, but their interpretations will vary, demonstrating many possible right solutions.

There are other ways to use imitation to teach poetry and songs. Often the focus of the lesson and the abilities of the children determine the process I choose for presenting new materials to them. Here are several examples of ways in which I have found imitation useful.

1   Sing a short song or recite a short poem, and ask the class for an immediate echo of the whole. This works well with material that includes repetitive phrases.
2   Perform the song or poem. Then, beginning with the first, ask the class to echo each line. Repeat, combining lines 1 and 2, then 3 and 4 before echoing the whole. This is a common way of presenting material and is most useful when teaching lengthier phrases. However, repeated use of this process may lead to dull, predictable introductions to potentially lively material.
3   Give the children a listening task. Do any of the words repeat? Do all the words in my song make sense? What movement does this poem or song suggest? Echo the phrases the children identify as solving the listening task. This approach can be an efficient way to focus on the purpose for using the material to meet the lesson's objectives.
4   After presenting the song or poem ask the students to identify the easiest phrase to learn. Often echoing all the correct student responses results in learning from one another.

The purpose of spending time to practice echo imitation is to establish routines that help children participate, giving them opportunities to listen carefully, to prepare skills, and to anticipate the lesson process. Skillful use of this tool can eliminate wordy directions and allow you to transmit music efficiently to your students.

Additional resources
Frazee with Kreuter *Discovering Orff*, p. 27
Orff and Keetman *Music for Children*, ed.
   Murray, Vol. 1, pp. 53, 141

Expression

1   Use dynamics — loud compared with soft, becoming louder then softer — illustrate poetry, stories, chants, songs, movement, and playing.

As we move from one lesson to the next throughout the day, it is easy for us to lose our sensitivity to the expressive qualities of the music we are making. Expressive elements, such as tempo, timbre, articulations and dynamics, should be used in every lesson to bring our music to life. While we call attention to expressive elements at the beginning of the year, this objective should always be present, for we want to convey musical meaning in each lesson.

Ask your children to think of a sound they can make with their mouths or hands to accompany your poem. Then recite to them:

CLASS:	Who has seen the wind?
SOLO 1:	Neither I nor you:
TEACHER or	But when the leaves hang trembling
CLASS:	The wind is passing through.
CLASS:	Who has seen the wind?
SOLO 2:	Neither you nor I:
TEACHER or	But when the leaves bow down their heads,
CLASS:	The wind is passing by.

Christina Rossetti

Invite the children to make their sounds, but only as you direct them. Create a gentle wind sound introduction and sound carpet, passing the opportunity to make their sounds from one group to another. Recite the first verse over their accompaniment. Ask the children what dynamic changes they heard, using the terms loud and soft, crescendo and decrescendo. Draw a picture, using the crescendo and decrescendo signs to describe the contrasts the children wish to create. I use the symbol *p* for 'piano,' *f* for 'forte' and *mp* and *mf* for 'mezzo piano' and 'mezzo forte.' The children enjoy knowing these Italian terms and symbols to describe their music.

When preparing the second verse, ask them to listen for changes in the dynamics required to interpret the words. Again, direct an introduction and sound carpet as you recite the poem. Using their suggestions, draw a second picture of their sounds. Encourage them to compare this setting with that of the first verse and then adjust the markings to achieve a good dynamic contrast.

You can also create contrast by using different voices, as suggested in the notes in the left margin beside 'Who Has Seen the Wind?' Movement, either from a sitting or standing position, may be added to illustrate their sounds. Finally, if you wish to enjoy a big production, transfer some of their sounds to hand drums, maracas and other shakers.

When teaching 'Bobby Shaftoe' later in the year, recall this experience with dynamics and timbre. Now, with the children's help, create a musical adventure for Bobby Shaftoe.

Bobby Shaftoe

adapted by AS

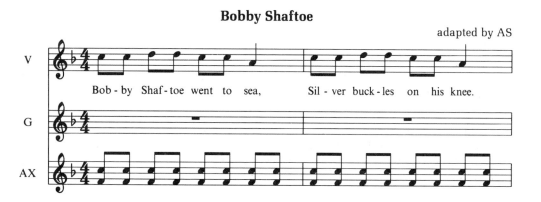

He'll come back and mar-ry me. Hand-some Bob-by Shaf - toe.

Bob - by Shaf - toe looked a - bout. All his rib - bons flew a - bout,

All the peo - ple gave a shout, 'Yea' for Bob - by Shaf - toe.

Between verses 1 and 2, tell the story of a sea voyage, complete with storm, the sighting of a sea monster, and a period of no wind before the ship sails into the harbor.

Between verse 2 and a return to verse 1, improvise the triumphant return of Bobby Shaftoe to his home port. Help the children use the terms and symbols to describe dynamic levels, and represent their musical story telling in ikonic pictures to order their ideas for performance.

2 Use articulation, smooth, detached, accented, short, to illustrate poetry, stories, chants, songs, movement, and playing.

Poetry and songs describing motions and feelings which are familiar to children can inspire their exploration of ways to make different sounds from the same source.

Jump or Jiggle
Frogs jump
Caterpillars hump

Worms wiggle
Bugs jiggle

Rabbits hop
Horses clop

Snakes slide
Sea gulls glide

Mice creep
Deer leap

Puppies bounce
Kittens pounce

Lions stalk...
But...
I walk!

Evelyn Beyer

Collect pictures of these animals to place in order on a board. Then ask your children to interpret typical movements for each animal, first with their hands and arms as they sit, and then in self space. Next guide their movements by reciting the poem. Return to the board and recite the poem again, pointing to the pictures in order. To extend the poem, ask the students to echo the action word for each animal two times, interpreting the movements they created in their sounds ('Frogs jump, jump, jump'). Then discuss their interpretations by using such words as 'smooth,' 'sharp,' 'accented,' as you or a student create symbols to record their ideas regarding articulation (see the illustration following each line above). When the children speak the poem again, with the extension of each line, ask a student to point from one ikon to the next, directing the articulations as represented in their drawings.

Articulation can be explored by interpreting the words in body percussion. Name the animal and then make the three sounds with snaps, claps, pats or stamps, using sharp attacks, brush strokes and other effects. Then you could ask your class if you have chosen the best sounds. The children may enjoy choosing an instrument to follow each body percussion part.

3   *Encourage artistry through the use of the child's ideas as spontaneous responses to musical stimuli. Extend and change music performances to explore and reinforce what is being taught.*

This is an opportunity for us teachers to remind ourselves and our students that attitudes toward instruction influence the way lessons unfold. To fulfill it requires us to know our material so well that we are willing to play with the children in exploring it, and to let our group music making guide us toward each lesson's final product. The following examples illustrate simple ways we can encourage participation and interaction.

1   Make a conscious effort to interact, one to one, with as many children as possible in each lesson. Include several solo echoes; acknowledge with a gesture or comment on an individual's responses to music activity; use individuals to play a part, to demonstrate, to conduct.

2   Ask for suggestions from your children for ways to use already taught materials, such as providing the introduction, changing the timbre to accompany a second verse, providing a bridge of music between repetitions, or creating a short movement motive to accompany the music. You can take a small idea and repeat or expand it. Even though class periods are short in many of our schools, and we teach many children at once, we can find small ways to include the child's suggestions in forming the interpretation of our classroom music performances. In this way we encourage the children to think and respond from their ability to perform artistically.

3   Use questions as a way to reinforce the focus of the lesson, giving children the opportunity and practice in identifying the importance of their involvement. 'Geoff, is there another way to perform this pattern?' 'Daniela, will you direct us with a new tempo?' 'Carlos, this song is about a bear. Select an instrument to play its footsteps'. 'Amy, did the class follow the map of our performance as we planned?' 'Rami, why did we not sing as beautifully this time?'

From small steps which recognize the musical judgement of our students we can develop the atmosphere required to encourage improvisation and creation.

Rhythm

1   *Perform durations equivalent to the length of the beat in speech and movement, on body percussion and instruments.*

This Old Man

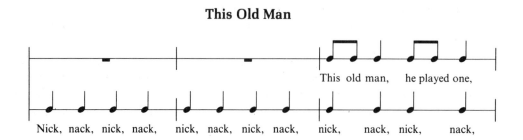

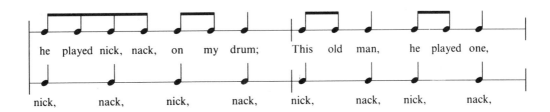

he played nick, nack, on my drum; This old man, he played one,

nick, nack, nick, nack, nick, nack, nick, nack,

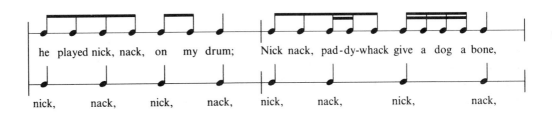

he played nick, nack, on my drum; Nick nack, pad-dy-whack give a dog a bone,

nick, nack, nick, nack, nick, nack, nick, nack,

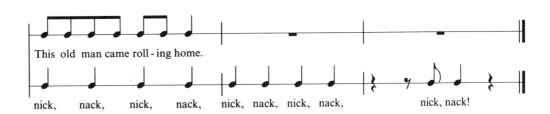

This old man came roll-ing home.

nick, nack, nick, nack, nick, nack, nick, nack, nick, nack!

This chant of lyrics from a familiar song your children may know from pre-school, reinforces the beat with the words, 'Nick, nack, nick, nack.' Have the children mirror you as you chant the accompaniment and pat both knees. Ask them to continue chanting and patting as you recite the words, either as you know them from the song or in this version. Change the patting pattern to another body percussion level and invite the children to recite the poem with you, determining with them the dynamic level for each phrase. After sufficient practice, divide the class into two groups, one to recite the poem and the other to provide the pattern on the beat. The children may choose to sing the song, rather than chant it to the beat accompaniment. Then create a bridge between each verse. Introduce each verse, chanting:

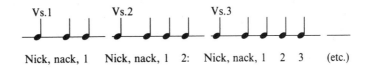

Nick, nack, 1   Nick, nack, 1   2:   Nick, nack, 1   2   3   (etc.)

Of course, you will need ten ways to perform the beat, one for each verse. You may also use this opportunity to guide the children to choose a untuned instrument to lead the accompaniment for each verse.

> Cindy Lee,
> Can't you see?
> If so, do so.
> Bounce your knees,
> Tap your toes,
> Twirl around and
> Away you go![2]

The children and I have enjoyed using this poem to reinforce and explore expressing the beat in movement. Chant the poem, with the children joining in as it becomes familiar. Follow the suggested instructions in the fourth and fifth lines, and let the class suggest ways to perform the last two lines. Use class suggestions or invite the children to turn to a partner to plan movements to fit the first three lines.

The poem can also provide the structure for further movement expressing the beat. My children have found this little 'Catch Up' game a fun and challenging way to extend 'Cindy Lee' because each person may use smaller or larger steps or may travel through space by different pathways. Have all the children learn a second chant.

> One, two, three, Partner, can you find me?
> One, two, three, You can't get away from me.

On 'go,' at the end of the poem, one partner can move into space, chanting the words of the first line. She stops on 'me.' The second partner bounces in place while the first moves and then moves to meet his partner, chanting the second line. The object is to meet the partner on 'me,' and then together move and recite 'Cindy Lee' again. Then the second partner may explore space and be 'found' by the first.

I find that there are many jump rope rhymes which may be adapted to provide practice in responding to the beat. Because there is one speech sound on nearly all beats of 'I Like Coffee,' the beat is reinforced. Place two instruments on stands, such as bongos, temple blocks or congas, in the center of the circle. Invite your children to chant with you:

> I like coffee
> I like tea,
> I'd like <u>Joey</u> to
>   play with me.

When the children can chant the rhyme accurately, play the beat on one instrument, calling one of the children to join you at another instrument. When the student is playing accurately with you, repeat the rhyme, but call a new player to replace the first one. Later, you may ask a child to replace you as well.

After the children become skilled at playing with you, offer a new challenge. Extend the rhyme with the chant, 'O-U-T, and that spells out!' You then join the circle, leaving the students to lead the chant and play. He chooses a new leader by filling in a new name to join him on the other instrument. They play together, establishing a steady tempo.

2   Derived from Edith Fowke *Sally Go Round the Sun* New York: Doubleday, 1969.

Help them chant, 'O-U-T, and that spells out!', and the new leader continues the game.

I have found familiar chants such as this one are useful because they do not have to be taught before the exploration of beat begins.

> Pease porridge hot,
> Pease porridge cold,
> Pease porridge in the pot,
> Nine days old.

In subsequent lessons, encourage children to share hand jive games from the playground and camp. This time accompany the ancient rhyme 'Pease Porridge Hot' with a patting pattern that connects the whole class. Have everyone chant, patting both knees as they do so. Then chant, patting your right knee with your left hand, and your right neighbor's left knee with your right hand. That leads the children to chanting and patting the left knee and other neighbor's right knee. Then my children enjoy sequencing these motions, changing each time the rhyme is repeated, or, perhaps, changing at the beginning of each phrase.

Take time to associate the concept of a regular beat with other familiar experiences, such as the pendulum motion of a clock, the quartz clock second hand moving, the drip of a faucet. Listen to several types of music, such as a John Philip Sousa march, the second movement of Vivaldi's *Spring*, from *The Four Seasons*, and Pavane from Ravel's *Mother Goose* Suite. Find the beat in each of these and compare the tempos, timbres and articulations found in each example.

During these activities, ask the children to draw the beat in the air. Comment on the variety of ways they choose to draw it. Then ask them to draw the beat on the board or on large pieces of construction paper as they chant one of their favorite rhymes. Repeat the chant again, retracing their markings to discover that they have a record of the number of beats found in their music.

It is an easy step for children to accept a common symbol for the sound on the beat, which can be compared to the quarter note, | (♩). Give the children many opportunities to draw the beats as a horizontal line as they chant or sing to connect the ikon with the feeling. They can show phrases as well by beginning a new line of beats with each one. Then 'fill' each beat by drawing | on each line. A chart with pictures of untuned instruments with four quarter notes drawn inside each is fun to play as you and then a student direct, moving from square to square.

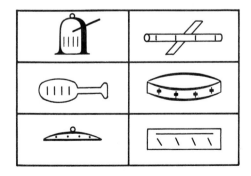

When you assign only one or two players to each square the chart can be used to direct an accompaniment for songs in duple meter.

Additional resources
Frazee with Kreuter *Discovering Orff*, p. 59
  Discussion.
Orff and Keetman *Music for Children*, ed. Hall,
  Vol. 1
  'Trom, Trom, Trom' (p. 69)
  Recite the poem, patting the marching
  beat. Later, the children can fill the rests
  with 'Trom' as others chant the poem.
  Trading parts as soon as the last 'Trom' has
  sounded in an exciting quick reaction
  challenge.

2   *Respond accurately to various tempos in movement, speech, song, and body percussion. Apply the terms 'fast,' 'slow,' 'faster,' and 'slower' to identify tempos and tempo changes.*

Hop Old Squirrel

Ruth Crawford Seeger

Hop old squirrel, eid-le-dum, eid-le-dum, Hop old squirrel, eid-le-dum, dum.

Hop old squirrel, eid-le-dum, eid-le-dum, Hop old squirrel, eid-le-dum dee.

The expressive nature of tempo becomes clearer to our children when they use it to alter materials to tell a story. For instance, this little song about the squirrel can be expanded to create a story about its adventures in the autumn of the year. I like to begin by singing the song to the children as they respond in movement to the lyrics. I change the tempo for each verse, and later ask the children if it was faster or slower than the verse preceding it. Guide the students to choose an untuned instrument to follow the motions for each verse. A second sound, playing on the first beat of each phrase, can signal a change in movement direction. The squirrel can run, stop, climb, peek or chase. You can develop a story about the squirrel, using the instruments the children choose to accompany each verse. Drawings to remind the children of the sequence and illustrating tempo may look like this.

1 Hop, old squirrel   ▪ ▪ ▪ ▪
2 Run, old squirrel   – – – – – –
3 Climb, old squirrel   _ _▬

We can frequently call attention to tempo and its importance in expressing the music for they will always feel the beat in every song, in every lesson.

Additional resource
Johnson *The Magic Forest*
   'Fire Stations' (p. 41)
   'To Market, to Market' (p. 51)

3   Discover and then identify, through speech and song, the quarter note (♩) and rest or silent beat (𝄽).

In and Out is one of my favorite jump rope rhymes for it appeals to all age groups and lends itself to all sorts of rhythm games. This is one of the ways I have used the poem:

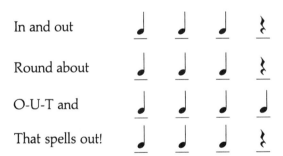

In and out	♩	♩	♩	𝄽
Round about	♩	♩	♩	𝄽
O-U-T and	♩	♩	♩	♩
That spells out!	♩	♩	♩	𝄽

The children learn the chant easily by using the ideas from the poem to find ways to express the beat. Then while half the group chants softly 'Beat, beat, beat,' the other half will recite the poem. They will discover that the first group speaks in places where group 2 does not. The following game illustrates this. With the children form a circle and place a hand drum, a triangle, and a wood block in the center. As you walk inside the circle, point to one person with each beat of the poem. The child speaks the chant and claps when you point to him on his beat of the rhyme. When you point to someone on a silent beat, that person goes to the center of the circle and picks up an instrument. At the end of the rhyme, each player in turn plays the rhythm of the line which precedes her rest. The students in the circle may make soundless gestures in the rests left by the instrumentalists. The last player becomes the new leader.

When the children return to the board, ask one of them to record the beats with horizontal lines as they chant. Then, another person fills the beats with quarter notes or 1 and crosses out the beats which are silent. Call this felt beat a rest, and present the symbol of the quarter rest. My children use either a squiggly line or a 'seven with a hat' to make the symbol.

Consider beginning your sequence of melodic objectives here ('Melody,' 1 and 2). Then continue with 'Rhythm,' 4.

4   *Identify a repeated pattern as an ostinato* ‖: :‖

This poem and the symbol ‖: :‖ is useful because children discover that the rhythm of each line is the same even though the words are different.

> Engine, engine, Number Nine,
> Going down Chicago Line.
> See it sparkle, see it shine,
> Engine, engine, Number Nine.

Your students may know this rhyme. Chant it, and then clap the word rhythms. After you have divided the class into four groups, invite each one to clap one phrase of the poem while listening for phrases which sound alike and those which contrast. They will discover that all four are the same. Identify the repeated pattern as an ostinato. Show your children this ostinato:

‖: ♪ 𝄽 ♩ ♩ :‖
Choo Choo Choo

Then perform it on sand blocks while one group chants the rhyme, and another chants with the ostinato. Ask the class to compose another ostinato to repeat as an introductory section, and a third to end the piece. The poem becomes a story when the tempo increases during first performance of the poem then slows as the poem is repeated and moves into the coda. 'Engine No. Nine' ostinatos may look like this.

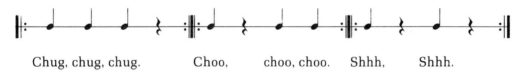

Chug, chug, chug.   Choo,   choo, choo.   Shhh,   Shhh.

Practice reading and using these symbols by performing the following little piece from notation.

5 *Perform, read and write patterns containing quarter notes and rests.*

Now it is time to practice patterns using the quarter note or *ta* with the soundless beat or rest in echo imitation, using a gesture for the rest, such as a wink, a nod of the head, or a wave away from the body. When you use a sound to identify the rest it often becomes a habit that is difficult to repress when silence is needed. If you use rhythm syllables, echo imitation should include aural dictation, echoing your body percussion pattern in the same body percussion and then with syllables.

This is also the time to use notation to record the patterns the children compose to accompany their songs and poems. It is wise in the first grade to use only one or, at the most, two parts to accompany speech and song activities to create a good balance between voices and instruments and to ensure accuracy in playing. Show the children this pattern to accompany their singing of a familiar song, such as 'Yankee Doodle:' When they repeat the song use another four-beat pattern suggested by a student.

Yankee Doodle

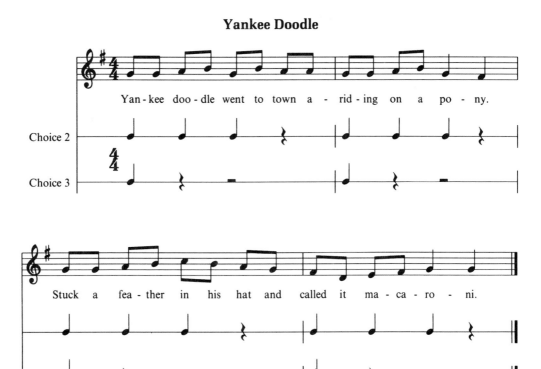

Chant 'Icky Bicky Soda Cracker' with the children until they are comfortable with it. Then introduce the body percussion ostinato, first from movement and then from notation. It will look like this:

99

Icky Bicky

Ask the students to work with a partner to create a new four-beat ostinato to accompany a familiar rhyme or song.

Rhythm dictation should be fun when it is introduced at this level. Your class will enjoy this little game. Place four benches in front of the students, and ask four children to fill them. The benches represent four beats and the children represent the four quarter notes or 'ta's that fill them. You clap a four-beat pattern which may contain a rest and quarter notes. The class then repeats the rhythm and the group has just a few seconds to figure out how they can change to represent the pattern. The children sitting on the rests usually decide to 'sit out' on the floor just behind their bench. The class then claps what it sees, and a 'music writer' places the pattern on the board. After two patterns have been dictated, choose a new group of four and a new music writer.

It is an easy step from this game to individual dictation. I use an idea first introduced in *Discovering Orff*, Grade Two (p. 86). The children are given a worksheet with this grid *without* x's or symbols.

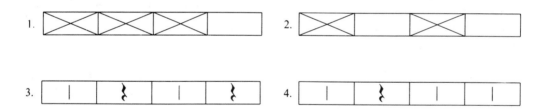

A first step is to fill the boxes for the sounded beats with an X, leaving the boxes for the silent beats empty. Then, in another lesson, place a quarter-note stem or 'ta' and rest in each of the appropriate squares.

Additional resources
Frazee *Orff Handbook for World of Music – 1*
   'How Do you Do?' (p. 19)
Steen *Orff Activities: Grade 1*
   'Sally Go Round The Sun' (p. 17)
   'Struttin' on Through' (p. 18)

Consider exploring rhythm patterns while introducing texture ('Texture,' 1–3).

6 Explore speech materials for inflection, rhythm, and timbre.

Descriptive words in poetry provide material for exploring vocal sounds and instrument timbre while practicing playing sequentially.

> Susie's galoshes
> Make *splishes* and *sploshes*
> And *slooshes* and *sloshes*
> As Susie steps slowly
> Along in the slush.[3]

You will want to put this poem on a board or newsprint. Ask your students to listen for special 's' sounds as you read the poem aloud. You may have to tell them that galoshes are boots, but they will have no trouble identifying the words that describe the sound galoshes make. Assign each underlined word to a group. As you read the poem again, invite them to speak their assigned words, experimenting with its special qualities. Guide them in choosing instruments and techniques of playing them that also illustrate the meaning of the words. The children can join you in reading the poem and the instruments will replace the underlined words.

Reciting just the underlined words in sequence becomes an ostinato. After the instrumentalists have played in lines 2 and 3, they may continue as an ostinato accompaniment and coda. Some children may enjoy creating movement which illustrates the same ostinato – for instance, pretending to walk in the slush while others read the poem and a third group plays the instruments. This poem is in triple meter and provides us with an opportunity to explore the beat and rhythms of threes.

By isolating a word within a spoken phrase the children become aware of its meaning and length of sound. First establish the rhythmic flow of 'Listen to the drums'[4] by asking the children to echo you. Then ask them to echo each other, speaking together at the end.

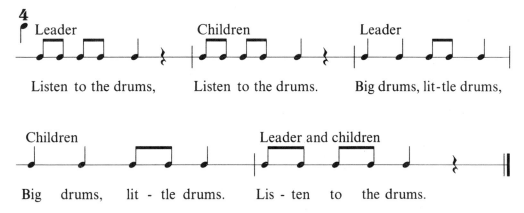

It is easiest to substitute a drum sound for the word 'drum.' The children should also be able to hear the rests which end three of the phrases. Fill these beats with a soundless gesture, such as cupping a hand back of the ear. The words 'big' and 'little' may challenge their thinking, for the obvious, but not most interesting, choice for sound would be more

3   From Rhoda W. Bacmeister *Stories to Begin* New York: E. P. Dutton, 1940.
4   From Carl Orff *Music for Children*, American edition, Vol. 1 (Preschool) (p. 44, no. 79)

drums. Encourage the use of contrasting timbres and dynamics. They may have suggestions for 'Listen to the,' such as a vocal sound or another instrument. Speak the poem first, and then play the poem with all the word rhythm substitutions. The objective is to hear and enjoy the interpretation of the words without losing the rhythmic flow of the poem.

New rhythms will be created when you assign three groups of children to perform each set of words. Do this by pointing to one group of players and then another in an order not found in the poem. My students love the element of surprise that results. Or the groups may be placed in a new order, playing as you direct.

Additional resource
Frazee with Kreuter *Discovering Orff* p. 60
  Discussion.

7   Use speech as a means to transfer words to rhythm and to distinguish beat from rhythm.

Since the beginning of the year our students have identified the beat and have listened for its tempo. Before we begin rhythmic notation using three symbols it is important that the relationship of beat, which we feel, and the rhythm, which we hear and perform, is clear.

The children may know a derivation of this jump rope rhyme. Ask the children to step the beat they feel as you chant it.

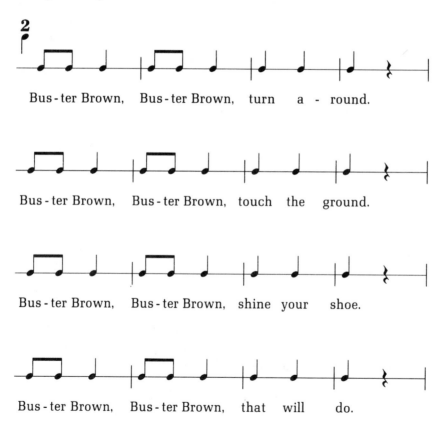

Bus - ter Brown,   Bus - ter Brown,   turn   a - round.

Bus - ter Brown,   Bus - ter Brown,   touch   the   ground.

Bus - ter Brown,   Bus - ter Brown,   shine   your   shoe.

Bus - ter Brown,   Bus - ter Brown,   that   will   do.

Divide the class into partners, one tapping the beat on the shoulder of the other who claps the rhythm of the words. Then trade responsibilities. The child who claps should feel the beat while performing the rhythm. Help them to describe what words last the duration of the beat and what words made two sounds to one beat. Now, facing their partners, have them clap 'Buster' on their partner's hands, clapping their own on 'Brown.' They can use the next four beats to move as the words suggest. They should be able to notate the rhythm of each phrase ending, for only quarter notes ('ta') and rests are used:

Another way to explore new rhythms is to use names of people and things. Ask your children to make a list of all the names of one syllable in their class. Next, have them make another list of two-syllable names which begin with an accent. Arrange eight of the children named in row to make a pattern which is then chanted by the class. Some classmates will accompany them by lightly patting the beat. Words from science and social studies can also be used to create a rhythm theme.

8   *Perform, read and write patterns using* ♩ , ♫ *and* ♩ .

The final step to reading a symbol is an easy one if there has been a variety of experiences preceding it. In this sequence reading began with two symbols, quarter note ('ta') and rest. Now we are ready to add eighth notes, or the division of the beat. 'One, Two, Three' is a rhyme which I have heard sung to several tunes. While you may choose to sing it, its rhythm is most important when meeting this objective. Ask the children to indicate how many phrases they hear as they chant:

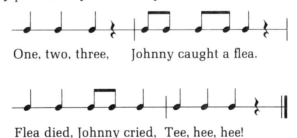

One, two, three,   Johnny caught a flea.

Flea died, Johnny cried, Tee, hee, hee!

Then ask them how many beats they felt in each phrase. Stepping in place, and turning for each phrase may help them find the answer quickly. Invite four children to stand before the class, each holding a large, colorful sheet of construction paper to represent the beat. Guide the children to find ways to represent the sounds of each phrase. For instance, they may choose to hide the fourth sheet for the first phrase. Write the conventional notation for this phrase on the board, for this should be review for them. Choose four more children to illustrate the second phrase. The problem now is to illustrate two sounds on one beat. The easiest solution is to divide the paper into two strips to represent two sounds on one beat. After the children have worked this out, show them notation ⊓ , with two stems beamed together. If this is confusing to some, return to the boxes, placing two Xs in one box.

Solving the problem of notating the last two phrases will be easy. Be sure to read the whole poem from the construction sheets and from notation.

The reading skills of your students will be reinforced when they use notation to compose and remember accompaniment patterns. Ask the children to create a new pattern of four beats not found in the poem. Use it as an ostinato to accompany the chant in body percussion or on instruments. Then write several patterns, each time encouraging the children to listen to the contrast between the rhythms of the ostinato and the rhythm of the poem. Your students will gain confidence in reading when they use the skill to learn new material and when you ask them to notate ostinatos or their rhythmic ideas in the lessons ahead.

In another lesson, lead the children in clapping four beats lightly, moving from left to right, moving at a moderately slow tempo. Four boxes on the board will help them visualize this. Ask them to put a rest on one beat, and then perform the new pattern. Return to four claps. Then ask them to put eighth notes ('ti ti') or two sounds in one box. Again, ask them to perform their patterns. When the children appear confident, hear individual improvisations, each clapped in order to create little pieces. This exercise can prepare a contrasting section for song settings.

Additional resources
Boshkoff *Ring Around, Sing Around*
  'Ring Around the Rosie' (p. 3)
Frazee *Orff Handbook for World of Music – 1*
  'Gogo' (p. 17)
  Teach BX ♩ as ₹.
Steen *Orff Activities, Grade 1*
  'Rain, Rain' (p. 19)

> You may wish to delay this final goal until late in the year as a preparation for the evaluation of rhythmic skills.

9   *Write four-beat patterns from dictation, using* ♩ , ♫ , *and* ₹ .

Written dictation is most successful when children have had many experiences leading up to this step. Our preparation begins with early echo imitation exercises which require a quick response that involves physical reaction rather than analysis. It is an important first step, because our memory often depends on our physical recall. A second step involves verbal analysis. When we ask children to use a system of rhythm syllables we are training their ability also to analyze what they hear. The value in this step is that we trade sound with sound, duration with duration. It gives the student time to hear twice, first the original source and then a translation of it into syllables. The syllables categorize the sounds into specific meanings in common with patterns from other experiences. Drawing our impressions of relative length of sounds is also helpful, especially when it happens at the same time it is heard. The next step is reading stick and conventional rhythmic notation. (The half note has not yet been introduced, making only the stems of notes relevant to rhythm reading.) Practice in reading, using physical and aural responses, also precedes dictation. Children need opportunities to write rhythms thoughtfully, composing or recalling without pressures of time. Just drawing symbols for many children is a time-consuming affair! Improvising in ways suggested in this chapter is meant to help children visualize as well as hear their early efforts at making their own music. Each child responds to several of these techniques of learning, but not necessarily to all of them.

Individual written dictation is a complex task for young children, and should be addressed only when you are sure that most of your students will feel successful doing it. There are several formats suggested here, each testing different aspects of analysis. For each example you clap the correct pattern which they echo clap before they record their answers. In the first example you perform one pattern and they select one of two notations. This eliminates the need to draw symbols.

The second example saves time for the student because she will draw only one or two symbols.

The third example helps the children remember the relative value of rhythm to beat by using boxes as they appeared in previous lessons.

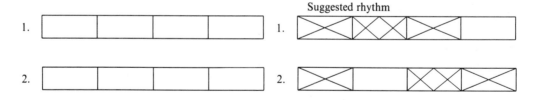

Either Xs or symbols may be placed in the boxes, illustrating a pattern you perform, they echo, and you perform once more. This final example requires the most from students, for they must remember the sound you perform, the symbol, and be able to draw it before they forget it!

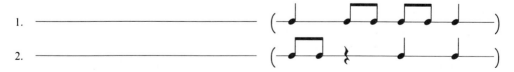

Melody

1   Extend the awareness of pitch by exploring expressive speech.

It may seem indirect to begin children's vocal training and melodic awareness with speech. Yet all children speak, though some children do not feel comfortable singing with a group. A second reason for beginning with speech is that our singing habits are influenced by our speech habits. Children who sing low or have a limited range often speak in the same manner. Finally, we want to build on a process of pitch awareness which we began in kindergarten.

Many Mother Goose rhymes lend themselves to speech exploration. Adding motions as the children sit or stand in place dramatizes the words and illustrates the range and quality of the voice. 'Little Boy Blue' is a very ordinary rhyme until it is acted out. I like to begin by examining each line for possible ways of expression.

> Little Boy Blue, come blow your horn! (*Perhaps the horn was used to sound an alarm when the shepherd was in trouble.*)
> The sheep in the meadow, the cows in the corn. (*Imagine that Boy Blue has lost his flock. The cows may become very sick if they eat too much corn.*)
> Where is the boy who looks after the sheep? (*Who would be looking for Boy Blue? How do they feel about him? Will he lose his job?*)
> He's under the haystack, fast asleep! (*His mother may feel one way when she finds him, but his employer may feel another way, and his best friend yet another.*)

After the children have set the scene and the characters, choose a soloist to act and say each line. Call attention to the various ways the children use their voices to express the words, referring to range (higher and lower), dynamics (softer and louder) and articulation (smooth, sharp, accented, short).

Introduce the words in parentheses as you discuss interpretations. After several sets of children have explored the possibilities, divide the class into four groups, one for each line. Encourage them to use gestures to illustrate their lines. One child may enjoy being Boy Blue, who snores for a coda to this little drama.

Your objective is to broaden your children's speaking range as well as singing range. These poems will help by encouraging high and low contrasts.

> Down goes the lamb,
> Up goes the lark,
> Run to bed, children,
> Before it gets dark!
>
> The wind blew low,
> The wind blew high,
> The wind touched everything
> As it passed by.

Imagine that we are to recite one of these poems to someone who does not understand our language. We can repeat words or make them sound longer, or say them in any way that helps us express the meaning. This time gestures can't be used. I usually write the words on the board, and then move them about to picture the children's suggestions. Here are two interpretations of these poems, but help the children to develop their own.

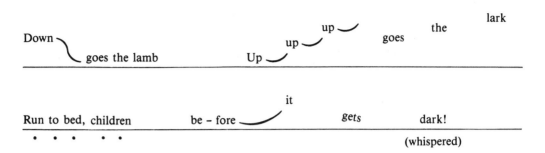

Sometimes my children have recorded their performances. Then I show the score to another class at their level and ask them to 'read' it. Sometimes we even compare tapes, not to find out who is best, but to marvel at how many ways the children can express the same words.

2   Identify melodic contours as moving upward, downward, or repeating pitches.

Describing melody as moving upward or downward is an acquired concept for, in fact, differences of pitch are differences in the speed of vibrations in air. Yet we conventionally describe relative pitches as higher and lower.

Throughout the year find and add to your collection of materials and activities stories and life situations which the children can describe in vocal sounds. Create stories about elevators, creatures that leave the ground, or about adventures on mountains, all of which reinforce the concept that our voices make melodies that move up and down.

Ask one child to assist you, forming a mountain by raising her clasped hands to chin height, keeping her shoulders relaxed. As you sing 'Yoo Hoo' to the class, trace the melodic motion up and down her arms. Ask the children how your actions related to your song. One child can then turn to another and, as you repeat the song, can follow the melody on the arms of the other who forms the mountain. Help them discover that the melody moves up in short durations, and moves down in longer durations. The student who formed the mountain may sing, 'Yoo, hoo,' and the other person echo. All join to sing the last phrase.

107

The barred instruments illustrate melodic motion. When you explored timbres you no doubt played glissandos which the children described as moving up or down. Prepare two alto xylophones to hold only d, e, f♯, g and a. Place them against a chair or box so that the left end boards are on the floor and the right end boards are in the air. Invite students to demonstrate how one can go 'up the hill' and 'down the hill.' Direct the first child to play the alto xylophone when we reach the top of the hill, and the second to play when we reach the bottom. Prepare two glockenspiels with only a and f♯ bars. Ask the children to identify which bar is high, which is low. Compare this sound with the calls in the song, and invite a child to play the mountain echo. Do not complicate the focus of this lesson with extended preparation of the pedal tone on bass metallophone, or insist on a marked tempo that restricts the playing ability of the instrumentalists. Focus primarily on guiding the children to sing and hear the relationships between their voices and the instrumental responses.

Yoo Hoo

adapted by AS

108

The children can explore melodic contour by mapping the shapes of familiar songs. Choose songs for this activity that move with direction that is easy to define. Here are two examples.

'All the Ducklings' is a melody which repeats pitches as well as moving up and down. Draw a picture of the melody in movement first, then on paper or the board. Your observations of their ability to draw the melody in detail will help you decide if some students are ready to add the challenge of playing each phrase on barred instruments. The setting for this song is easy, for the xylophone plays high, low, high, and the bass may play a tremolo, imitating water, or on the first beats of each measure. Sing with an introduction played by a student, following by the song and setting, followed by instruments playing the melody unaccompanied. Return to the song with the instrumental setting and the coda.

All the Ducklings

German folk song/arr. AS

See the lit - tle duck - lings swim-ming here and there.

(Swim, lit - tle duck-lings swim . . .)

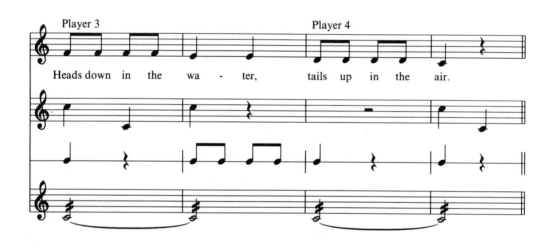

Heads down in the wa - ter, tails up in the air.

Introduction (optional)

CODA

gliss.

Additional resources
Boshkoff *All Around the Buttercup*
   'The Snail' (p. 6)
Boshkoff *Ring Around, Sing Around*
   'See Saw' (p. 1)

110

Frazee, *Orff Handbook for World of Music — 1*
  'Hickory, Dickory, Dock' (p. 7)
Steen *Orff Activities, Grade K*
  'Humpty Dumpty' (p. 2)

> Consider finishing the melodic sequence while applying and practicing the remainder of the 'Rhythm' sequence (3–9).

3   Identify two pitches in chants as higher and lower, then sol and mi, with gestures, vocally, and on instruments.

First we guided our students to explore the range and expressive qualities of their voices. Next, they explored shapes that melodies formed. Now they are ready to hear and compare definite pitches. It is easy to become absorbed in these little songs with limited pitches, for they are important to developing vocal accuracy and to attaining music reading skills. However, balance these little songs by singing rote songs with wider ranges and longer phrases, and help the children discover the motives they have studied in the first-grade sequence.

  1   Wide to narrow intervals.

I like to anticipate our pitch-matching sequence of activities by exploring wide intervals which become gradually narrow. Ask your students to clasp their hands and raise them above their heads, taking in breath as they move. Then raise their hands and sing a pitch as high as they imagine their hands to be. Then sing the pitch that is as low as the sound they imagine when their hands are at their sides. To encourage internalized pitch, ask them to think a high and a low sound as they move up, then down. Then ask each child to move and sing again. As they listen to themselves compare the sound produced with the one imagined. They will be amused when you walk among them and match their pitches. Sing octave c's for them, moving your hands as well, before inviting them to echo you, calling one high and the other low. Sing intervals, each one smaller than the preceding one, bringing hands closer together as well.

  Later, sing *sol–mi* on a neutral syllable, asking them to show this relationship with their hands before they echo you. After they have identified wide leaps and then smaller ones, play a game of guessing which one you are singing or playing. They can respond with their hand gestures. Now it should be easy for them to find the octave and minor third intervals in the song 'Ding Dong Bell'. Continue to use hand gestures as they sing and add instrument parts. Each part was constructed to continue the comparisons of high and low. Use the untuned parts to challenge secure rhythm readers.

  Draw pictures of several common melodic motives and ask the children to select the best representations of 'Ding, Dong, Bell.'

(Ikons of melody fragments)

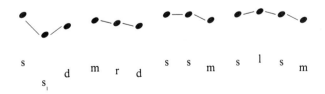

111

Ding Dong Bell

Words: Mother Goose
Music: AS

2   Sol–mi

The next step is to identify a narrow interval as high to low or low to high. The 'Flower Song' was written for this purpose. Prepare the lesson with echo singing and have your class gesture the shapes as well. Then when you sing this song on a neutral syllable they should be able to give you a gesture of appropriate distance. Make a list of flowers (pictures will help) then practice chanting them in turn. When they can recite smoothly, challenge them to sing the flower names, first by groups of students and then by soloists. Return to the song, adding the words, then the accompaniment. Bridge the return of the song by having solo singing of the flower names.

Flower Song

Words: Mother Goose
Melody: AS

Now label the high sound as *sol* and the low as *mi*. Draw the rhythm of the song, and place the beginning letter of each syllable below it. Read it by singing:

s m m s s m m

Aunt Dinah

Words: Shotwell
Melody: AS

'Aunt Dinah' is an attention-getting tension reliever, that provides lots of practice on *sol–mi*. Make a little game of identifying speaking voices and singing voices. Ask your children to echo you only if you sing. As you give each phrase, alternate between singing as written and speaking the phrase. The children will enjoy making a movement game to fit the song. After the song is learned and enjoyed, ask the children to sing the most common melodic motive in syllables (*m s s m*).

Additional resources

Boshkoff *All Around the Buttercup*
   'Star Light' (p. 7)
Boshkoff *Ring Around, Sing Around*
   'See Saw' (p. 1)
Steen Orff Activities Grade 1
   'Star Light' (p. 11)

4 *Identify three pitches in chants as* sol, mi, *and* la, *with gestures, vocally and on instruments.*

Begin the lesson with a review of the singing game, 'Buster Brown.' Perhaps the class can guess what song you have in mind by reading the rhythm.

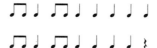

After they have enjoyed playing the game, ask them where to place the *s–m* syllables below the rhythmic notation. They will, of course, discover the need for *la*.

Take turns leading another game. You will sing all syllables on 'loo'. If they think it is *sol*, place their hands on their chins; if it is *mi*, on their waists; if it is *la*, on their heads. Take turns leading the game. If you wish to raise the challenge level, ask them to point to you if you sing anything other than *sol*, *mi*, and *la*.

Most *sol–mi* songs also contain *la*. This will become clear to your class as they review, Johnny Caught a Flea (*s–l–s*) (p. 102), 'Oliver Twist (p. 85), 'Bluebird' (*s–m–s–m–s l–s–m*) (p. 72), 'Bobby Shaftoe' (p. 89), and 'Wee Willie Winkie' (*s–l–s–m*) (p. 61). All can be reviewed or taught to illustrate typical patterns.

After a new pitch has been introduced I like to use it in many combinations. Improvisation vocally and on the instruments also leads the children to internalize the new pitch in many patterns. The melody below was composed to practice the interval of *mi* to *la* and to lead to improvisation. Begin preparation for the lesson with aural dictation, singing in syllables as you point to the letters. I like to use a ladder which I fill in as pitches are introduced. Then hold an alto xylophone up, with only c', d' and a pitches on it. The children now sing the notes you play in syllables.

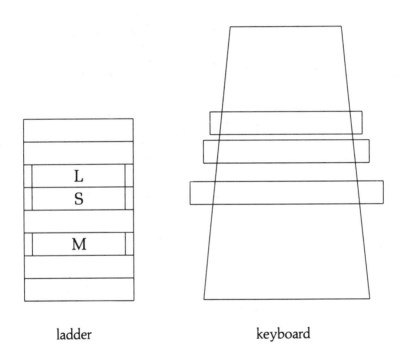

ladder   keyboard

Then, when you sing the first phrase of the song on 'loo' it should be possible for the children to respond in syllables. The first verse accompaniment gives you an opportunity to review up and down, while the second can be taught by reading rhythmic ostinatos.

The children can create contrasting melodies by playing the rhythm of each phrase on the instruments. Two players on glockenspiels can make snow melodies on *s–m–l* bars, and two more can make rain melodies on soprano xylophones.

Weather

adapted by AS

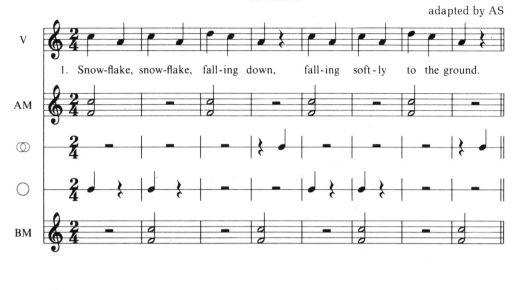

1. Snow-flake, snow-flake, fall-ing down, fall-ing soft-ly to the ground.

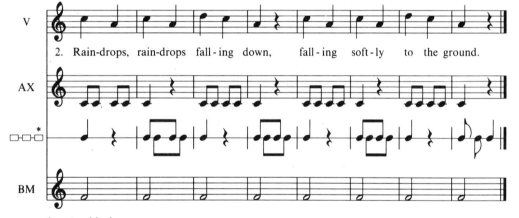

2. Rain-drops, rain-drops fall-ing down, fall-ing soft-ly to the ground.

*use top blocks

Additional resources

Boshkoff *All Around the Buttercup*
   'Bounce High' (p. 8)
   'The Mill Wheel' (p. 10)
   'The Clocks' (p. 17)
Frazee *Orff Handbook for World of Music – K*
   'Rain Dance' (p. 9)
   Mi may be considered the tonal center.
Ladendecker *Holidays and Holy Days* Vol. 1
   'Witch, Witch' (p. 3)
   Game with solos.
Orff *Music for Children*, American edn., Vol. 1
   'Wee Willie Winkie' (p. 4)
Orff and Keetman *Music for Children*, ed. Hall
  and Walter, Vol. 1
   'Bell Horses' (p. 7)

5 *Sing chants and pentatonic songs with simple ostinato accompaniments.*

There are many rhymes and chants in compound meter in the English and American tradition. There are also melodies our children enjoy singing which we do not wish to analyze or put into notation. By introducing them at this level we prepare our students for more conscious learning in second and third grade. These settings are composed to reinforce understandings and skills our first graders are developing. A possible lesson focus is discussed for each song which also contains musical elements that anticipate learning that follows. The orchestration parts should be taught through body percussion or movement before actually playing them on the instruments.

'Charlie Over the Ocean' is a favorite game because of the chase at the end. It's so much fun the leader who anticipates being chased forgets he is singing a solo, my objective for teaching the song. The children sit in a circle, accompanied by finger cymbals and hand drum players in the center. Write the two instrument parts on cards to remind the players. They will play for two games and then choose others to take their places. The leader sings as he walks around the outside of the circle and the group responds. When he sings 'Can't catch me!' he taps the nearest person in the circle who then chases the leader back to the empty position. If the leader is caught, he must circle again. You may change the key to match the range each leader can sing in most successfully.

Charlie Over The Ocean

118

First graders often study signs of spring and the following song invites them to share their observations with the class. Teach the song with the 'hole' filled with the beats patted on knees. Then tell the children that they are to fill the phrase with their own ideas. They practice this by imagining how they will sing it and then they join you in singing the other phrases. I always caution them to have several signs of spring in mind, though it is fine to have the same sign in several vocal responses.

'Santa Maloney' is an old English singing game that moves at a moderate pace which most children can match as they walk in a circle. Ask the children to decide what movement should mark the last phrase, 'As we go round about.' One child walks around the inside of the circle, in the opposite direction. She moves to the music, and, led by the teacher, the children sing words that describe her actions. Return to 'Here we go Santa Maloney,' and she picks someone to replace her.

An adaptation of the game will review quarter note–rest patterns, using the boxes for notation.

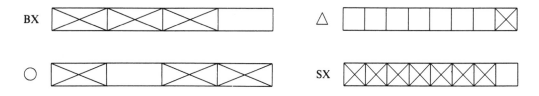

Place the instruments in the circle, with children facing the center. The class sings and walks around the circle, stopping to 'go 'round about' in self space. If a child is standing in front of an instrument, he picks up the mallets during the last phrase and prepares to play. You may play the melody on recorder, or the class can sing the melody on 'loo' to their accompaniment. The players return their instruments to the edge of the circle and the game repeats.

Santa Maloney

England

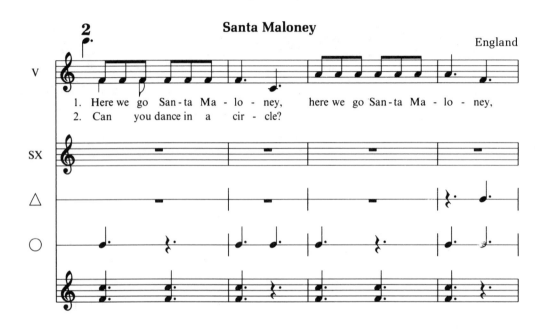

1. Here we go San-ta Ma - lo - ney, here we go San-ta Ma - lo - ney,
2. Can you dance in a cir - cle?

here we go San-ta Ma - lo - ney, as we go 'round a - bout.

Over in the Meadow

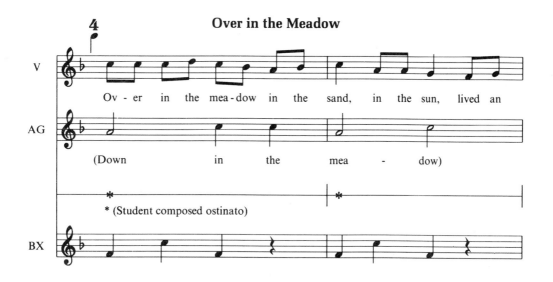

V: Ov - er in the mea - dow in the sand, in the sun, lived an

AG: (Down in the mea - dow)

* (Student composed ostinato)

V: old mo - ther tur - tle and her lit - tle tur - tle one.

V: 'Dig,' said the mo - ther, 'I dig,' said the one, So they

sang and were glad in the sand in the sun.

There are several picture story books that illustrate 'Over In the Meadow.' Our school's favorite is edited by John Langstaff.[5] My children have enjoyed composing ostinatos for unpitched instruments to describe the setting and the animals featured in each verse. The bass xylophone part can be played by a second person on alternate verses. If you have a bass and alto metallophone, you may choose to use a level bordun on alternate verses. The alto glockenspiel and soprano xylophone parts may trade with pitched ostinatos created by the children, played on *sol* or c bars. Short improvisations on *sol*, *mi*, and *la* will make effective introductions to some of the verses. This project will review notation in a practical and meaningful way. Consider recording the end result so your students can hear their creation from the point of view of an audience.

Texture

1   Perform patterns over the beat using a body percussion sound or an instrument, while speaking or singing.

It has been a goal of Orff teachers to train their students to perform more than one musical task at a time. When you sing or speak and accompany yourself you are totally involved in making music.

This involvement is not possible for younger students until they are able to feel the underlying beat as they perform. Begin by having the students pat their knees while you recite:

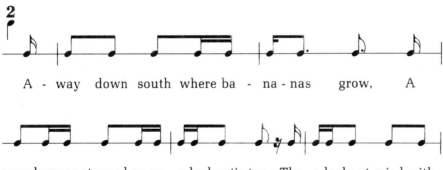

A - way down south where ba - na - nas grow, A

grasshopper stepped on an e-lephant's toe. The e-lephant cried with

5   John Langstaff with pictures by Feodor Rojankovsky. New York: Harcourt, Brace Jovanovich, 1957 and 1985.

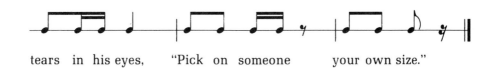

tears in his eyes, "Pick on someone your own size."

Ask them to listen, joining you on the last phrase. Add lines, moving backwards, until the poem is learned. Next, alternate the patted beat with a clap, and chant the poem. For this last challenge you need to stand or sit in a circle. Pat your knees, clap your hands, pat your knees, but then clap the hands of both neighbors. It makes a lively accompaniment for the clap with neighbors is reinforcing for those who move with less conviction.

The lyrics of an old hymn tune set the mood for feeling the beat in a gentle rock of three beats. Ask the children to pat one knee, then the other, then clap lightly. Read the words from the board or chart, pointing where the beats fall.

Now the day is ov-er, Night is draw-ing nigh. Sha-dows of the even-ing Steal a-cross the sky.

2. Now the darkness gathers,
   Stars begin to peep.
   Birds and beasts and flowers
   Soon will be asleep.

Divide the group in four and assign one measure of accompaniment to each group while all perform the poem. When this is secure, assign pats to hand drums and triangles with finger cymbals to the claps. When you line up all four measures the children will be able to watch the beats pass as they chant and direct with their body percussion pattern.

2   Perform accompaniments on barred instruments, using the tonic note and chord, level and broken borduns.

3   Learn these accompaniments by preparing with body percussion, speech, and reading notation.

These goals may be integrated with rhythm and melody goals, as you apply rhythmic reading skills while accompanying songs and chants.

Tonic and bordun accompaniments are basic to the texture of Orff instrumental settings.

Because your students will be using them throughout their elementary music program it is well to take time to identify and practice playing these accompaniments.

Sally Go Round

AS derivation

'Sally Go Round' has stirred visions of space travel for my students. Imagining travel in the sky and beginning the song on *sol* has helped them sing with a light quality. It also provides an opportunity to identify *sol* and *la*. Prepare the bass metallophone for this tonic orchestration by patting 'one, two, three, (wink!)' on one knee. Review the children's awareness of high and low by hiding the instruments before you play the alto and soprano metallophone parts. The one who names the timbre correctly gets to play. The glockenspiels play a glissando, prepared by hand motions that go up, down, up, while the finger cymbal plays on the name. The ending is nearly the highest sound we have on Orff instruments.

My children have enjoyed a game Lynn Johnson describes in *The Magic Forest*. The children sit scattered throughout the room. One (or several) person carries a wand, and wanders through the 'sky.' On the final rest, she lightly taps the nearest person who then takes the wand. The first person places her hand on the new leader's shoulder, becoming part of the satellite. Soon all are roaming through space!

The chord bordun, first and fifth degrees of the scale, is the basic drone sound characteristic of Orff settings. It is also the easiest accompaniment for young children to play. Use speech ostinatos to teach the setting for 'Pat-a-cake.' The parts are presented here in the way I would introduce them before transferring them to the instruments. (The students do not see the notation.) You may use one or more to accompany the song.

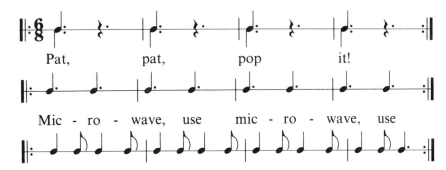

Bake a cake and bake it fast, oh, bake a cake and bake it fast.

Pat-a-Cake

Words: Mother Goose
Melody: AS

125

A contrasting section is instantly cooked up by just speaking the ostinatos!

The level bordun interests first graders because they can see as well as hear it move. 'Juan Pirulero,' a Spanish singing game, can be accompanied by one player, moving the chord up to another octave on the same instrument. The part can also be shared by two players at the same instrument or between the bass and alto xylophones, both playing in the lower octave. Prepare these parts from body percussion. Pat and clap the metric accents for the bordun, so that your children can see the levels changing. As you learn the song, clap the beginning of each phrase, drawing the hand out until the next phrase begins. This prepares the glockenspiel part. The temple block part may be prepared by patting the rhythm on the knees. Simplify this part or eliminate it if it interferes with the enjoyment of the song.

There is a little game that can extend the enjoyment of this song as well, as the children experience another song in triple meter. Form groups of four or five children. Each group decides quickly what kind of work they will imitate for just eight metric beats. Each group can demonstrate as B sections, returning each time to the song. Perhaps you can guess what work each group pantomimed.

Juan Pirulero

New Mexico

The most demanding bordun for first graders is the broken chord, particularly if it has an ostinato rhythm. In 'Who Built the Ark?' the bordun just rocks from left to right. Practice patting and then walking in place, stopping on the last 'ark.' A cluster of notes begins each phrase. Practice the wood block part from notation. Ask the children to write a four-beat rhythm which repeats once to begin and end the song.

Who Built The Ark?

4   *Perform a rhythmic ostinato as accompaniment to a theme.*

Throughout the year the emphasis in orchestration has been placed on beat/rest patterns, for this parallels the skill level of most first graders. Some settings have included four-beat rhythms with eighth notes, always for untuned instruments, to be played by those of your students who are ready for the challenge. By the end of the year most students are ready to speak and perform an ostinato at the same time. Here are two examples which you may employ to practice this skill and then use for evaluation purposes.

Chant the poem 'Dr. Foster,' and, with the children, decide what dynamics should be used. Then practice the ostinato for body percussion. Draw attention to the eighth notes which are clapped, and quarter notes which are patted. To test their stability carry on a conversation with them as they practice, expecting replies, of course. If needed, use the speech ostinato to reinforce their performance. Then chant the poem to its accompaniment.

Doctor Foster

The poem contains durations the children are not ready to learn, yet they experience them in speech. Some of your more dexterous students may wish to play the poem on temple blocks or bongo, while others perform the ostinato on hand drums and triangle.

Near the end of the year your children will be reading rhythmic notation quite easily. Practice the little rhythm piece, reading from notation. Half the class can clap the top line, while the others pat the ostinato beneath. Be sure to switch parts. It may be orchestrated, using the suggestions in the score or those of your students.

Rhythms

Timbre

Place this objective early in the year, perhaps after 'Skill in Group Instruction,' 3.

1   Learn the names of classroom instruments and the techniques of playing each.

At the beginning of the year, make a point of introducing each instrument and the requisite playing technique. Let the children imitate you and then try other ways of producing sound. Sometimes I will use the instruments of one family, such as drums, for one block of lessons, making sure that each child gets a chance to play. Then another family of instruments will be introduced.

Some instruments are challenging to play well. Consider playing hand drums with soft mallets until the children's coordination is more mature. If the wood block is difficult to play, place it on a music stand and use two glockenspiel mallets. Finger cymbals may be played by suspending one and using the other as a mallet. The goal is to find ways to help the children play with good control.

The children will learn to recognize specific timbres from quick-reaction games. Place a variety of untuned instruments before the class, and hide a group of the same instruments. (I put my collection on the bench behind my upright piano so I can see the children and play.) You will play a pattern on one of the instruments and they will raise their hands when they recognize the sound. Call the name of one person who then picks up the instrument and joins you. If he guesses wrong, he may pick another person to play.

2   Identify aurally the orchestral instruments according to family, range, and name.

This objective reminds me to review the music listening experiences my children have had during the year. Very often assembly programs, field trips, and listening lessons have exposed the children to music beyond the sounds of the classroom. If not, you may wish to take time to invite guest players to demonstrate for your students. There are also excellent filmstrips and pictures accompanying recordings to aid you in meeting this goal.

Form

1   Identify repeated rhythmic and melodic motives and phrases in speech and song.

Words give children the first clues to identifying alike and different patterns in music. However, careful listening often leads us to discover surprises. Consider two short examples the children learned earlier in the year. First, chant:

> Engine, engine, Number Nine
> Going down Chicago Line.
> See it sparkle, see it shine,
> Engine, engine, Number Nine.

Ask the children to chant the lines that are the same (1 and 4). You will say the remaining ones. Next have them clap the word rhythms and say your lines. When one group claps lines one and four which are alike, and the other group claps lines two and three, they will discover that the rhythm is the same in all four lines (aaaa). They are on their way to becoming good music detectives.

Now sing 'Bobbie Shaftoe' from page 89. Ask your children to guess which of the four lines are alike. Give them a little time to review the song in their minds. Then ask four children to each sing one phrase of song on 'loo.' Have them hold up as many fingers as there are phrases alike. (There are four (aaab).) For a challenge, review 'Hop Old

Squirrel,' page 96. It is easy to identify four 'Hop old squirrel' phrases, but the 'eedle drum, eedle dum's' will require some very careful investigation (abac-abac). Continue to play little detective games each time the children learn new songs. It not only helps them learn more quickly, but, hopefully, they listen with greater understanding.

Your children now have some models on which they can base an improvisation. Tell the class you have an idea you would like them to echo twice. Clap a four-beat pattern, listen to their echoes, and add a new pattern to end it. When the class repeats the next pattern, invite another child to end with a new four-beat pattern. The next step is to use student ideas to begin and end the theme.

2   *Identify sections as same or different (i.e. AA or AB).*

We return to a song learned early in the year to explore AB form. Sing 'Clap, Clap, Clap Your Hands,' (page 84) and ask the children to accompany the singing with their own body percussion ostinatos. Now they can share their ideas with a partner, making sure the hand jive supports good singing. Then play the new melody on a recorder or barred instrument, and ask them to listen for the last 'Clap your hands together.' Their next task is to listen to compare this music with the song they sing, joining with you on the cadence.

Practice both bordun parts to illustrate sections. The soprano xylophone part plays on 'clap,' while the glockenspiel announces each four-beat motive. The tambourine outlines the phrases, and is the only part that plays in both sections. The partners remaining will perform their hand jives as they sing. The singing partners now have a problem to solve, that of showing two sections with their movement. It can be as simple as swinging in place for the second section. Be sure all are together for the ending.

This song parallels other songs found in music over several centuries in AB form, or simple binary form. If your third or fourth graders have played the little march from Volume 1 of *Music for Children*, (adpt. Murray, p. 95) the first graders will find their dance fits the music. Bach used this form for the marches found in *Notebook for Anna Magdalena Bach*. The March in G major and March in E major are especially clear examples. The 'Horn Pipe' marked 'Allegro Vivace,' from Handel's *Water Music* is another good example of this form.

Clap, Clap, Clap Your Hands

Clap, clap, clap your hands, clap your hands to - ge - ther.

Take time at the end of the year to check your goals for first grade. Check off those you have accomplished and make a note of those which you want to pick up in second grade. It is particularly important to assess your students' rhythm and melody skills. You will want to know both the level of their performance skills in singing, movement and playing, as well as their ability to use rhythm and tonal syllables and rhythmic notation.

These objectives represent a full year of growing. Your students have begun to read and write music, just as they have begun to read and write in the classroom. They have communicated their own ideas through movement, story telling and improvisation. They have begun to be an ensemble of musicians by sharing the responsibilities for melodies and accompaniments. This music has become their music and hopefully they are excited about how much they know.

5 · Second Grade

Many children who begin second grade appear to be very mature compared to their first grade classmates. They know what is expected of them when learning in a group and they feel comfortable moving from one activity to another. They remember more complex instructions, enabling them to work on tasks in groups or independently. Rhythm symbols, while still simple and of limited number, are easily understood. Yet it is important to maintain their enthusiasm for reading skills by introducing only as many new symbols as they can assimilate while maintaining their existing vocabulary. Because second graders have finer control of gross and small motor skills they enjoy the challenge of instrument playing. Consequently, the more they are directly involved in making music the better will they learn about music.

During this year lessons will be planned to help the children become conscious of pitch relationships, both aurally through solfege and in staff notation. Practice in rhythm skills should be kept simple the better to concentrate on melodic literacy. As more children become accurate singers ensemble singing will become a rewarding activity that also builds a spirit of community. Two-part singing may be introduced through melodic ostinato accompaniments, and later, two-part canon.

Music depends on listening skills in order to be understood. You will want to guide your children to make a habit of listening to each other and themselves. Listen for accuracy of performing rhythmically on the beat and for singing tunefully together. The use of ostinato is exciting when shadings of loud and soft are applied. Help them to use dynamics, timbres and articulations to draw out their interpretations and to use their awareness of phrase structure to keep the ensemble together. Children find it easy to be critical, so center discussions on the review and evaluation of the music's interpretation rather than on behavior. This helps children establish their own, rather than your, standard of expectation for individual and group musical performance.

Goals

We begin with a review of the rhythm symbols introduced in first grade. From this work the beat will be extended rather than divided. Then it is an easy step to explain 2/4 meter. Practice performing rhythms from imitation and with notation following as you prepare accompaniments for the songs which are used to present melodic concepts. The children can use rhythmic notation to conserve their own introductions, codas and contrasting sections for pentatonic songs that prepare for pitch notation which follows.

Experiences in movement, playing the barred instruments and opportunities to draw melodic contours all help prepare children for melodic notation. From a review of chants on two notes in the first grade it is now an easy step to add *la*, then *do*, and fill in *re*. The process may go quickly if the children have been singing patterns with syllables since first grade. After much practice in F, you may review the pentatonic scale in C, and then in G. The instruments are very helpful tools in explaining transposition to children.

In the second half of the year the children are introduced to 4/4 meter and the whole note. This is an easy step, allowing us to give more attention to rhythm analysis skills. Your children can now be expected to remember and perform 4- and 8-beat patterns in activities and song settings. After many opportunities to read and perform rhythms, we can test their understanding through dictation and composition activities. Their understanding of melody can be evaluated by using the same process. Each time a new concept is introduced what children already know is temporarily challenged by their new learning. When we give careful attention to opportunities to analyze and apply new concepts the children can make these transitions smoothly, demonstrating confident musical independence for their skill level.

Also in the second half of the year I like to introduce experiences and materials that preview the children's third grade instruction. I use 3/4 and 6/8 meter materials for objectives other than rhythmic notation and writing, drawing their listening awareness to groups of three as well as two. While reading and writing of melodic motives will be limited to the octave *do* to *do*, I use *la* pentatonic songs and songs of a wider range to encourage and expand the children's vocal range, and to give them an awareness of accuracy in rhythm and melody and a sensitivity to interpretation or expressiveness.

Once again our objectives are organized according to the elements of music. As my class becomes able to use more complex materials, the integration of those elements of music becomes more obvious and sometimes more troublesome to both me and my students. When I consider my lesson objectives in relationship to curriculum objectives, I want to be aware of three things. First, I want to keep my lesson objectives clear. Second, I am aware that because music is all elements at once, my curriculum objectives often include what I want students to learn consciously and what I want them to experience as preparation. Consequently, and third, I should integrate objectives when it can be done effectively, and move from one element objective to another to take advantage of the children's abilities and interests, to address program issues, or to take better advantage of the materials chosen. My objectives list then becomes an invaluable check list that helps me record what has been covered and to what degree my children may be held accountable.

Second Grade Objectives

Rhythm

1 Perform, then read and write, a duration twice the length of one beat, ♩♩ = ♩, using the tie.

2 Identify and conduct in 2/4 meter, observing the down beat as beat one and the metric accent.

3 Identify 2/4 meter in notation by placing bar lines in notation of songs and rhythms.

4 Perform, read, and write ♩ ♫ and ♩ _ in 2/4 songs, rhythms and instrumental pieces.

> Consider moving to 'Melody,' 1–5, combining those objectives with a continued application of the known durations ('Rhythm,' 4, 5). Then, continue with the rhythm objectives (6–10).

5   Improvise and compose pieces using the known durations.

6   Write four-beat patterns from dictation, using the known durations, ♩ ♩ ♩ — .

7   Perform rhythms while walking the beat, and then while walking and singing.

8   Perform, then read and write, rhythms using the whole note as ♩ ♩ — o .

9   Identify 4/4 meter by placing bar lines in rhythms and melodies.

10   Perform, read, and write o and — in 4/4 rhythms, and instrumental pieces.

Melody

1   Review and practice *sol–mi* chants in singing, movement, on instruments and in notation.

2   Identify *la* in *sol–mi–la* patterns in songs, on instruments, and in notation.

3   Identify *do* as a tonal center in performance and then in notation.

4   Identify *mi–re–do* patterns in performance and notation.

> Rhythm objectives ('Rhythm,' 5–7) may be alternated with 'Melody,' 6–7.

5   Practice reading to perform songs and accompaniments in pentatonic.

6   Improvise and write melodies using the motives typical of pentatonic songs (e.g. *sml, mrd, dms, dls*).

7   Analyze four-note motives vocally. Take down sequences of up to four notes from dictation.

> Rhythm objectives 8, 9 and 10 may be placed here.

8   Identify the pentatonic scale in F, then in G and C, on instruments, then in notation.

Texture

1   Build an awareness of accuracy when singing in unison (an ongoing objective).

2   Perform settings involving a melody and a melodic ostinato.

3   Perform rhythms and melodies in two-part canon.

4   Perform a moving bordun with a partner.

Timbre

1   Compare timbres and registers of barred instruments using the chord, level, or broken bordun.

Form

1   Analyze songs based on motives. Improvise from these models (for example: a a' b a, a b a c, or a a' b –).

2   Analyze songs with question–answer phrases that together create a section. Improvise, based on the model.

> You may link these objectives with 'Rhythm,' 5 and 'Melody,' 6, as they occur.

3   Identify ABA form as two contrasting sections followed by a repeat of the first.

In my experience it's wise to take the first few days of school to review the rhythm symbols introduced in first grade: the quarter note, quarter rest and paired eighth notes. I use some favorite settings from the previous year, mixed with some of the new pentatonic songs I will use later when introducing melodic symbols. Then, when nearly all the students are comfortable moving to the beat at various tempos, echoing familiar four-beat rhythm patterns, and performing them from notation, I move on to the first new concept.

Rhythm

1 Perform, then read and write, a duration twice the length of one beat, ♩‿♩ = ♩, using the tie.

My children have often used the beat–rest pattern to accompany their chants and songs. The new task for our class is to discriminate between that familiar pattern and a duration which is sustained through two beats. You might introduce this concept through a demonstration using untuned instruments. Show the children several untuned instruments and ask them to guess which may make the shortest and longest sounds. Then ask your students to pat the beat at a moderate tempo and listen for the length of sound each instrument is capable of making. First play a hand drum on each beat and compare this to beats on the board. Then play a triangle on every other beat. Your students will probably have little difficulty in hearing the sound continue through two or even more beats. Next, tell the children to walk to the beat of your drum, and to continue to walk at the same tempo even after you stop playing the drum. After they are walking without the support of the drum, play a triangle in half notes. Ask them to clap with the triangle, but to be careful not to lose the beat in their feet. Discuss with them how to make their clap motion of the half note describe the difference between it and a beat–rest pattern. Practice once more, responding to the drum, (♩ 𝄽) or the triangle (♩).

When you return to look at the beats drawn on the board, lead them to conclude that beats representing the triangle will be tied together while a beat–rest pattern represents the sound of the hand drum. Give the new duration the name, half note, and a rhythm syllable, if you use them. I find it helpful to use the boxes and Xs introduced in Frazee's *Discovering Orff* (p. 86) at this time, for it parallels the introduction of ikonic notation leading to stick and conventional notation begun in first grade. Use boxes to illustrate the rhythm of the first phrase of 'Old Mother Brown.'

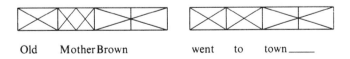

Old   Mother Brown   went   to   town_____

'Old Mother Brown' is an old hand-clapping game song that my classes enjoy. Ask partners to use a familiar hand-clapping pattern of quarter notes to accompany the song.

When this is comfortable, ask them to listen for the half notes and adjust their pattern to illustrate the longer duration each time it occurs. Their motions must show the length of the half note, and not the length of beat—rest. Your children may decide to use ♩ ♩ ♩ as an ostinato. Others may use the rhythmic outline,

2 Identify and conduct in 2/4 meter, observing that the down beat is the first beat and the metric accent.

I have found that 'Angel Band,' with its strong emphasis on numbers, is easy to conduct. As the children sing have them pat their knees on the numbers. Ask them what happens to their hands between pats. When their hands come up they may clap, then pat. Sing the song and make the same motions, this time with both hands in the air; down, then up.

Your class can mirror the same motion on hand drums, stroking down with the thumb on the lower fourth of the drum and stroking up with finger tips on the top fourth. Name the first beat the down beat, the second the up beat. Half the class may conduct the verse and play drums on the refrain, while half play, then conduct the others.

Angel Band

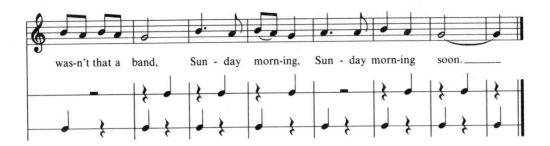

was-n't that a band,   Sun - day morn-ing,   Sun - day morn-ing   soon._____

Additional resource
Frazee with Kreuter *Discovering Orff*, p. 87
   Examples to be conducted and read from
   notation.

3   *Identify 2/4 meter in notation by placing bar lines in notation of songs and rhythms.*

After the children hear and conduct music organized in 2 we introduce them to symbols of meter. We can return to familiar material, 'Old Mother Brown,' and sing it while conducting. Then ask one row to face the second row. The first row will conduct while the second row sings the song, lightly clapping the word rhythms as they watch each other.

When I introduce a new rhythm symbol I like to repeat the process I have used before as a means of associating the new note with previous knowledge. As your children sing the first phrase, draw each beat on the board. Then ask them to show all divided beats or eighth notes (there is only one pair in phrases one and two). Next, identify the sounds that last two beats and 'tie' them together. Replace the tied beats with the half note symbol. As your students pat the down beat, have one student mark the notes which fall on the down beat or metric accent. The class can now see that the half notes take up all the space between metric accents. Next, have students place bar lines in front of the accented notes and define the bar line as dividing the music into measures of two beats. Then introduce the meter signature: the top number defines how many beats of rhythm are in each measure, while the bottom figure identifies the duration of the beat.

In my classes 'Old Mother Brown' has other uses as well. For instance my students use the song to review rhythmic notation and practice their new skills to conduct their ensemble. Begin with the bass metallophone part and place this ostinato on the board:
Ask your students which bass instrument will sound half notes most easily, and how they recommend preparing the part. Next, demonstrate the wood block ostinato and ask them to clap it and then write it on the board ( ). The alto xylophone part gives you an opportunity to introduce the half rest, filling two measures. Place the rhythm of the pattern on the board and ask your children to put in bar lines. After the setting is prepared ask several students to take turns conducting the ensemble.

4   *Perform, read, and write   and   in 2/4 songs, rhythms and instrumental pieces.*

It is virtually an axiom of teaching that once you have introduced a new symbol to your students you must have them use it in many new contexts. Children should see the symbol and perform its meaning through movement, singing and playing. They should also be able to hear the duration in the music they perform and write what they hear in notation. The transitions between hearing, seeing and performing should be clear before your children move on to a new task.

Ducks in the Millpond

arr. AS

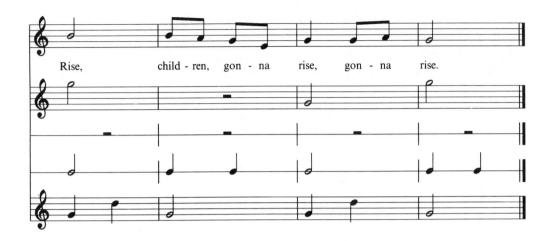

Rise, child - ren, gon - na rise, gon - na rise.

I arranged the setting for 'Ducks In The Millpond' to give my class experience in using notation. The students read some parts while others are heard and then written. Start by putting these two rhythms on the board:

As you sing the B section melody on a neutral syllable, ask the students to select the correct rhythm. Now clap the correct rhythm and then chant the words before singing them. Then ask a child to circle the notes where the word 'rise' occurs. The soprano metallophone plays the rhythm of the circled words. Your children will be able to write it. The bass xylophone and finger cymbal parts are mirror images of each other and can be taught from notation.

Ask your children to listen for the half notes in the A section. They will discover there are none. A level bordun will add half notes to this section. The untuned ostinato is written for tambourine, but the students may wish to change the timbre of the part; that may necessitate changes in the notation as well.

The little piece for untuned instruments which follows uses the rhythmic outline from the soprano metallophone part of the B section. You might begin by chanting 'Rise, children, gonna rise, rise,' for that will help introduce the theme. The guiro and hand drum parts should be taught from notation.

140

All body percussion sounds are short, but continuing the gesture helps us feel the half note duration. I find it helpful to use the following body percussion ostinato to prepare a little instrumental exercise that you may use to explore the pentatonic pitches in C while practicing reading this rhythm.

Prepare instruments in C pentatonic.

When the pattern is secure, play the clapped eighth notes on xylophones, the snapped quarter notes on glockenspiels, and the patted half notes on metallophones. You may add an accompaniment of a familiar rhythm on an untuned instrument to complete the ensemble. The piece will have a strong ending when all students play the tonic c on the last measure.

Additional resources

Boshkoff *All Around the Buttercup*
    'The Clocks' (p. 17)
Frazee with Kreuter *Discovering Orff*,
    pp. 89–90
    More activities to explore half notes in
    rhythmic patterns.

> Consider moving to 'Melody,' 1–5, combining those objectives with a continued application of the known durations ('Rhythm,' 4, 5). Then, continue with the rhythm objectives (6–10).

141

5 Improvise and compose using the known durations.

I look for two kinds of responses to tell me the children have assimilated the meaning of half notes, as compared to quarter and eighth notes. First, they have the ability to write a short pattern, using the symbols correctly when they record rhythm patterns. The second response is the ability to perform a four- or eight-beat pattern, which includes a half note, read or improvised over a steady beat. The first response is controlled by thinking of the value of each note. It does not require a timed reaction. The second response depends on an internalized store of patterns as well as an ability to think quickly. Both are important in achieving musical independence.

These are some games I have used to encourage quick reaction skills. Begin by placing a four-measure rhythm on the board, leaving one measure empty.
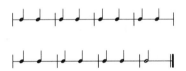 Then ask your class to read the rhythm silently, filling the empty measure. Now clap the rhythm, with each person filling the measure as she chooses. After you have practiced, listen to individual solutions. Then erase another measure as well. Again, prepare with silent reading, followed by practice before hearing more solos.

Another time, place the following framework on the board.

Then invite a child to change one measure to make the rhythm more interesting. Now ask your class to perform it. Another child may change another measure but keep the first child's change, and have the class perform the results. Proceed until all but the last measure have been changed.

Now give each student an opportunity to write his own rhythmic theme; you may choose to use boxes, each representing one measure. Prepare the class by placing a duplication of their worksheet on the board.

Establish the tempo, and then point to each measure as they think a rhythm pattern in their minds. Next, have them perform their patterns in body percussion, again as you point to the boxes. Encourage your students to modify their patterns until they have one they like. Then ask them to write a rhythm on their worksheets. You might conclude by choosing a group of their compositions, arranging them on the board for the class to perform.

6 Write four-beat patterns from dictation, using the known durations, ♩, ♫ ♩, ♩, ⅓, and ♩.

If you use rhythm syllables, it is important that your class practices them in aural dictation exercises before introducing written dictation. This means that when you perform a four-beat pattern, each student is able to repeat the pattern and then chant it in the correct syllables. When they respond confidently to this task and other class dictation activities, they are ready for individual evaluation.

Of course, nothing makes learning more fun than a good game. Here's one that works well with my class. Give each student an envelope containing rectangles. Four rectangles have half notes written on them, four have half rests, eight have quarter notes, four have quarter rests, and eight have pairs of eighth notes.

Now have your children separate their squares into five piles. You begin the game by performing a four-beat pattern which the class echoes, and then 'writes,' by selecting the correct boxes and placing them in order. Give them many patterns to practice, practice, practice!

Now when you present individual dictation your children will have a number of experiences to draw upon. The first example uses boxes, paralleling the game described above. The second uses the line and bar lines, as the children find in music scores.

The rhythms which appear here would be appropriate examples for evaluation.

7 Perform rhythms while walking the beat, and then while walking and singing.

You have probably noticed that some children can walk in place and clap the rhythm of a poem accurately, but when they walk through space their concentration is challenged. These poems can be chanted and then clapped as they walk.

1 2 3 O'Leary, 4 5 6 O'Leary, 7 8 9 O'Leary, 10 O'Leary more

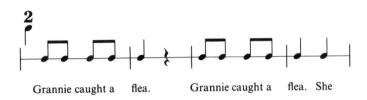

Grannie caught a   flea.   Grannie caught a   flea. She

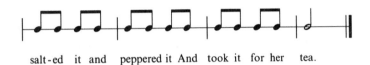

salt-ed it and peppered it And took it for her   tea.

The next challenge is to have your students chant a poem and clap an ostinato. First have them clap on beats one and three while walking the beat and chanting. Then have the class clap ‖: ♩ ♪ ♫ ♩ :‖ with each poem. Perhaps the children can suggest other four-beat patterns to clap as they walk and chant or sing.

Additional resources
Frazee with Kreuter *Discovering Orff*, pp. 92–3

8 Perform, then read and write, rhythms using the whole note
as ♩♩♩♩ = o, ♩♩ = o.

To introduce the whole note let's return to a variation of a familiar game. Set up a drum (♩), a triangle (♩), temple blocks (♪) and a suspended cymbal (o) so that you can play all four. Divide the class into three groups, assigning each one a duration, quarter, eighth or half notes. They are to determine how they will move through the room when they hear their signal. Introduce one duration at a time, allowing each group to move for eight beats. You may choose to have two groups move at once. Surprise them by playing the whole note, helping them to conclude that a fourth group is necessary. Again, play two durations, each against the whole note.

Your children are familiar with half notes and will enjoy telling you now how many quarter, eighth and half notes must be tied together to equal the length of the whole note.

The following rhythm piece will help them apply what they have just experienced and discovered. They will be able to learn this piece from notation.

9 *Identify 4/4 meter by placing bar lines in rhythms and melodies.*

Ask your students to listen for whole notes in the following very old version of 'Three Blind Mice.' Prepare them by having them 'compose' a pattern of four quarter note arm/hand movements. It is easy to maintain their patterns if the first of the four gestures goes down. Now sing the melody with mock seriousness and then ask them how many whole notes they heard. Then sing the phrases containing whole notes, which they echo.

Three Blind Mice

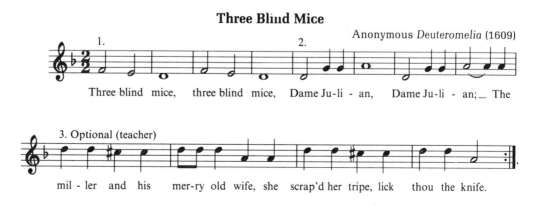

Your students should be able to write the melodic rhythm on the board. They will see that 2/4 will not be a likely meter because the rhythm falls into groups of four beats. Because they are familiar with the concept of meter from their experiences with 2/4, they will have little difficulty in placing bar lines and writing the symbol for the new meter. Measure eight will require careful listening to determine whether they wish to sing 'an' as ♩ 𝄽 or ♩ ♪ .

10   *Perform, read, and write* 𝅝 *and* ▬ *in 4/4 songs, rhythms, and instrumental pieces.*

When my children perform their songs they find it challenging to internalize the beat during rests and long durations without rushing. They will improve if they practice rhythms such as the one in 'Three Blind Mice.' First clap the rhythm from notation. Then practice it by clapping the half notes to prepare finger cymbals, patting the whole notes to prepare suspended cymbals, stepping the quarter notes to prepare drums, and snapping the eighth notes to prepare claves. Have them play from notation, and then play from memory as you conduct them in four. Challenge them to test their rhythmic independence also by performing the melodic rhythm with body percussion in canon at the interval of four beats.

Finally we practice what we know by learning 'Crawdad Hole,' which contains whole notes. This derivation is interesting because phrases one, two and four are three measures long, while the third phrase is two measures long. Prepare your students for this unusual length through rhythmic echo. Give them patterns that are eight beats long with the addition of the whole note,

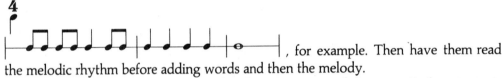

, for example. Then have them read the melodic rhythm before adding words and then the melody.

The moving bordun parts follow the phrase structure of the song. Each ostinato is eight beats long, with an extension of four beats for phrases one, two and four.

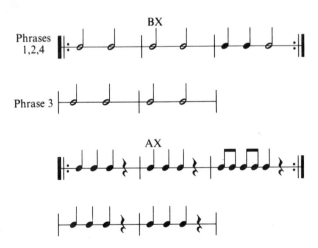

The glockenspiel plays on 'ice,' and the finger cymbal part begins on 'Babe'.

146

4

Crawdad Hole

Adapted *Just Five*

V

G

AX

BM

1. Stand-ing on the ice till my feet got cold, Sug-ar Babe:
hot,
numb,

Stand-ing on the ice till my feet got cold, Sug-ar Babe:
hot,
numb,

Stand-ing on the ice till my

feet got cold, watch-ing that Craw-dad go to his hole, Sug-ar Babe.
hot, rock and trot,
numb, go and come,

Additional resource
Frazee *Orff Handbook for World of Music – 2*
  'The Big Corral' (p. 14)

Melody

1   Review and practice sol–mi *in singing, movement, on instruments and in notation.*

Your children should have a spatial sense of melodic line from their experiences with movement and ikonic notation in first grade. I like to begin their melodic studies by leading them to recall their understanding of melody through a review of some of the songs and games I presented then. Then I follow this with a review of *sol–mi* and *sol–mi–la* patterns in aural dictation. Begin by singing a short pattern, using a neutral syllable – then ask the class or a student to respond, singing the syllables which name the pattern. When your children respond with ease, ask them to answer on the neutral syllable and then write the first letter of each syllable in the order they appear in each pattern.

    Throughout these lessons on pitch you will find it helpful to have a syllable ladder placed where all the students can see it. Place only the syllables the children are using on the ladder. Draw attention to the parallels of up and down and to empty spaces that are in common with the instruments, and then with the staff.

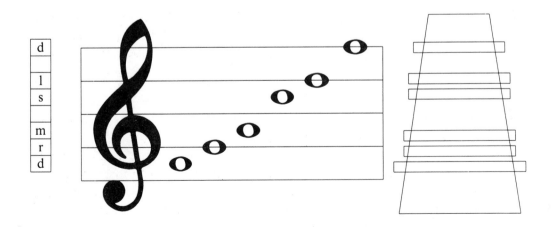

When beginning pitched notation I find it is helpful to have materials which children can manipulate easily to help them visualize what they are learning about pitch relationships. I laminate a staff for each child that fills an 8½″ by 11″ page. In a separate envelope there are noteheads, colored black, cut out to fit between the lines of the staff.

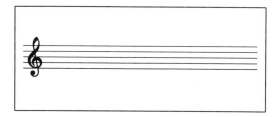

First, explain to the children that lines and spaces are always counted from the bottom up. Practice placing circles on the third and second lines, the third and second spaces, the fifth and fourth lines, and so forth, until the children become accustomed to counting in this way.

Also review *sol–mi* patterns, using hand motions to indicate the higher and lower pitches. In this lesson *sol* will always be in the third space, and *mi* will be in the second or lower space (c–a of F pentatonic). After they echo four pitches, using solfege, have them place the circles on the staff to represent their pattern. Some of the patterns may be *s–s–s–m, m–m–s–s, m–s–s–m.* Let the children suggest others which you may write and then sing.

'Gonna Sing a Song' has only two *sol–mi* patterns which repeat several times. Ask the children to identify them as they listen to the song. Then ask them to chant 'Oo-ah' with you as a response. As they join you in singing the song, have them follow the melodic patterns with their hands, and then put the syllables of each pattern on the board, as you did in first grade: *mm^{ss}m*. The bass xylophone and tambourine may be prepared from rhythmic notation, practiced in hand jive movements worked out with a partner.

Gonna Sing a Song

2

Gon-na sing a song, Ooo - ah,___ And it won't take

long, Ooo - ah,___ A lay-uh, lay-uh, lay-uh, lay-uh,

Ooo - ah,___ A lay-uh, lay-uh, lay-uh, lay-uh, Ooo - ah!___

When your class reviews the song, pass out staff charts and note heads. Have them practice placing the note heads on the staff and then write the two motives found in the song. Then add the alto xylophone after notating its pattern. You can add a little surprise by inviting the xylophone player to choose which way to play 'Oo-ah,' using *sol–mi* or *mi–sol*. After the class has heard the first 'Oo-ah' they sing with the player in syllables.

Additional resource
Boshkoff *All Around the Buttercup*
    'Star Light' (p. 7)

2   *Identify* la *in* sol–mi–la *patterns, in songs, on instruments and in notation.*

You may find it very useful to begin by reviewing several of the three-note songs your children learned in first grade ('Oliver Twist,' 'Bobby Shaftoe,' 'Bluebird,' 'Buster,' Brown,' 'Weather,' for example). They will enjoy the games and accompaniments as you take time to draw attention to the comparative high and low pitch relationships in each melody.

After your class is comfortable with this review, present 'Rain' from stick notation with syllables written beneath, reading this notation before adding the words. Then show your students an alto metallophone or xylophone with only c and a (*sol* and *mi*) present. Ask them to determine what bar should be placed on the instrument to play *la* for this melody; relate this to the placement of *la* just above *sol* in staff notation. Now place four alto-range instruments on the floor for four players. Assign each to play one phrase of the song, perhaps as an unaccompanied B section to the song setting. Your students can play the phrases in other orders. Place each phrase on a card. Shuffle the cards and then give each child a card in the new order to be played or sung.

Rain

151

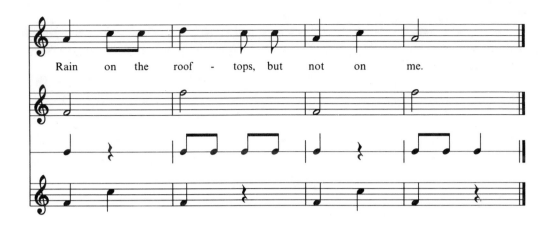

Rain on the roof - tops, but not on me.

I wrote 'Old Mother Witch' to give children an opportunity to practice *l–s–m*, a pattern that is not heard frequently. All accompaniment parts can be learned from stick notation in body percussion as preparation for instrument playing.

Old Mother Witch

Nursery rhyme

Old Mo - ther Witch   fell   in   a   ditch.

152

Picked up a pen-ny and thought she was rich.

Additional resources
Boshkoff *All Around the Buttercup*
  'The Snail' (p. 6)
  'Bounce High' (p. 8)
  'Ding Dong Bell' (p. 9)
  'The Mill Wheel' (p. 10)
Ladendecker *Holidays and Holy Days*, Vol. 1
  'Witch, Witch' (p. 3)

3   Identify do *as a tonal center in performance and then in notation.*

Your children will have the tonal center in their ears for they have been playing it in their accompaniment patterns and singing it in melodies and echoed patterns. Now ask them to sing 'Ring Around the Rosie' on a neutral syllable, and then in syllables. You and they will discover that most of them sing *sol, sol, do* at the end. Explore their ability to hear the tonic, *do,* in relationship to the syllables they already read and write. Then ask the students to stand on the outside perimeter of the room, while you stand at the center. You will improvise melodies using *sol, la* and *mi,* singing or playing the recorder. They may step toward the center, or home, only when you play *do.* Watch the students' responses and improvise to encourage their success while challenging them to respond accurately and quickly.

Because they know *sol* and *mi* and can identify *do,* the children can be introduced to melodic patterns that outline the tonic chord. 'Weather Report' outlines the tonic chord, which in notation is space to space to space, as it also appears on barred instruments with only *sol, mi,* and *do* present. Introduce the idea of tonic or tonal center by using body placement for each syllable.

Top of head (*la*)

Waist (*mi*) – – –

Shoulders (*sol*) –

Arms down, fists closed (*do*)

You should sing this melody with syllables, and then with body signs, before introducing *do* or the tonic on the staff. The simple accompaniment is prepared through body percussion.

Your children will probably enjoy taking turns playing one of the phrases in the song. However, the song is deceptively simple, for each phrase begins with the same motive, but ends differently.

Weather Report

AS

1. Red sky at night is the shep - herd's de - light.
2. Sun - shi - ny show - ers won't last an hour.

strike

*3 cymbals, large to small, played by drawing ratchet handle against rim.

Red sky in morn - ing the sai - lor's warn - ing.
Soft A - pril show - ers will bring May flow - ers.

154

4   Identify mi–re–do *patterns in performance and notation.*

The last syllable, *re,* completes the pentatonic scale. It is also the syllable which, by placement on the metric accent, gives cadence to melodies. *Re* occurs in each phrase, but is most obvious at the beginning of the last phrase of 'Black Snake,' dictating a change of harmony. Prepare the students by asking them to read the following melodic line.

Black Snake

Southern childrens' game

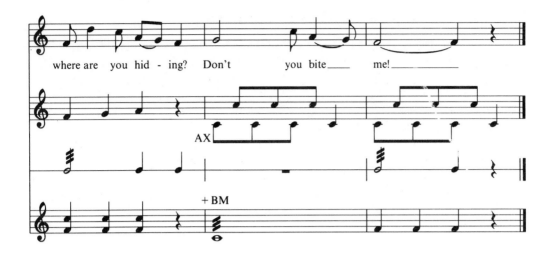

where are you hid - ing? Don't you bite___ me!___

Erase the first *mi*, replace it with *do* and sing again. Then remove the first *sol* and replace it as well with *do* and sing the line. Ask them to compare this melody with your performance of the first phrase of 'Black Snake.' Your students may not hear *re*, until they sing it back to you, for it is hidden as a passing tone. Then guide them in deciding where to place *re* in the melodic outline just presented. The glockenspiel part may be taught from notation, practicing the same sequence of pitches in reverse. A maraca part suggests the hissing of a snake, but your children may have other suggestions for unpitched color and ostinatos.

Next draw your students' attention to the form of the melody. The first phrase is repeated three times. Ask them to notate the syllables of the pitches in the fourth phrase, beginning on *re*. It dictates a change in orchestration, highlighting the new syllable and melodic pattern. Ask your children to listen for *re* as a way of anticipating the changing of accompaniment patterns.

It is important to take time to practice *mi–re–do* melodies by learning several three-note melodies of a variety of patterns before moving on to more pentatonic literature.

Additional resources

Frazee *Singing in the Season*
  'Sing a Lamb' (p. 2)
Frazee with Kreuter *Discovering Orff*
  'The Boatman' (p. 99)
  'Long-Legged Sailor' (p. 100)

  Rhythm objectives ('Rhythm,' 5–7) may be alternated with 'Melody,' 6, 7.

5 *Practice reading to perform songs and accompaniments in pentatonic.*

It appears that children can read chants of two notes, adding new pitches quickly, to arrive at the point of reading the pentatonic scale fluently in a short period of time. While they absorb the logic of notation with some ease, my children develop the ability to write melodies over a longer period. It is the work of second graders to read and write pentatonic melodies within the octave of *do* to *do*. If you are sure of their reading and writing skills, you may choose to present the principle of transposition, or you may wish to expand the range of pitches they read to include the pentatonic syllables below *do* and above *do*. While you are guiding them to develop their reading and writing skills they are also developing aural analysis skills that include recognition of pitches beyond the range they read and write.

My children have helped me create games that help them practice the skills of reading and writing pitched notation. One game is an old-fashioned spell down. Place a felt or magnetic staff before the class, with four noteheads prepared to attach to the staff. Ask the children to number off to form two teams. I establish *do* or *sol* as the beginning pitch, and show the children where this pitch is on the staff. Then I sing it and a second pentatonic pitch, using a neutral syllable. The team echoes me but provides the name of the second syllable. The first 'writer' may consult with the team before recording the motive on the staff. The first team member of the second team may correct the recording of the interval or, when the answer is correct, will receive a new interval, beginning again on the same pitch. There are several ways to raise the challenge level. One is to echo sing only on neutral syllables, requiring the 'writer' to identify the interval independently. Another way is to dictate three, and then, after considerable practice, four syllables. I like to guide the children to become aware of ways to use mistakes to lead to correct answers by using each dictation as an opportunity to listen, remember the pitches, compare the pitches and pattern, and then write.

Another more creative way to practice notation is to give partners or small groups of children a barred instrument, two cards, each containing a four-beat melodic motive, and paper containing four staffs of lines widely spaced. Ask each group to compose a melody of four measures, using only two motives, and record their composition on their staff paper. Ask each group to sing and play the results. Some groups will use the motives given, while others, more sure of their melodic skills, may wish to alter the motives they are given to make a more interesting melody.

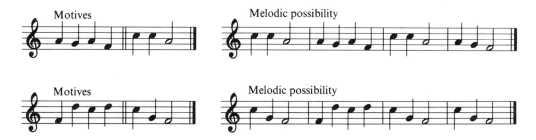

While each of these activities helps the children practice reading and writing skills, the most musical way to practice is to perform music. The following settings and songs have been chosen to encourage practice in singing and playing of typical pentatonic melodic motives.

'Arre, mi burruto' is a *sol–la–sol–mi* melody which my children played as well as sang. In the setting for voices the instrumental accompaniment is very easy to support accurate singing of the simple melody. Adding a melodic ostinato, based on *mi–re–do*, provides your students with an opportunity to practice singing two familiar melodic motives to create harmony.

Arre mi burrito (Giddy Up, My Burro) I

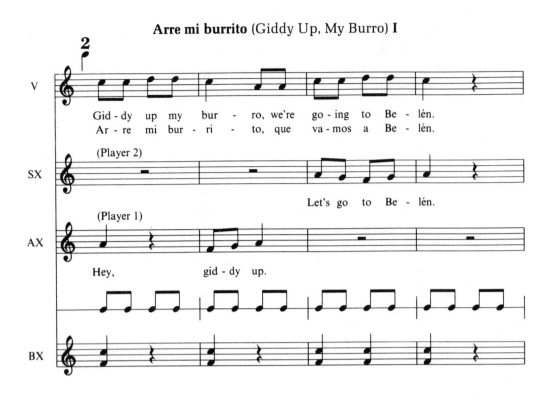

V: Gid - dy up my bur - ro, we're go - ing to Be - lén.
Ar - re mi bur - ri - to, que va - mos a Be - lén.

SX (Player 2): Let's go to Be - lén.

AX (Player 1): Hey, gid - dy up.

Fie - sta is to - mor - row, and one next day a - gain.
Que man - an - aes fie - sta y el o - tro tam - bien.

Let's go to Be - lén.

Hey, gid - dy up.

The second setting gives children the opportunity to match their sung melody to barred instruments so as to make an instrumental piece. It will indicate musical independence when your students sing and play in canon with you on recorder or a barred instrument for the experiences challenges them to perform this otherwise simple melody with rhythmic accuracy.

Arre mi burrito II

'Babylon's Falling' gives our second graders an opportunity to review *mi–re–do* patterns. Notice that the bass part is also a pitched ostinato, not a bordun.

Your students should also practice melodies which center around *do–mi–sol* in order to prepare them to hear thirds, the basis of chordal harmony. 'Bow Wow Wow' is one of my second graders' favorite singing games. To play the game they stand in a circle, facing a partner. During the first measure they clap their partner's hands and during the second measure they shake their fingers. Then as they sing the third measure they join hands and rotate to exchange places. On 'Bow, wow, wow!' they swing their joined hands up and down, but on the fourth beat they jump 180 degrees to face a new partner. I like to divide the class into several circles so that the children can rotate around the circle to return to their original partners. This game never fails to delight the children as they discover who their new partner is with each turn. It is a wonderful way to practice these important intervals.

Bow Wow Wow

4

V
1. Bow, wow, wow, who's dog art thou?
2. Now, now, now, who's pet art thou?

SX

AM

BM

or
C. bass
bar

Lit - tle Tom - my Tuck - er's dog. Bow, wow, wow.
Sec - ond grad - er's di - no - saur. Wow, wow, wow!

'Willowbee' is a singing game with many derivations. This version begins with a *do–la–sol–la* motive and ends with the familiar cadence of *mi–re–do*. When you guide the children to notate the melodic ideas and the accompaniment melodic ostinatos, do not use stems or rhythmic notation. Rather, place the noteheads on the staff, letting the space between each indicate the rhythm. My children perform this game by forming a set of two equal lines, partners facing each other. During the refrain partners face each other with hands joined, and make a see-saw motion with hands and feet, as though sifting. On the last phrase they step back to form the alley. During the verse the head couple can decide how they wish to come down the alley, or the group can determine these actions before they play the game.

Willowbee

Southern singing game

This way we wil-low-bee, oh wil-low-bee, oh wil-low-bee, oh,

This way we wil-low-bee___ All night___ long. Oh, long.

Danc - ing down the al - ley, the al - ley, the al - ley.

with brush

162

Danc - ing down the al - ley_____ All night_____ long.

2. Singing down the alley . . .
4. Swinging down the alley . . .

3. Skipping down the alley . . .
5. (Students' idea)

Additional resources
Boshkoff *All Around the Buttercup*
  'All Around the Buttercup' (p. 15)
Boshkoff *Ring Around, Sing Around*
  'Deta, Deta' (p. 6)
Earley *Something Told the Wild Geese*
  'White Sails on the Sea' (p. 4)

6   Improvise and write melodies using the motives typical of pentatonic songs (e.g. sml, mrd, dms, dls).

I like to begin melodic improvisation activities by recalling patterns familiar to the class. Ask your students to recall four familiar four-beat melody patterns and ask them to assist you in writing each one so that all can see the notation. Assign a small group of children to be responsible for performing each one. Then ask one of your students to direct, choosing any two or more groups to sing in any order. Second graders may need help to find patterns that end their songs best. Encourage them to repeat motives, becoming aware of repetition and contrast as elements of form and frameworks for improvisation.

The same game may be played with instruments. Place four barred instruments of the same timbre, set in F pentatonic, before the students. Ask a student at each instrument to improvise a four-beat melody. Again, students may take turns deciding how the patterns are to be ordered to making new melodies.

The following poems were chosen because the words encourage our children to think about repeating melodic motives and contrasting ideas. Begin by echo singing short melodic motives in syllables. Ask your students to describe the form of one of the poems. Then you may ask if there is a little melody for the first line. After the class has sung it together guide the class to determine a melody for the second line, and so on. You may begin the project together and then ask partners or small groups to finish the song. Comparing the results will illustrate to your children that there are many possible musical solutions for each melody. Another time you may give your students one of the following poems and a melody for the first line. Then in partners they are to finish the melody by singing it or playing it on a barred instrument.

> Go to bed, Tom,
> Go to bed, Tom.
> Tired or not, tired or not,
> Go to bed, Tom.
>
> Mr. East gave a feast,
> Mr. North laid the cloth,
> Mr. West did his best,
> Mr. South burned his mouth
> While eating cold potatoes.
>
> Swan swum over the sea,
> Swim, swan, swim.
> Swan swum back again,
> Well swum, swan!
>
> Diddle, diddle, dumply,
> Cat is in the plum tree.
> Half a crown to bring her down,
> Diddle, diddle, dumply.

You and the children can make a little songbook from these improvised melodies. Prepare an $8\frac{1}{2}'' \times 11''$ sheet with four staffs. You can write one measure of the melody, inviting the class to help you write the remaining measures. These sheets can then be duplicated and made into students' songbooks.

Additional resources
Boshkoff *All Around the Buttercup*
   'The Squirrel' (p. 16)
   'Little Black Bug' (p. 18)
Frazee with Kreuter *Discovering Orff*,
   pp. 104–5
   For other improvisation activities.

7   Analyze four-note motives vocally. Take down sequences of up to four notes from dictation.

After considerable practice in reading, writing and improvising, your students will now be ready to analyze pitch relationships through dictation exercises. This is an important step, for I have found through this activity that some students sing well but cannot connect the correct solfege syllables with the pitches, while others cannot sing the pitches accurately but can identify the melodic patterns on instruments and in writing. These activities, then, give me information concerning my students' understanding of pitch relationships which helps me evaluate the effectiveness of my instruction for each of them.

164

Begin with aural analysis. Start your class warm-ups by singing a few melodic motives of three or four pitches, identifying the first syllable, but finishing on a neutral syllable. The children, together or as individuals, should echo with syllables. At other times ask your class to sing and then find ways to change these motives. Playing the instruments seems to help reinforce the concept of higher and lower pitches, which needs to be checked each time new pitches and patterns are added to their vocabularies.

You may wish to use the laminated staffs used at the beginning of the year to take dictation before you test the children individually. When most of the class is comfortable with group dictation you may begin with short tests. Prepare sheets for each child.

A Student fills in the syllable letter, then the note head.

B Fill in two syllables and place note heads above them.

C Fill in three syllables and place note heads above them.

You should begin by singing the pattern on a neutral syllable, then ask the class to echo, also on a neutral syllable. You may sing the pattern once more as they write the first letter of the syllable in each blank. Then they may go back and place the pitches on the staff. I like to give only four or five examples, and devote only five to ten minutes of any class period to this kind of activity. When the children are successful in taking two-note dictation, give them three, and then, perhaps, four notes. I do not ask them to add rhythm to these patterns in second grade.

Rhythm objectives 8, 9 and 10 may be placed here.

8 Identify the pentatonic scale in F, then in G and C, on instruments, then in notation.

Children understand transposition when they find that the pentatonic scale of three bars, space, two bars, space, is a pattern that repeats and can be found in several positions on their instruments.

Canon

Sol mi re do   sol sol mi re do.

Sol sol la la do do la la sol mi re do.

When presenting an instrument piece I often begin with the rhythm. Place the melodic rhythm of this piece, one line for each phrase, on the board. Ask the students to star the lines that are alike. Next teach the melody with syllables and ask the children to add the syllables below each line, observing that the starred lines continue to be alike, and that the second line is nearly the same. Now ask your class to tell you how line three is different in rhythm and in melody.

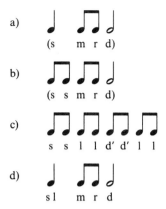

(*Canon preparation rhythm*)

a) (s   m r d)

b) (s s m r d)

c) s s l l d' d' l l

d) s l m r d

Next give each child a barred instrument, or place two children at each instrument so they may take turns playing. Ask them to remove e and b bars, and then identify which bars are *do*, *re*, and *mi*, and which are *sol*, *la*. At this point refer to the syllable ladder where the syllables are also grouped in the same way. Ask the class where the melody will begin, noting that since the melody moves down, the high c is the beginning bar. Give your students a moment to tap out the melody, using their finger tips. Then hear several children play the melody before hearing the group play together. If the children are having difficulty playing the melody review each line by singing it to them before asking them to play it back. Add the accompaniment, and if the children need more practice, save the transposition experience for the next lesson.

Now ask your children to describe again the direction and syllables used in each measure. Then have them replace all the bars and remove the f and c bars, setting the instruments in G pentatonic. Again, ask the children to play the melody, based on the pattern of three and two bars they see on their instruments. This always delights them. Ask them to describe what happened. The melody is the same, but it has changed position, or it has been transposed. Replace all the bars again, and remove f and b bars, or set up C pentatonic. It is easy for them to play the melody again.

At this point, I show the children the same melody written in three keys, noting how the relationship between notes has remained the same, but the placement of the five notes as a unit has changed. Conclude your instruction on transposing by having your students read pentatonic songs in each of these tonal centers.

Texture

1 Build an awareness of accuracy when singing in unison (an ongoing objective).

Every lesson should have the objective of encouraging children to sing in tune. You may consider devoting a lesson to it periodically to refocus the children's attention to its importance. The child's ability to sing tunefully affects his ability to hear the texture that results when his singing is accompanied. Also, a child may sing in tune alone, but may be unable to do so within a song setting. When textures become more than one voice thick children may become distracted causing them to sing with less awareness of pitch accuracy. There are several ways we can help children become aware of this ensemble skill.

One way to help children become aware of tuneful singing is to record them. Ask them to sing a favorite song followed by a student soloist or yourself also singing the song. Ask them to sing again with awareness of being in tune. Play the recording for them and help them identify when they were most successful.

Playing recordings of other children singing well in unison is another way to help them identify tuneful singing. You may also demonstrate the difference by comparing a good unison sound to a piece of yarn or string. We see one thread when the strands are twisted tightly together, but the thread loses strength when it is frayed. Voices focused together are like the single strand, while out-of-tune singers lose their effectiveness by being like the frayed cord.

Resist tedious work on this goal, but call attention to it frequently and encourage tuneful singing by individuals and groups.

2   *Perform settings involving a melody and a melodic ostinato.*

Take this opportunity before the end of the year to review your students' ability to read pentatonic melodies. When the children are singing tunefully, add the challenge of performing melodic ostinatos, which is the first experience they have of singing in harmony.

When you introduce these songs you may wish to practice the children's reading skills by learning the ostinato from notation. Or, you may sing the ostinato and ask them to write it or even play it as practice in dictation. It is also good to use these ostinatos spontaneously to enrich a lesson when the melody is used to highlight some other objective.

If the children achieve a good balance between the melody and the ostinato, they may also create a complimentary unpitched rhythm ostinato. When you do this, be sure to make a visual of their ideas so that the music may be recalled in a later lesson.

My second graders enjoyed singing these two-part settings which they recorded. We listened to the song carefully and commented on the clarity of each melody and ostinato when they were sung alone and in harmony.

Run, Children, Run

168

Run, child-ren, run, it's al - most day.

Run! child-ren, run. Run! child-ren, run!

Down in the Meadow

4

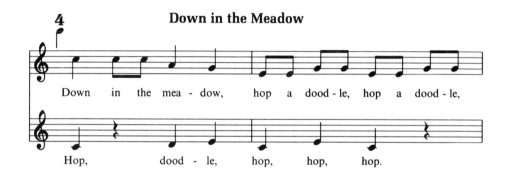

Down in the mea - dow, hop a dood - le, hop a dood - le,

Hop, dood - le, hop, hop, hop.

Down in the mea - dow, hop a dood-le doo! Down in the mea - dow, the

Hop, dood - le, hop, hop, hop. Hop, dood - le,

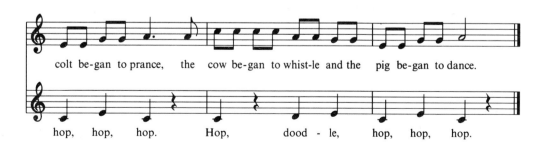

colt be-gan to prance, the cow be-gan to whis-tle and the pig be-gan to dance.

hop, hop, hop. Hop, dood - le, hop, hop, hop.

2

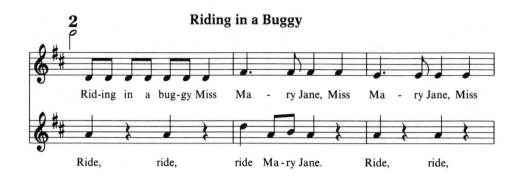

Riding in a Buggy

Rid-ing in a bug-gy Miss Ma - ry Jane, Miss Ma - ry Jane, Miss

Ride, ride, ride Ma-ry Jane. Ride, ride,

Ma - ry Jane. Rid-ing in a bug-gy, Miss Ma - ry Jane, I'm a

ride Ma-ry Jane. Ride, ride, ride Ma-ry Jane.

long way from home. Who moans for me? Who moans for

Ride, ride, ride Ma-ry Jane. You moan for me, you

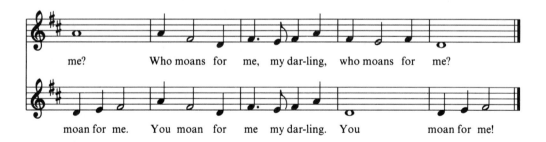

me? Who moans for me, my dar-ling, who moans for me?

moan for me. You moan for me my dar-ling. You moan for me!

3   Perform rhythms and melodies in two-part canon.

Each of these canons may be used to practice rhythm reading and playing skills introduced during the year. Canons will test your students' ability to perform with increased independence. Consider playing a voice canon on drums, or a body percussion canon in untuned percussion. The instrument canon may be sung in syllables first, and then played.

Often my children appreciate seeing each canon in score, thereby providing an excellent opportunity to practice music reading. Help them to avoid the trap of over singing in an effort to maintain their part. Sometimes it helps to write the canon out in two parts to demonstrate the play between them.

Using these canons as models, ask your class to compose their own rhythm canon in 4/4 meter, of four measures length.

A body-percussion canon. Transfer to untuned instruments.

Rhythm Canon

Canon for voices or instruments

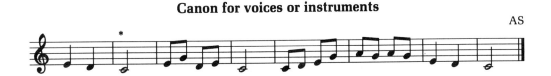

Canon for voices,

White Sands

White sand and gray sand; Who'll buy my white sand? Who'll buy my gray sand?

4 *Perform a moving bordun with a partner.*

Your second grade children have been using chord, level and broken bordun accompaniments throughout the year. They have also become skillful at singing with melodic and rhythmic ostinatos. The moving bordun, divided between two players, becomes a new accompaniment possibility, based on these skills. When you present 'Echoes,' teach the bordun as a partner accompaniment, and compare it to the following simple bordun ostinato which is the basic pattern.

Echoes (with moving bordun)

Traditional

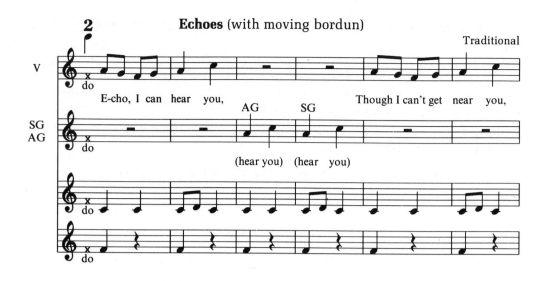

E-cho, I can hear you,   Though I can't get near you,

AG   SG

(hear you) (hear you)

You're so far a - way.

AG   SG

AG

SG

(near you) (near you)   (a - way)   (a - way.)

Echoes (with simple bordun)

Traditional

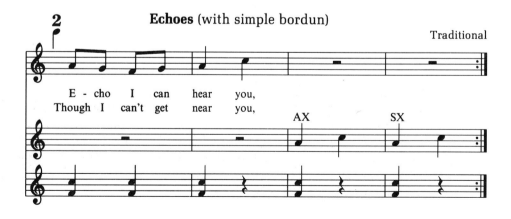

E - cho I can   hear   you,
Though I can't get   near   you,

AX   SX

172

you're so far a - way.

Timbre

1 Compare timbres and registers of barred instruments, using the chord, level, or broken bordun.

I have found that children need repeated opportunities to review basic music concepts. Though they are using the instruments almost daily, they are not asked consciously to compare the quality and range each represents. Let this simple setting of 'Echoes' provide a basis for your students' exploration by beginning with the orchestration possibilities suggested here and in the previous lesson. Use one of the bordun possibilities for each variation. Then ask your students to find three ranges of *mi–sol* on alto and soprano xylophones, or bass, alto and soprano metallophones, for instance. Encourage them to try other sequences than low to high, such as xylophone to glockenspiel.

This may be an excellent time to listen to ways in which composers have used timbre and range to increase our listening pleasure. Stravinsky's *Greeting Prelude*, for instance, divides the melody between timbres and ranges. *The Cuckoo in the Woods* from *Carnival of the Animals*, by Camille Saint-Saëns, is another easily accessible recording that demonstrates 21 cuckoo calls in different ranges and timbres.

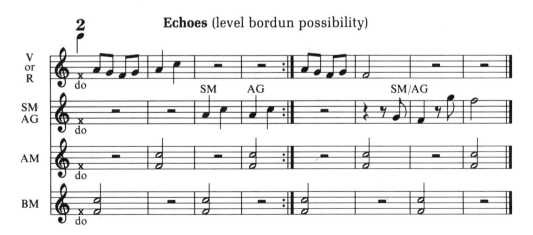

Echoes (level bordun possibility)

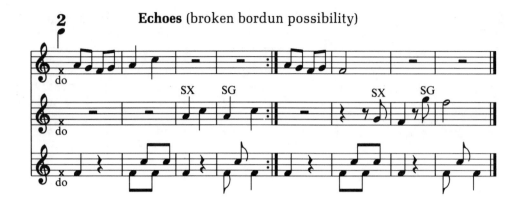

Echoes (broken bordun possibility)

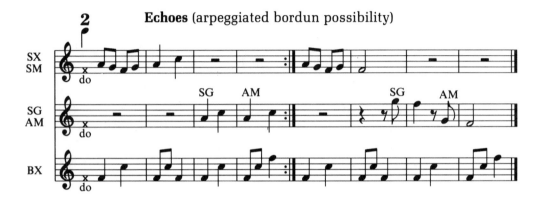

Echoes (arpeggiated bordun possibility)

Form

1 Analyze songs based on motives. Improvise from these models (for example: a a' b a, a b a c, or a a' b –).

I have found that children improvise most freely through movement. Singing games, such as 'Oliver Twist' and 'Willowbee' have prepared the children to improvise many ways, responding to the same musical material. The following little game will help your class refine these skills. Ask one child to demonstrate one way to move four beats, and then have the class repeat it. A second child will perform the same action, but change it slightly. Again, the class will imitate the changed motion, and the first child will end with the first motion. When the class performs each set of motions in order the result is a little movement composition. Try other small forms, such as a b a c, or a a' b (eight beats), using new leaders.

Now ask the children to review familiar songs, such as the 'Canon,' (p. 171 or 166) (a a' b a), 'Shoo Fly', A section (p. 176) (a a' a b) and 'Black Snake' (p. 155) (a a a b). Together, create movement sequences which illustrate these small forms.

Next divide your class into four groups and choose a leader for each. Then present the first leader with a card with a four-beat rhythm, such as ♫ ♩ ♫ ♩ ♩. The student may perform the rhythm with any body percussion she chooses. The next leader will perform the same pattern, but change it slightly, either by choice of body percussion level, or by changing the rhythm of one beat. The third leader may improvise a completely new four-beat rhythm, while the fourth leader must remember the first leader's performance and repeat it. The group will echo each leader in sequence, and then will follow the leaders, performing without the echo. This variation of the movement preparation may be repeated, using four families of untuned instruments.

Experimenting with melodic motives is more demanding, for the dimension of pitches moving up and down is added to the forward motion of rhythm. Ask your class to sing a melodic motive, such as one of the following examples.

Motive example 1   Motive example 2   Example 3

Ask the children to think of a way to change it, or create a'. The class can then sing the first, followed by the second. Continue, using the same process to complete one of the small forms listed above.

2   Analyze songs with question–answer phrases that together create a section. Improvise, based on the model.

After you have taught the following Mother Goose rhyme, ask your children to act out the poem with a partner, one asking and one answering.

> 'How many miles to Babylon?'
> 'Three score miles and ten.'
> 'Can I get there by candlelight?'
> 'Yes, and back again.'

When the children repeat the poem, ask them to speak with their hands rather than their voices. Experiment by substituting gestures, such as elbows, eyebrows, or nonsense syllables to indicate similarities and differences between questions and answers.

Look for other question–answer song phrases by reviewing songs your class has already learned, such as 'Babylon Is Falling' (p. 160) 'Bow, Wow, Wow' (p. 161) and 'Willowbee' (p. 162). Each has the form of a question phrase followed by an answer phrase. The children will observe that questions frequently fill all the beats of the phrase with rhythmic motion, while answering phrases frequently end with a long duration or rest. They will also hear that melodies move away from the tonic during the question phrase, but return to *do* by the end of the answering phrase.

The following activities may serve as frames for exploring rhythmic and melodic questions and answers. Begin by asking the class to perform four beats. You respond with three beats and a rest. Then ask half the class to clap a four-beat rhythm, filling all beats. Ask the other half to respond, placing a rest on the fourth beat. After this group practice ask the students to turn to a partner and repeat the exercise. Be sure to let several pairs perform for the class so others can hear examples and from them learn what sounds more like questions and more like answers. Alternating this activity with movement and chanting 'How many miles to Babylon?' not only extends the musical experience, but frames the length of the improvisations. Unpitched percussion may be used when the body percussion preparation seems secure.

You may link these objectives with 'Rhythm,' 5, and 'Melody,' 6, as they occur.

3 Identify ABA form as two contrasting sections followed by a repeat of the first.

I like to use 'Shoo Fly' as an example of ABA form because it is already familiar to my second graders and they hear the contrast quickly.

After we have sung the song together I invite them to walk around the room as they sing 'Shoo fly don't bother me....' They are to show me that they hear a new section by moving in place. They may walk again when the refrain returns. When the children have agreed when to stop to provide contrasting motion, form a circle and, using their suggestions, decide how they will move for the A section. It may be as simple as walking to the right for eight beats, and then to the left for eight beats. Now contrasting movement must be improvised, and this is easily achieved by turning to partners or trios. Give them a few minutes to solve the problem of providing contrasting movement, drawing, perhaps, on the ideas they used when they moved alone. Now when you and the class sing the song and move, the ABA form will be very obvious.

Your children have a structure to compare to other examples of ABA form. For instance, Edvard Grieg's *Norwegian Dance*, opus 35, no. 2, is a clear three-part form, but the children will be delighted to discover that each section has three phrases of eight beats. The A section is repeated at once, an octave higher, followed by a three-phrase B section which also repeats before returning to A. My second graders have enjoyed adjusting their movement to fit Grieg's music.

Norwegian Dance Opus 35, No. 2

Edvard Grieg

This form is used by many familiar composers in short to complex and lengthy compositions. Some frequently recorded examples which my children have enjoyed are: *Dance of the Sugar Plum Fairy* (ABA) from *The Nutcracker* by Peter Ilyich Tchaikovsky, *March* (AABA) from *The Comedians* by Dmitry Kabalevsky, *Ballet of the Unhatched Chickens* (AABA) from *Pictures at an Exhibition* by Modest Moussorgsky, and *Elephant* (ABA) from *Carnival of the Animals*, by Camille Saint-Saëns.

Additional resource
Frazee with Kreuter *Discovering Orff*, p. 115

During the second grade our students have been introduced to reading melodies and have strengthened their rhythmic performance and notation skills. They have had opportunities to analyze music and to apply what they heard to the music they played and sang. They have tested their skills and new knowledge as they made music while moving, singing, and playing. It has been a year of growing independence which should provide ample preparation for the challenges of third grade.

Before the year ends, record your evaluation of each student's ability to use rhythmic and melodic notation, to match pitch and sing in a group, and to use the instruments. Though these records are subjective, they help you to assess where your instruction should begin next year, as well as help you to determine what changes in the curriculum outline for second grade need to be made.

6 · Third Grade

In grade two, our students acquired basic rhythm and melody skills which provide the foundation for our goal of guiding them toward musical independence. Because these basic skills and knowledges are so important, I begin the third grade with a review of rhythmic durations, 2/4 and 4/4 meter, and the pentatonic scale; *do, re, mi, sol* and *la*. Through a review of singing games and favorite settings I can quickly assess what the children remember and what they may need to be taught again before moving on. Each year the time needed to complete this re-evaluation and the content of the review may vary, due to the changes in our school environment. Yet the effectiveness of continuing instruction is dependent on being aware of what our students actually know. When this evaluation is complete, we are ready to move on.

Goals

I like to begin third grade rhythm studies with the introduction of triple meter, for this allows the children to use durations that are familiar while being challenged to place them in new patterns. Later in the year syncopation will be introduced and improvisation in known durations and meters will broaden their ability to use rhythm musically.

Third graders are stronger singers and have an increased vocal range, often from c to e′ or f′. They will be reading an expanded pentatonic scale to match this range, introducing *la* and *sol* below *do*. When we present and explore *la* as a tonal center we introduce the children to the potential of modalities, to be presented in later grades.

Expanded range and stronger voices contribute to the children's enthusiasm for melodic ostinato and canon singing. Our success is dependent on our combined efforts to be always conscious of singing in tune, alone and with the group. Third graders need our help in learning to listen for what is accurate and beautiful in their vocal performance so that they become able to set their own standards for a musical performance. As mentioned earlier, hearing other children through live performances and recordings is one way to help students understand the quality of sound you wish them to attain. If children are to enjoy singing in more complex textures they must have the skills to sing, hear and analyze as they perform.

Near the beginning of third grade I like to introduce the letter names of the lines and spaces of the staff. In second grade the students were introduced to syllables on the staff, and playing barred instruments has already labeled pitches with letters as well as solfege names. It is important to take time now to learn the letter names of pitches on the staff and to practice identifying them by both letter and syllable as a way of linking classroom music to the music they may be learning outside of school.

Not only are third graders singing with a wider range and stronger sound, they are more dexterous. Instrumental accompaniments can be more challenging, and they can learn these parts more quickly with the increased use of notation. They are capable of playing instrumental pieces, and the more complex ones may be taught from aural dictation, preparing them for reading skills to be introduced at higher grade levels. Because they are physically ready, it is important to plan for their skill development, both in singing and playing.

Throughout the year the children will enjoy opportunities to improvise as a way to practice and demonstrate what they know. Musical problems requiring several steps may be solved more enjoyably in pairs or small groups because of their increased literacy and skill level.

There are several objectives which I save for the second half of the school year. First, *fa* will be introduced, signalling our departure from pentatonic melodies. This will be more meaningful for the children if they are skilled in performing and analyzing pentatonic melodies. Then notation of syncopation will be presented and practiced through improvisation. And, finally, experiences in performing sixteenth notes and compound meter will be introduced in preparation for notation in fourth grade. Before taking these steps I must evaluate the ability of the children to perform these patterns accurately. This is an important step from Part I, you will remember, because our literacy objectives follow our performance objectives. Consequently, echo activities and aural dictation become important preparations as well as a means for me to assess the pace of our progress through the year's objectives.

Using the Curriculum Outline

From this discussion we are aware that the selection and arrangement of our objectives may be dictated by our appreciation for the children's fine motor coordination and their ability to give attention to tuneful singing. There are influences outside our classrooms that can affect our ordering of objectives. In our desire to work with other teachers and school programs it may be more efficient and effective to begin with melody objectives, for example. Or an opportunity to hear an orchestra performance may prompt us to deal with texture and form earlier in the year. In each case, having a curriculum structure within which we can move blocks of objectives becomes invaluable, for it prevents us from losing direction as well as appreciation for what we have already accomplished. When you see the suggestions in smaller type in the curriculum order you will remember that these are only to help you respond with a flexibility that acknowledges the unique conditions of each year's instruction.

Third Grade Objectives

Rhythm

1 Compare duple with triple meter through movement, song, speech, and instrumental activities.
2 Identify ♩. as ♪ ♪ ♪
3 Define 3/4 meter and determine bar line placement in rhymes and songs.
4 Perform, move, read, and conduct music in triple meter.

Consider moving to melody objectives 1–4. In this way, you can practice known rhythm skills while presenting new melody objectives.

Consider developing improvisation experiences based on 'Form,' 1 before taking dictation.

5 Take dictation in 2/4, 4/4 and 3/4 meters.
6 Identify the anacrusis (upbeat) as duration(s) which anticipate the downbeat.
7 Perform syncopation in movement, song, and instrumental activities.
8 Read and write syncopation as ♪ ♩♩ ♪ and ♪ ♩ ♪ .
9 Improvise and/or compose using the durations already known to the class.
10 Take dictation, in duple and triple meter, using the known durations.

> Consider moving to melody objectives 5 and 6, while practicing these durations and preparing to introduce the notation of sixteenth notes.

Melody

1 Add reading and writing low *la* to the tonal vocabulary (*l   d r m   s l'   d'*).
2 Add reading and writing low *sol* to the tonal vocabulary (*s l   d r m   s' l'   d'*).
3 Identify *la* as a tonal center in d, e, and a.

> Consider moving to your place in the rhythm sequence, or to 'Texture,' 1–3, 'Harmony,' 1, or 'Form,' 2 while practicing music in the pentatonic scale and before evaluating through written dictation.

4 Take three- and four-note dictation, using *s, l, d, r, m, s', l'*.
5 Add *fa* to the tonal vocabulary to make a six-note or hexatonic scale.
6 Read, write, play, and improvise or compose melodies using the hexatonic scale, *d r mf s l   d'*.
7 Take dictation of four pitches from the hexatonic scale.

Texture

1 Sing and play one part in textures of up to four complementary lines.
2 Perform an instrumental canon with the group, and then with one or two other players.
3 Sing and/or play a melodic ostinato with a melody.
.4 Sing two- and three-part canons with the class and in small groups.

Harmony

1 Play the arpeggiated bordun and melodies requiring cross-over hand motions.
2 Perform moving bordun accompaniments with a partner and alone.
3 Perform bass ostinatos to prepare for the recognition of chord roots.

Timbre

1 Develop percussion techniques necessary to play accurately syncopations and sixteenth notes on classroom instruments.

> This may be integrated through settings with rhythm and melody objectives. It must, however, be presented before reading and writing syncopation and sixteenth notes.

Form

1 Improvise rhythmic themes in question-and-answer phrases in 2/4, 3/4, and 4/4 meters, using the known durations.

> This may be integrated with improvisation objectives of rhythm 9.

2 Improvise melodies, using texts and question-and-answer phrases in 2/4, 3/4, and 4/4 meters, in pentatonic scales on *do* and *la*.

This may be integrated with the improvisation objectives of melody 6.

3 Improvise or compose sections to extend known materials to include rondo form.

Rhythm

1 Compare duple with triple meter through movement, song, speech, and instrumental activities.

Your children have become well acquainted with duple meter and common or 4/4 time through performing, reading and writing in second grade. They have sung and moved to music in compound meter as well, responding primarily to the duple accents. Be sure to include experiences in triple meter during your review at the beginning of the year before moving to this next step.

Because I want to base their understanding of triple meter on an internalized physical response, I like to begin our study with movement. Use two rototoms, temple blocks or piano to guide this activity. As you play ♩ ♪ ♪ ♩ ♪ ♪ (low, high, high), have the children respond with motions that pantomime activities from home or the playground. Respond to their motions by chanting descriptive words, such as 'down, up, up,.' or 'Toss, wait, catch,' which may help to clarify and refine their motions. Let them watch each other and describe solutions that match your tempo and accents. Then change to duple, or ♩ ♪ ♩ ♪ (low, high, low, high), and repeat the exercise. This time your discussion will lead to a comparison of the motions of each meter.

From the motions created by the students, select one for each meter (you may want to add a third in 4/4.) Perform each in a series of four-measure sets. To increase their consciousness, I like to have the children count the beats in each measure aloud as we move from one meter to the next. Words may also be used.

Have the words of 'Piping Hot' visible to the class. As you chant the rhyme in three, ask the children to discover the meter and illustrate it with a simple body percussion accompaniment.

Piping Hot

Piping hot, smoking hot,	(♩ ♩ ♩ |♩ ♩ ♪)
What I've got, you have not.	(♩ ♩ ♩ |♩ ♩ ♪)
Hot grey pease, hot, hot hot,	(♩ ♩ ♩ |♩ ♩ ♪)
Hot grey pease, hot!	(♩ ♩ ♩ |♩ 𝄽 𝄽)

After they have chanted it with you and their accompaniment, ask them to notate the poem placing stress marks below the appropriate beats in each line.

Now ask the students to pat-clap as they read the poem silently in duple. They will create several rhythmic solutions which they will enjoy comparing through performance and notation. A little piece can be created by chanting in three, followed by a solo in two, then returning to threes. Another way to compare is to work with a partner or small group to transer the word rhythms to body percussion pieces. Over the page are ways your class may notate this poem.

The children will hear the result of their analysis when a group of children play each version on different unpitched instrument timbres.

In order to prepare for the presentation of triple meter in notation, take a few minutes each lesson to practice echoing body percussion patterns in duple and triple. Ask the children also to echo using rhythm syllables, as this helps them aurally analyze what they hear.

Additional resource
Frazee with Kreuter *Discovering Orff*, p. 120
    For additional games comparing meters.

2   *Identify ♩. as ♩ ♩ ♩*

Place the words of this poem, 'Growing,' in front of the children, with the notation of quarter notes for each line beside it.

Growing
Go to bed late,   ♩ ♩ ♩ ♩ ♩ ♩
Grow very small,   ♩ ♩ ♩ ♩ ♩ ♩
Go to bed early,   ♩ ♩ ♩ ♩ ♩ ♩
Grow very tall!   ♩ ♩ ♩ ♩ ♩ ♩

Ask the children to listen for long durations as you speak the poem, being careful to sustain the last syllable of each line. Now they can tie these beats or quarter notes together. Then write the tied quarters as ♩ ♩ ♩ and finally as ♩.. After chanting the poem together, repeat it in canon at the interval of one measure. The children will be able to hear one group chant three syllables as the other chants one.

The poem may be played by having one group perform the quarter notes on drums and half and dotted half notes on triangles, while group two plays the quarter notes on woodblocks and half and dotted half notes on finger cymbals.

3   *Define 3/4 meter by determining bar line placement in rhymes and songs.*

From the notation the children worked out for 'Piping Hot' and 'Growing,' it is an easy step to defining the meter and placing the bar lines in rhythmic notation. Help them remember that the bar line falls in front of the metric accent, and that the rhythm of both poems falls in groups of three beats.

Place the accompaniment for 'My Horses Ain't Hungry' on the board as unbarred ostinatos. Ask the students to put in the bar lines to help them see each pattern more clearly.

As they perform the accompaniment in body percussion you can present the song vocally or on recorder. When the melody is whistled a lovely effect results, the makings of an introduction or coda. One by one, transfer the body percussion to the timbres called for in the score as the children learn the song.

My Horses Ain't Hungry

2. I know you're my Polly,
   I'm not going to stay.
   So come with me darlin',
   We'll feed on the way.

3. With all our belongings,
   We'll ride 'til we come
   To a lonely little cabin,
   We'll call it our home.

Additional resources

Hamm *Crocodile and Other Poems*
   'The Icicle' (p. 19)
Orff *Music for Children*, American edn., Vol. 2
   'Cotton-Eyed Joe' (p. 170, no. 218)
   'Bed Is Too Small' (p. 171, no. 219)
   'American Lullaby' (p. 171, no. 220)

4   *Perform, move, read, and conduct music in triple meter.*

Dalcroze Eurhythmics teachers frequently suggest conducting exercises that use large motion responses which may be refined to conventional conducting patterns later. My children have enjoyed these activities and they have understood my function as conductor better after practicing being conductors themselves. To conduct in two, the children bring their arms down on beat one, hands closed, opening them on beat two and moving up, pointing fingers above the head. The first and last beats of every meter are conducted in the same way. Walking to the music you provide while conducting in two is quite easy for third graders. To conduct in three, move arms down on beat one, hands closed; for beat two, move arms out to the side, hands relaxed and palms facing up; and on beat three, move arms up, pointing fingers up. It is sometimes a challenge for my students to conduct and walk in three, and it helps to walk in place first. When conducting in four, the first, third and last beats are the same as in triple meter. Bring hands down on beat one, up to chest level on beat two, and finish by moving out on three, up on four. These large motions may be refined to parallel our conventional conducting patterns. However, our purpose here is to help build another physical response to meters, and to give our children one more comparison of them.

Tossing a bean bag or ball between partners is another good way to illustrate meters. Each pair or each small group is to find a way to demonstrate triple meter by moving the ball in a pattern of three motions with the strongest stroke on one. Ask them to sing 'My Horses Ain't Hungry' as they demonstrate the meter.

Ask the children to internalize their motions as you sing 'How Long, Watchman?' They should be able to identify what words fall on dotted half notes. When the song is learned, form a circle of partners. As they sing, add the motion of clapping their partner's hands on beat one, and their own hands on beats two and three. Then ask them to turn to the person at their backs to clap the next phrase. In this way they will discover that this song has three-measure phrases, a special delight when the meter is three as well.

When I prepare the setting I review the song first by having the children sight-read it in solfege. Then each part is taught from notation. Sometimes I ask the children to teach me a part through body percussion motions they determine by reading it. This spiritual has three verses of Bible stories that demonstrate that sometimes we have to wait a long time for results. We like to use soloists who speak expressively over a tremolo on F on a bass metallophone or timpani. We respond as the score indicates. You may want to use student ideas and add percussion color to dramatize each verse.

How Long, Watchman?

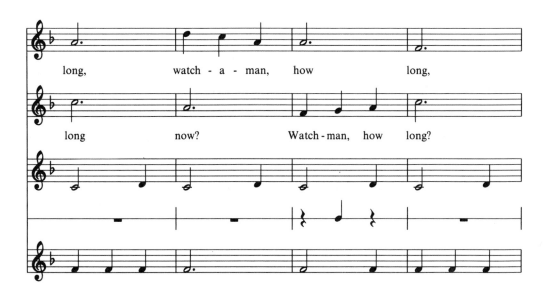

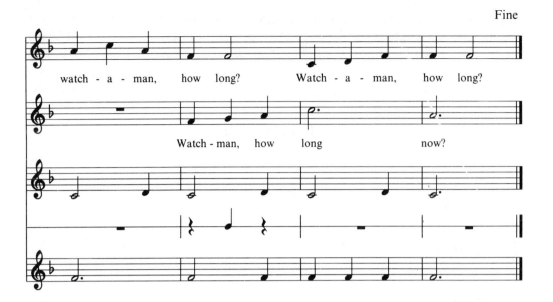

watch - a - man, how long? Watch - a - man, how long?

Watch - man, how long now?

Chant: no meter

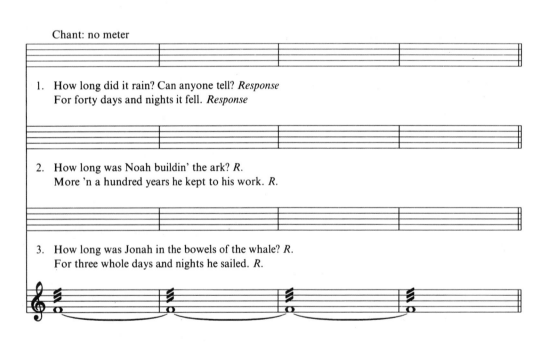

1. How long did it rain? Can anyone tell? *Response*
   For forty days and nights it fell. *Response*

2. How long was Noah buildin' the ark? *R.*
   More 'n a hundred years he kept to his work. *R.*

3. How long was Jonah in the bowels of the whale? *R.*
   For three whole days and nights he sailed. *R.*

Response to chant

V

How long, watch - a - man, how long?

BM

Because we tend to teach fewer songs and pieces in triple than we do in duple, it is important to provide sufficient time to practice rhythms in this meter. 'Calliope' gives your students practice in reading and performing on both barred and unpitched instruments. The melody was written to be played by alternating hands up and down the pentatonic scale. The bass xylophone part is best played without alternating hands, and outlines the meter clearly. The glockenspiel part will give your better coordinated players a challenge, for each measure should begin with the right hand.

'No Tune Calliope' is like 'Calliope' in many ways. Ask the children to compare the theme's rhythm in each, and then ask them to point out the ways in which the rhythms are the same, and ways they are different. If all children prepared 'Calliope' with body percussion, there will be no need to prepare the children to play this piece, for they are nearly identical rhythmically. You may perform 'Calliope' as an A section, with 'No Tune Calliope' as a contrasting B, or you may perform both pieces as an ABA piece. Parts of 'No tune Calliope' may serve as an introduction or coda for 'Calliope.'

No Tune Calliope

Now that your children have discovered that the rhythms of the percussion piece used patterns from 'Calliope,' it will be easy to use it as a model for improvisation. Just erase measures, as illustrated in the model below. Tell the children you want to hear different rhythms in these measures. After they have practiced silently, and then lightly with body percussion, ask for solos. First, have the wood solos followed by drum solos, using the metal instrument accompaniment. The children may enjoy improvising on woods and drums at the same time, a test of their rhythmic security in triple meter. More measures may be erased for each solo until they are improvising on the model they have in their minds and kinesthetic memories.

These pieces may inspire your students to compose a poem or story about a calliope that becomes worn, rejected, and then perhaps restored by your class. They may also enjoy creating a movement piece to perform to a recording of their calliope music.

Additional resources

Carley *Recorders with Orff Ensemble*, Bk. 1
    'Fairy Lullaby' (p. 23, no. 15)
    Use recorder, or substitute alto
    glockenspiels.
Frazee *Orff Handbook for World of Music – K*
    'We Give Thanks' (p. 21)
    This is written in 2/2, but if counted in four
    it gives a wonderful opportunity to
    practice dotted half notes in 4/4.
Ladendecker *Tunes for Young Troubadours*
    'Song of the Donkey' (p. 2)
Orff and Keetman *Music for Children*, adpt.
    Murray, Vol. I
    'Canon exercise' (p. 91, no. 2a)
    'Rondo' (p. 111)

> Consider moving to melody objectives 1–4. In this way, you can practice known rhythm skills while presenting new melody objectives.
>
> Consider developing improvisation experiences based on 'Form,' 1 before taking dictation.

5   *Take dictation in 2/4, 4/4, and 3/4 meters.*

The purpose of dictation at this point is to test each child's understanding of rhythmic values, rather than testing the strength of their memories. For this reason I begin dictation exercises with two measures, and then give them one longer example as an extra challenge.

The process we use is important, for we are helping them internalize and analyze a pattern before they write it down. I have found the following process works well for my children. I stand where the children can see me perform. First, I perform the example, usually on a drum. The students clap back the example. Then I repeat it, and this time they echo clap as before, and then repeat it in their minds, using rhythm syllables. Now the children are prepared to write. The following examples are drawn from materials presented under previous objectives. (The boxes contain suggestions for dictation.)

At another time, test the child's understanding of meter by asking her to place bar lines in a score. There is no performance for the child reads the meter signature and places the bar lines in the correct positions.

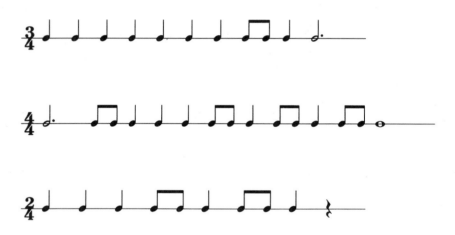

And, finally, they are to identify the meter by counting the number of beats in each measure and placing that number in the time signature.

6   *Identify the anacruiss (upbeat) as duration(s) which anticipates the downbeat.*

When triple meter was introduced, your students were introduced to conducting motions. After you and they have begun to conduct in two, ask them to join you in singing 'Angel Band,' a song they learned in second grade (p. 137). 'On what beat do the numbers fall?' you may ask. 'The first beat,' they will reply. 'What words are sung between the numbers?' you continue. 'There was,' they should respond. 'What conducting beat fell on these words?' From this question they will observe that this is the second beat which moves up, consequently called the upbeat or anacrusis. Walk, stepping only on beat one, but conducting and singing 'Angel Band.' The song begins on the upbeat, borrowed from the ending.

Next, review 'My Horses Ain't Hungry', (p. 185) and again, review the conducting for triple meter. On what beat does this song begin, and what conducting gesture do we use? Again, they will identify the upbeat, this time in triple meter.

When you review the conducting pattern in four, introduce the children to 'This Old Hammer' which begins on an upbeat. When the children imitate swinging a sledge hammer, they will feel the upward motion to the swing, as well as the strong downbeat. The setting can be taught by relating each part to the conducting beats.

This Old Hammer

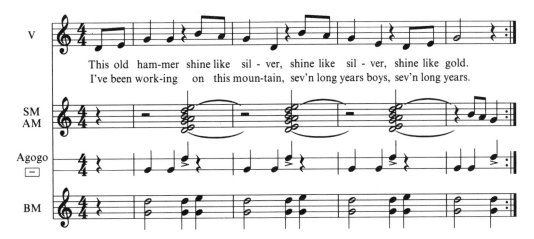

193

To reinforce the meaning of anacrusis, I ask my students to look through a songbook for other songs that begin with an upbeat. They may recall other songs they know as well.

7 *Perform syncopation in movement, song, and instrumental activities.*

We can begin our study of syncopation with a familiar melody, 'Black Snake,' which they learned in second grade (p. 155).

Black Snake

Black snake, black snake, where are you hid - ing? Black snake, black snake, where are you hid - ing? Don't you bite____ me!

Sing and clap it with your students as you walk to the beat, turning with each phrase. Ask them what durations are in each rhythmic phrase and then demonstrate this by walking forward with the four quarter notes, turning to step on eighth notes for the second half of the phrase.

Practice this movement pattern while singing before introducing the next step. Then clap the melodic rhythm of phrases one, two and three with the movement pattern to discover where the longer sounds are in the second measure. When they step this rhythm again they will be more conscious of the short–loooong–short durations they are clapping.

One other experiment may help demonstrate the off-beat accents caused by syncopation. One partner claps on the down beat, and snaps on the up beat, making large gestures as he moves his hands and arms down, then up. The partner stands facing him and claps the melodic rhythm, moving left to right. The snaps of the second beat should be clearly audible, and some will see the snap in relationship to the clapped quarter note.

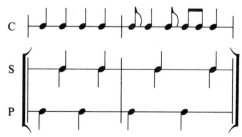

The melodic rhythm of 'Black Snake' makes a pleasing two-part rhythmic canon at the interval of one measure. Help your students choose distinctly different timbres for each part to illustrate the relationship of syncopation to the quarter notes. This rhythm can also be used as a basis for melodic exploration while giving a little practice in syncopation. Ask the children to change melodic pitches on measures 1, 3, 5, and 7, but repeat the rhythm on *do*, *mi*, or *sol* in measures 2, 4, and 6, ending on *do* in 8.

8 *Read and write syncopation as* ♩♪♩♩ *and* ♪♩ ♪ .

Now your students are ready to use notation to picture these experiences. First, draw the eight quarter notes that define the length of the phrase, and draw the bar lines for 4/4 meter. Next, on the line below, write the rhythm of the movement pattern used in 'Black Snake,' and ask the children to place a stress mark below each eighth note that was present in the melodic rhythm. The final step is to show the two eighth note sounds tied. This cuts the linked eighth notes in half, and the children are introduced to the convention of placing flags on the right side of the note stem.

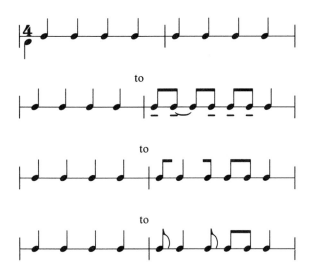

For notation practice have your students write the rhythm of 'Black Snake' in canon at the interval of one measure, for it again illustrates the sound of syncopation against the beat.

'I Heard the Angels Singing' can now be taught by reading the melodic rhythm. Place it on the board in stick notation with the syllable letters below. For comparison, place the notation of each accompaniment part you add below or above the melodic rhythm. Let the students choose the timbre for the unpitched rhythm which echoes the syncopation of the song.

195

I Heard the Angels Singing

One morn - ing soon,____ one morn - ing soon,____

One morn - ing, one morn - ing,

one morn - ing soon I heard the an - gels sing - ing.____

one morn - ing I heard them sing.

2. Down on my knees   3. One day 'bout noon

The class may enjoy composing an introduction using syncopation, and a coda as well, using timbres that set the mood and dynamic level to fit their interpretation of the song.

It will be important next to present a number of songs that include syncopation, either in the melodies or in the settings. 'The Poor and the Rich' may be taught for practice in reading syncopation and other durations. In addition, the setting also prepares the 'student for other learning, since the bass ostinato outlines tonic–dominant harmony, and the melody presents the pentantonic scale in a new key, D.

The Poor and the Rich

Josh-ua sat down in the tem-ple of Gil-li-um, Al - li - al - li il - li - um

yu - az - u - ray. He had a bad at-tack of spi-nal men-en-gil - li - um,

Al - li - al - li il - li - um   yu - az - u - ray.   Yu - az - u - ray,

yu - az - u - ray.   Al - li - al - li il - li - um,   yu - az - u - ray.

Your children will enjoy listening to *Golliwog's Cakewalk*, from *Children's Corner Suite* by Claude Debussy. Its primary theme is the familiar syncopated theme your students have just studied.

Additional resources
Boshkoff *All Around the Buttercup*
  'Canoe Song' (p. 21)
Carley *Recorders with Orff Ensembles*, Bk. 1
  'Miniature Suite and March' (p. 8)
Earley *Something Told the Wild Geese*
  'Whistle, Daughter, Whistle' (p. 9)
Fuoco-Lawson *Street Games*
  'Down, Down, Baby (p. 8)

9   *Improvise and/or compose, using the durations already known to the class.*

Your children will be able to write the rhythm of the nonsense words of the response in 'The Rich and the Poor'. By determining the meter and the length of the response they can also predict the length and number of measures in phrases 1, 3 and 5, which function as the question phrase. Give them time to compose question phrases of eight beats in their minds, using patterns they know, especially syncopation. Then call on a number of students to perform their solutions.

Their improvisations may be taken a step further. Place a conga or bongo drum in the center of the circle and invite as many as eight students to line up to perform their question phrases on the drum. The class then responds in body percussion, using the response rhythm they wrote from the song.

I have a set of flash cards of four-beat patterns we have read and performed in class. Sometimes we use them for sight-reading practice, flipping through them at a set tempo. I also use the cards for small group writing projects. Give each group four cards. Be sure one card makes a logical ending, and that one has a syncopation. The group is to arrange a two-measure question and a two-measure answer, using two or more cards. (They do not have to use all the cards, for motives may be repeated.) When their composition is finished they must decide how to perform it, using body percussion, movement or vocal sound.

Then ask the groups to turn over one card and perform their composition, replacing the pattern with a new rhythm.

10   *Take dictation, in duple and triple meters, using the known durations.*

I like to repeat the use of a format for dictation, for my students respond favorably to mechanics that they already know. To test the children's understanding of durations they have read so far, use the model of 'Rhythm,' 5 or one of these two variations of written exercises or quizzes which I have used with my third graders.

Testing Example 1

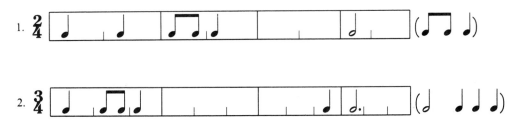

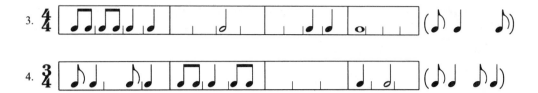

To complete the first example the children must listen and analyze the rhythmic phrase for missing durations. I perform the rhythm, they echo, and I repeat the rhythm before they fill in the missing notes. Example 2 does not require aural analysis. Rather, it tests their familiarity with the symbols and meter. Instruct the students to compose a rhythmic phrase. You determine the length of the phrase and the meter. You may choose to specify that it contain syncopation or certain durations in order to find out their ability to use the symbols you have just introduced. After checking their examples I often ask my students to perform them.

You may use the following:

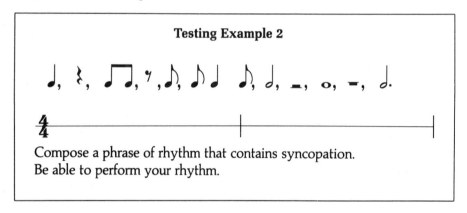

Consider moving to melody objectives 5 and 6, while practicing these durations and preparing to introduce the notation of sixteenth notes.

Melody

1   Add reading and writing low la *to the tonal vocabulary (*l   d r m   s l'   d'*).*

Before proceeding with the year's melodic objectives, I find it important to be sure the children are singing and reading the syllables *do, re, mi, sol, la,* and high *do,* accurately. This may be checked by sight-reading songs I used earlier to teach rhythmic objectives. If the children are reading well as a class I continue the sequence with assurance that they are ready for the next step.

I like to teach 'Grinding Corn' by rote, introducing the simple percussion accompaniment first as I sing. Then I ask the children to look at three cards which represent the melody.

From this the students can identify the melodic outline as b a b a c c. If they are good detectives, they will inform you that low *la* is missing. Once again, I like to use the alto xylophone, set in F pentatonic, so that children can compare the bars and spaces to the syllable ladder and the staff.

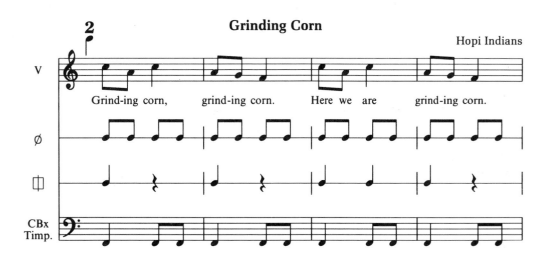

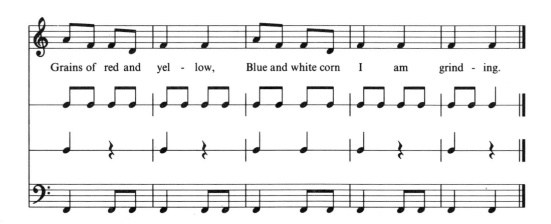

When the notation has been completed, return to the song and setting. Instrument players may sit in the center of the circle while others move around the circle, using a simple toe–heel step.

'Crawdad Hole,' which was used to perform and read whole notes in second grade, repeats the same *mi–do–la* motive the children discovered in 'Grinding Corn,' and uses all the other pentatonic notes. The alto xylophone part contains *sol*, the syllable to be presented next in the familiar role of the fifth of the bordun. You may wish to review the song here.

2   Add reading and writing low sol *to the tonal vocabulary (s l   d r m s' l'   d').*

When working with melodic notation it helps children achieve the objective if they use only note heads. Write the melodic outline of 'The Squirrel' on the board, and ask your students to sing it in syllables. The low *sol* is purposely left out. Then ask them to check the outline against your melody, two measures at a time. In this way they will hear and be able to place *sol* below *do*. Again, they may test their notation against the bars and spaces on an alto xylophone.

Melodic outline: **The Squirrel**

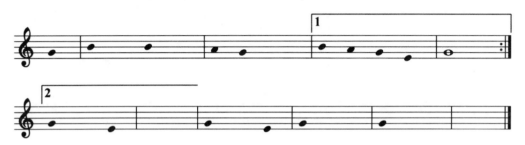

Singing *sol,–la,–sol,* immediately prepares the alto xylophone, which can accompany you as you teach the words of the song written on the board. The two woodblock parts should be on two different pitches, as though chattering to each other. Ask your students to make an introduction, which they will sing, beginning with low *sol–la–do*, and notate the results for them.

The Squirrel

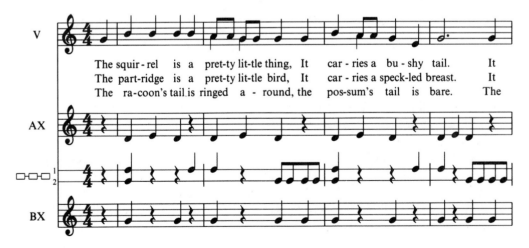

The squir-rel is a pret-ty lit-tle thing, It car - ries a bu - shy tail. It
The part-ridge is a pret-ty lit-tle bird, It car - ries a speck-led breast. It
The ra-coon's tail.is ringed a - round, the pos-sum's tail is bare. The

202

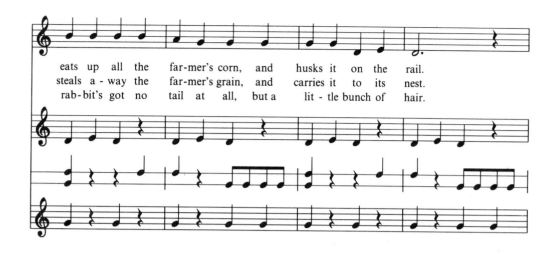

eats up all the far-mer's corn, and husks it on the rail.
steals a - way the far-mer's grain, and carries it to its nest.
rab-bit's got no tail at all, but a lit - tle bunch of hair.

Ho! Ho!_____ Ho! Ho! And husks it on the rail.
Ho! Ho!_____ Ho! Ho! And carries it to its nest.
Ho! Ho!_____ Ho! Ho! A lit - tle bunch of hair.

Now third graders will be able to sight-read many pentatonic songs with low *sol* and *la*. Many of these songs will begin with *sol–la* on an upbeat ('Rhythm,' 6). For example 'Angel Band' (p. 137) and 'This Old Hammer' (p. 193).

Additonal resources

Frazee *Orff Handbook for World of Music – 4*
   'Harvest Time' (p. 7)
Orff *Music for Children*, American edn., Vol. 2
   'Miss Susan Brown' (p. 172, no. 221)
Orff *Music for Children*, American edn., Vol. 3
   'Smile in Your Pocket' (A section only)
   (p. 10, no. 5)
   'How Many Miles to Bethlehem?' (p. 25,
   no. 11)
   'The Little Black Bull' (p. 27, no. 12)

Orff and Keetman *Music for Children,* adpt.
  Murray, Vol. 1, p. 95
  An instrumental piece.
Steen *Orff Activities,* Grade 3
  'Lone Star Trail' (p. 14)
  'Sing About Martin' (p. 11)

3   Identify la *as the tonal center in d, e, and a.*

Though your third graders have sung songs of minor character, their second grade studies of pitch notation focused on songs centered on *do* as the tonal center and lowest pitch. In third grade they have also had practice in playing, singing, analyzing and improvising melodies which revolve around *do* as the tonal center, with *sol* and *la* above and below it.

One way to present *la* as the tonal center is to introduce songs in which *la* is the most predominant note. Place this melodic fragment on the board and ask the class to sight-read first the rhythm, and then the melody, using syllables.

Ask your students what syllable seems most important and why. They will observe that there are four pitches on *do* or f, and that these pitches begin and end this phrase. Next, ask them to tell you how many times the phrase occurs in 'Sioux Lullaby.' As they hum a sustained *do* you will sing or play 'Sioux Lullaby'. If they have difficulty sustaining the pitch, support it by asking a child to tremelo on an alto xylophone f bar. Does their sustained *do* seem to be the tonal center? Is the phrase correctly written? Let the children correct the notation. Ask another student to circle all the notes that are the tonal center or, in this case, *la*. The children will discover that it is more comfortable to hum 'la' as you perform the melody again.

Sioux Lullaby

arr. AS

Now ask your children what note should be most important in our orchestration, since *la* is the tonal center. The answer may lead you to add instruments for the B section first. After teaching the instrument parts ask the children to conduct themselves in three and discover that this pattern does not fit the B section. Then, when you return to the first theme, they will be prepared to discover that it is in three. The arpeggiated bordun supports a strong feeling of three, so have all children practice by patting the right knee with the right hand, then left hand on left knee. Raise right hand on rest, then pat right knee, left hand pats left knee, right hand goes over left hand. Then the pattern begins again. My third graders asked to play and sing the first melody in canon. While not in the style of Native American music, it was a challenge my students enjoyed. The song is also pretty without this part, substituting woodland sounds of the children's invention for an introduction, section B and a coda. Verses are made by singing the names of various family members who could care for the small one.

Though our American folk music has fewer songs of *la* pentatonic tonality than of *do*, becoming familiar with it is the foundation for minor and modal experiences to follow in fourth and fifth grade. Take time to sing several *la* pentatonic songs, preferably in several meters and styles.

'I'll Sing You A Song' is in e pentatonic, giving the children another opportunity to test their knowledge by comparing the notation of e to d pentatonic. The word rhythms anticipate our study of sixteenth notes, while the melody and accompaniment patterns practice typical melodic patterns in this scale.

I'll Sing You a Song

arr. AS

I'll sing you a song and it's not ve - ry long, it's a - bout a young man who would-n't hoe corn. The rea-son why I can-not tell, for this young man was al-ways well.

Additional resources
Boshkoff *All Around the Buttercup*
  'Far Too Much Noise' (p. 20)
Carley *Recorders with Orff Ensemble*, Bk. 1
  'All Hands Round' (p. 24, no. 16)
  You may play the melody to inspire
  children's movement which identifies
  la- and *do*-centered melodies in this ABA piece.
Frazee *Orff Handbook for World of Music — 4*
  'Leatherwing Bat' (p. 14)
Goetze *Simply Sung*
  'My Good Old Man' (p. 6)
Steen *Orff Activities*, Grade 3
  'Debka Hora' (p. 22)

Take time, before moving on to the next melodic objective, to insert an opportunity for improvisation, using low *sol* and *la* in both *do* and *la* pentatonic. The discussion of this objective under 'Form,' 2, will give you materials and procedures to guide improvisation.

> Consider moving to your place in the rhythm sequence, or to 'Texture,' 1–3, 'Harmony,' 1, or 'Form,' 2, while practicing music in the pentatonic scale and before evaluating through written dictation.

4 *Take three- and four-note dictation, using s, l, d, r, m, s' l'.*

One way to help children become familiar with melodic dictation is to give them a little mystery to solve. First prepare them with aural dictation, by pointing to a typical pattern, such as *s l s m d* on the syllable ladder. Ask them to sing it back to you in syllables. After success with several of these, repeat the patterns but point to the staff instead.

These sheets contain the first phrases of four familiar songs. After they write the letters of the syllables below the notation, they may place the title of the song or the words of the phrase below the notation. (Since you have warmed up their tonal memories before giving them the sheets, and all four examples are in the same pentatonic, you have helped them to hear the examples in their minds.)

Staff and scale on the board

Mystery Song Quiz Examples

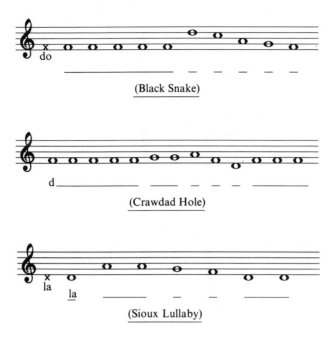

(Black Snake)

(Crawdad Hole)

(Sioux Lullaby)

Another way to test their reading skills is to give them a sheet with two possible answers. They just check the example you sing. The results of this quiz helps me to evaluate whether the students hear general contours of melodies or precise movement from interval to interval.

I also use evaluation tools like these to help me decide whether my students are ready to move the the next step, adding *fa* to their tonal vocabulary. If a significant number of children are unsure of pentatonic notation I postpone the introduction of *fa* and spend additional time applying and practicing what we already know.

5   *Add* fa *to the tonal vocabulary, to make a six-note or hexatonic scale.*

Sometimes my students have wondered aloud when we would 'get to sing *fa*.' Of course, we have been singing this syllable in rote songs, and, for several weeks before presenting *fa* in notation, we have introduced it into our echo singing of familiar melodic motives.

I like to introduce *fa* into notation through a song with scale-step phrases. 'By'm Bye' introduces *fa* in a *mi-fa-sol* motive in a song that requires only a simple orchestration to be effective. The children may already know the song from previous years, or it is easy to teach by rote, preparing the exploration in the lesson by asking the children to echo you as you count stars. The setting for the introduction and the bordun may be taught next, for these are familiar accompaniment patterns.

By'm Bye

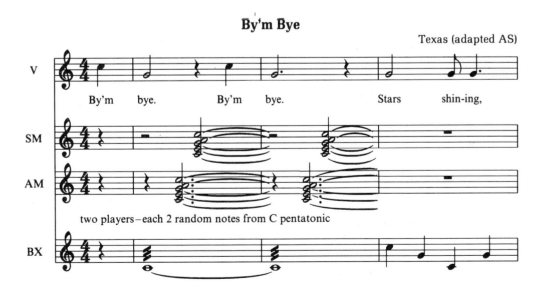

num-ber, num-ber one, (num-ber   one) num-ber two, (num-ber   two) num-ber three, (num-ber

(explore combinations of mi fa sol)

three) num-ber four, (m - f - s)   num-ber five, (m - f - s)   num-ber six. (m - f -

s) There are more! Oh   my,   by'm bye, by'm bye, good Lawd,   by'm bye.

Next, invite the children to choose a barred instrument set in C pentatonic to echo each star. Of course, they quickly discover that they now need *fa* or f to complete the pattern. The first time through the song each child should echo the pattern as it is sung. In another lesson, invite each child who echoes to use only *mi, fa* and *sol*, in the same rhythm, but in any order, giving each star its own unique sound. A third time the children may enjoy a little ear teaser. Each instrument soloist plays *mi-fa-sol* in any order, followed by a singer or singers who echo, using the correct syllables. At first it will help the children who echo to be able to see the instrument they echo. It will also help them to perform the song at a moderate tempo to allow the children to listen carefully before responding in syllables.

The second step is to give the children chances to read *fa* in melodies and accompaniment lines that are not in scale order. The second model lesson in Part I, Chapter 2, deals with this step. Here is a second setting, 'Ching-a-ring,' that will give your students this practice while providing a preliminary experience with sixteenth notes. Since our goal is to practice reading *fa*, we begin this lesson by placing the melodic outline of each phrase on the board, in mixed-up order. Ask your students to label each note by syllable, and after singing each, have the class arrange them in the correct order.

Melodic outline: **Ching-a-ring**

Now teach the rhythm of the words by rote and add this to the melody. The children may be able to think of the musical instrument that this song imitates, the banjo. The bass part should be taught by singing it in syllables, and both it and the tambourine parts may be taught from notation. Teach the alto xylophone part by imitation. Help the children to draw the conclusion that when *fa* is in a phrase it is prudent to listen for changes the accompaniment may require.

Ching-a-ring

Ching-a-ring a-ring ching ching!   Ho - a-ding cum lar - key!

A final step is to hear, sing, play and identify the need for a lowered fourth or b flat in the key of F. 'The Grand Old Duke of York,' in the key of F, is easy to teach, for the students will hear that the melody goes up the scale and down. After they have learned the song and the setting, invite one child to play the melody. That child or members of the class will be perplexed when hearing the b natural; you then introduce the b flat bar to replace b natural. The children will then realize the need for a key signature. From now on when you present pitched instrument parts in F use the key signature.

The Grand Old Duke of York

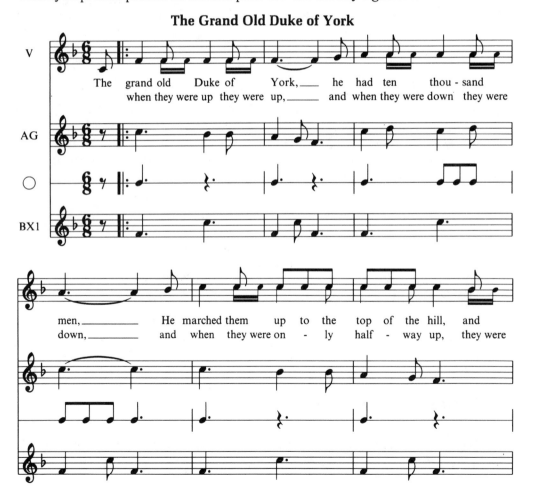

The grand old Duke of York, ___ he had ten thou-sand
when they were up they were up, ___ and when they were down they were

men, ___ He marched them up to the top of the hill, and
down, ___ and when they were on - ly half - way up, they were

marched them down a - gain. _____ And Hunt-ing we must go, a - hunt-ing we must
nei - ther up nor down. _____ A -

AM

BX2

go. We'll catch a fox and put him in a box and then we'll let it go.

Additional resources

Boshkoff *Ring Around, Sing Around*
  'Cut the Cake' (p. 11)
  Fa in song and accompaniment; game also.
Carley *Recorders with Orff Ensembles*, Bk. 1
  'Quiet Song' (p. 46, no. 31)
Earley *Something Told the White Geese*
  'Whistle, Daughter, Whistle' (p. 9)
Frazee *Ten Folk Carols for Christmas*
  'Look Away to Bethlehem' (p. 5)
  Melody adaptable to instruments.
  'Jesus the Christ is Born' (p. 22)
  La hexatonic.
Steen *Orff Activities*, Grade 3
  'Sarasponda' (p. 17)

6   *Read, write, play, and improvise or compose melodies using the hexatonic scale,*
d r mf s l d'.

Once we have introduced *fa* many hexatonic songs should be taught to practice patterns
containing that syllable in F, G and C. With each song find ways to highlight the new

melodic patterns, such as using the pattern to introduce the song, playing the melody, or adding *fa* as a passing tone in phrases where it does not appear and use this variation in a contrasting section.

Children who study music outside of school can be a valuable source of music which can be performed for their classmates. Not only can I draw parallels between what they play and know from their lessons with what we are learning to our classroom music, but I can also use their performances as examples for our classroom exploration. Nearly every year someone in third or fourth grade plays Minuet in G from *Anna Magdalena's Songbook* by Bach, and the children respond with enthusiasm, for many recognize the melody. For this lesson, ask a student to play. If this is not possible, you can play it, or you may use a recording.

After the children have heard the melody, ask them to sing the first two measures in solfege to discover if Bach's theme included *fa*. Next, one student can play this motive on an alto xylophone or metallophone. Since we do not have enough bars on our instruments to complete the theme, suggest that we can make a similar melody, beginning with Bach's idea. When my students began this activity, we used the following framework, experimenting together, and then hearing individual solutions before deciding a final melody.

After the class had performed and then written the melody, I provided a setting which they learned in the next lesson.

Here is their composition which you may use as an example. Let your students assign timbres to the melody and accompaniment.

Blake Flirts with Bach

You may prefer to divide your class into small groups, giving each a melody outline, pencil and a barred instrument. I find it important to set time limits to help the children focus and finish the project within class time. Allow time for the groups to play for one another. You may also consider sending the outline home with those who seem especially interested in the project. Invite them to play their compositions for the class when you have seen the written score and heard them perform.

7   Take dictation of four pitches from the hexatonic scale.

Any of the formats for dictation used earlier can be adapted to be used when the students have become comfortable in reading and writing melodic motives containing *fa*. A simple way to find out if the children recognize *fa* is to sing a short phrase, giving them the name of the beginning pitch. Ask them to fill in the blanks with the appropriate syllables.

1   s *(f)* *(m)* *(r)* *(d)*
2   d *(m)* *(s)* *(f)*
3   f *(s)* *(f)* *(m)*
4   d *(f)* *(r)* *(d)*
5   s *(f)* *(m)* *(d)*

Texture

1   Sing and play one part in textures of up to four complementary lines.

Throughout this year our students have been involved in ensembles which include one or more pitched ostinatos or melodic lines and unpitched percussion ostinatos. This objective then becomes integrated with rhythm and melody goals. It is a strong temptation to find ways to have all the children play and sing at once, and there are times when this may be the best way to give instruction. However, we do not always help children become independent performers when we limit them to working in large and often inaccurate groups. Sometimes it is helpful to use only one instrument for each part, trading players with every verse or repetition. I like to keep a roll call book, where I record instrument players each day. Then I am able to assign each child to a variety of instruments and parts.

2   Perform an instrumental canon with the group, and then with one or two other players.

To play in canon is another way of challenging children to perform accurately and independently. In addition, when you provide notation the children have a practical reason to read and interpret the music. These rhythmic and melodic canons have been performed by my third graders. First, the class sight-read and practiced the example as a single line and then they played in canon. To help clarify the parts and to recognize individual players, I asked several to play together in unison and then in canon. Finally, one to three children become responsible for each entrance. When I use a process like this which calls for individual responses, I am careful to choose volunteers, giving praise to those who accept the challenge.

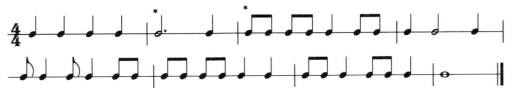

The children will enjoy choosing the entrances and the number of entries for these rhythm canons. I often give the children several choices of timbres for body percussion or instruments, and then ask them to decide if their choices made the performance of the canon clearer or confusing. In this way the children become aware of how the parts work together, rather than competing with each other.

The melodic canons are composed to give the children practice in alternating mallets. I have found, however, that some children become confused about melody direction if I insist on alteration. I then accept the solution that gives each child the most musical and accurate results.

Additional resource
Frazee with Kreuter *Discovering Orff*, p. 133–4
   Six canons.

3   Sing and/or play a melodic ostinato with a melody.

Singing a melodic ostinato as a way of practicing vocal independence began in second grade. Since that introduction, our orchestrations to accompany songs have often included an instrumental descant that can be prepared best by singing before playing it. Since the melodic ostinato most often moves in contrasting, contrary motion to the melody, you may discover that children often sing it with greater accuracy than two- and three-part canons. When a song has several verses, or you repeat it several times, consider playing the melodic ostinato first and then dividing the class to sing it with the melody on the repetition. Sometimes it is fun to appoint a listener who then tells the class whether both parts are heard clearly. My children enjoy recording their performances so they can hear the balance of voices themselves. The melodic ostinatos for the two sections of 'Hop Up, My Ladies' can be taught quickly by rote. However, reading the ostinatos will be valuable sight-reading practice and will help your children concentrate on their part as they sing in contrast to the melody.

Hop Up, My Ladies

arr. AS

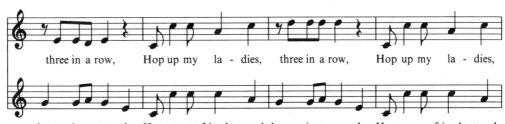

three in a row, Don't mind the wea - ther so the wind don't blow.

three in a row, oh, Hop up my friends, stand three in a row!

Additional resources

Boshkoff *All Around the Buttercup*
  'Far Too Much Noise' (p. 20)
  'Canoe Song' (p. 21)
  Both are *la*-pentatonic melodies with
  melodic ostinatos which can be sung. Let
  the children help you decide which words
  fit best.
Goetze *Simply Sung*
  'Shoo Fly' (p. 13)
Frazee with Kreuter *Discovering Orff*,
  pp. 131–2
  Four songs with melodic ostinatos.

4   *Sing two- and three-part canons with the class and in small groups.*

Learning these canons may serve several purposes, depending on how you introduce
and develop the lesson for each one. For instance, both the rhythm and melody of 'Lady,
Come Down' can be read by the students after *fa* is presented. It may also be played on
barred instruments. The harmony that results from the canon gives the children an
experience that prepares them for the recognition of tonic–dominant harmony in fourth
grade.

   'What a Goodly Thing' is one of my third graders' favorites because it became our
theme song when our school was engaged in projects concerning world peace. To
illustrate this theme the children chose a quiet, stately tempo. This gave us an
opportunity to work on sustained breathing and a strong phrase line. Movement may
be added to illustrate the meaning of the song and to mark each canon entry. First teach
the movement to the whole class as you sing in unison. Then arrange the class in
concentric circles, one for each canon entry. On the first two measures, on half notes,
walk four steps to the left. Then each child steps in his own circle to the left in place for
measures three and four. When they return to the larger circle in measure five, place arms
on neighbors' shoulders and rock left, right, left, right. Then drop arms and step in,
balance, step back and balance.

   In fourth grade we will learn to read in 6/8 meter. 'The Frogs' may be presented in rote
for experience in this meter. The canon is most fun at a brisk tempo with slightly
exaggerated diction.

   When singing in canon, take time to be sure the melody is clearly sung in unison first.
There is little musical value in singing in parts if the harmony is not clear, so divide into
only the number of parts your children can sing accurately. I like to record these class
performances so they can evaluate the canon's clarity themselves.

Lady Come Down

from *Pammelia*

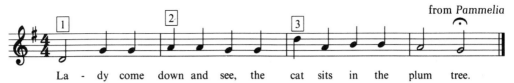

La - dy come down and see, the cat sits in the plum tree.

What a Goodly Thing

Words: Jean Richie

What a good - ly thing If the child - ren of the world

★ one possibility
□ another possibility

Could live to - geth - er In_____ peace.

The Frogs

Hear the live - ly song of the frogs in yon - der pond.

Crick, crick, cric - ki - ty crick. Brr - ump!_____

Additional resources

Orff *Music for Children*, American edn., Vol. 2
  'Where is John?' (p. 132, no. 180)
  'Three Blind Mice' (p. 133, no. 183)
Frazee with Kreuter *Discovering Orff*,
  pp. 134–4, 140–41
  Discussions and canons.

Harmony

1   Play the arpeggiated bordun and melodies which require cross-over hand motions.

Several factors will determine when you introduce this goal. The first factor is the physical readiness of the children to play patterns which require cross-over hand movements. I find that children this age want to play melodies as well as accompaniments, and, that as we introduce the diatonic scales, the instruments are helpful in visualizing pitch. However, the children's coordination abilities vary. A few of my third graders have always seemed able to play an arpeggiated bass pattern while some find these motions difficult in the second semester of third grade.

A second factor is the number of instruments and the amount of space you have, determining how many children can actually play in each lesson. If you have a limited supply of instruments and your primary performance source is song literature, you may choose to introduce only the arpeggiated bordun as another possible accompaniment. If you have an instrument for each child and you want to include instrumental performance, then giving the children an opportunity to deal with the technique of playing melodic patterns is necessary. While some children will continue to need to learn melody direction with one hand, I find that when the melody is familiar, they can switch to alternating hands. It is important to make it clear to the children that this is a physical skill, and each child is unique, just as they have observed when comparing handwriting or physical education skills. Assure them that with time and practice all will acquire the skill of alternating hands smoothly.

In 'Crossing Mallets', we introduce melodic sequence, or a pattern which repeats at another level. When you prepare the children to play this piece, practice sequences on imaginary or sketched keyboards and the syllable ladder, and demonstrate on a barred instrument as well. Plan your teaching process to guide your students to discover sequences as well as patterns in their motions and melodies.

Crossing Mallets

AS

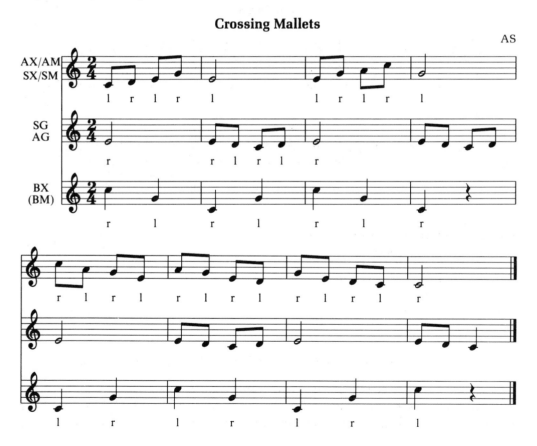

2 *Perform moving bordun accompaniments with a partner and alone.*

When the fifth degree of the scale is played by one student in an ostinato with pitches on either side, half the bordun is present. The tonic of the bordun is played by a second person. 'How Long, Watchman' (p. 187), 'The Squirrel' (p. 202) and 'Crawdad Hole' (p.147) are examples of this bordun. However, both notes of the bordun can be played by one person, using both hands as found in 'Mr. Rabbit.' The two-part form of the song is outlined by two borduns, a moving bordun for the verses and an apreggiated bordun for the refrain, as well as changing timbres in the other parts.

Mr. Rabbit

It is fun to make up new verses, changing the timbres of the unpitched and pitched ostinatos for each of them.

Additional resources
Steen *Orff Activities*, Grade 3
   'Lone Star Trail' (p. 14)
   'Zudie-O' (p. 23)

3   Perform bass ostinatos to prepare for the recognition of chord roots.

Several of the songs already presented in this chapter are accompanied with harmonic ostinatos: 'Blake Flirts with Bach' (p. 214) 'The Poor and the Rich' (p. 197) and 'Ching-a-ring' (p. 211). 'One More River' is accompanied by the same harmonic pattern in the verse and refrain. It should be taught as an ostinato. Facing partners, clap and pat this pattern as they sing:

clap partner's hands
pat own knees

Then ask each pair to find another way of moving the rhythm of the hands for the refrain. In the setting the bass line remains the same, but the other parts draw attention to the verse and refrain, or AB form.

The children will enjoy substituting and adding parts to reflect the content of each verse. Assign pairs or trios to create movement for each verse and others to play the orchestration. With the instruments in the center, the class will move in a circle during the refrain, while each small group, in turn, steps to the center of the group to act out the next verse.

One More River

19th-century college song

Old No-ah built him-self an ark, there's one more ri-ver to cross.____ He

built it out of hick-or-y bark, There's one more ri-ver to cross.____

One more ri - ver, and that wide ri - ver is Jor - dan. ____

One more ri - ver, there's one more ri - ver to cross. ____

2 The animals went in one by one,
  The elephant chewing a caraway bun.

3 The animals went in two by two,
  The rhinoceros and kangaroo.

4 The animals went in three by three,
  The bat, the bear and the bumblebee.

5 The animals went in four by four,
  Old Noah got mad and hollered for more.

6 The animals went in five by five,
  Old Noah hollered, 'You look alive.'

7 The animals went in six by six,
  The hyena laughed at the monkey's tricks.

8   The animals went in seven by seven,
        Says the ant to the elephant, 'Who are you shovin'?'.

9   The animals went in eight by eight,
        Old Noah hollered, 'It's getting late.'

10   The animals went in nine by nine,
        Old Noah hollered to 'Cut that line!'

11   The animals went in ten by ten.
        Old Noah blowed his whistle then.

Additional resource
Frazee, *Orff Handbook for World of Music − 3*
   'T'se the B'y' (p. 12)

Timbre

1   Develop percussion techniques necessary to play accurately syncopations and sixteenth notes on classroom instruments.

> This may be integrated through settings with rhythm and melody objectives. It must, however, be presented before reading and writing syncopation and sixteenth notes.

Much of our percussion technique is developed through body percussion. Through delayed echo work the children learn to listen for the complement of their response against the leader's next idea. The following rhythms are to be taught initially with body percussion and then on drums and woods. First, watch and compliment those who alternate hands lightly. Second, give the children a chance to hear themselves alone. I find that many children play the bongo, conga and hand drums with a dull thud. They will need help in putting the weight of a sharp, but light attack in the tips of their fingers. In fact, none of the percussion instruments needs to be played loudly with force. Rather, practice strokes which keep the fingers strong, the wrists flexible, and the touch light.

The word rhythms of two familiar canons are useful in preparing our students to play these less familiar durations accurately. I like to teach 'Kookabura,' a familiar Australian round, and 'Ding, Dong, Diggidiggidong' by rote at this point, and re-introduce them in the fall for the purpose of teaching notation of sixteenth notes. It is fun to sing them first and then play the word rhythms as percussion exercises. Experiment with different canon entrances to find the ones that provide the most contrast.

The rhythms which follow are to be taught from body percussion rather than notation. When the rhythms are clear in body percussion, play them on untuned instruments. Each rhythm may be played with an accompaniment or in canon.

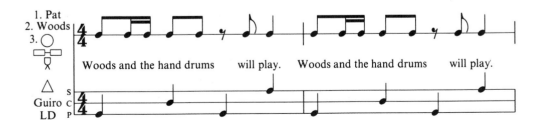

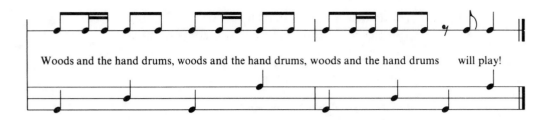

Woods and the hand drums, woods and the hand drums, woods and the hand drums   will play!

Drums

(to scrape
and
shake)

Additional resources

Orff and Keetman *Music for Children*, ed. Hall
    and Walter, Vol. I
    'Ding, Dong, Diggidiggidong' (p. 35,
    no. 31; p. 56, no. 47)
Orff and Keetman *Music for Children*, adpt.
    Murray, Vol. I
    'Ding, Dong, Diggidiggidong' (p. 24,
    no. 30; p. 136, no. 44)

Form

*1   Improvise rhythmic themes in question-and-answer phrases in 2/4, 3/4, and 4/4,
meters, using the known durations*

> This may be integrated with the improvisation objectives in rhythm 9.

When children echo us in these meters they are internalizing the length of a rhythmic
idea as well as the durations within the length. The next step is to have them fill the same
lengths or measures with their own ideas.

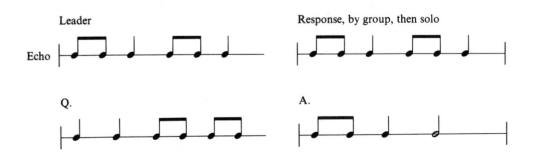

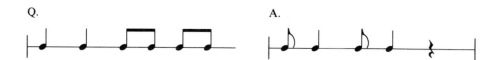

This is all an aural experience, and should be practiced when each meter is presented.

The next step is made easier if you again use boxes for measures. First the children read the boxes, filling in the missing beats, performing with body percussion. Exploration can then begin with half the group performing the questions, half the answers. Then have individuals respond by dividing the class into groups of four, one for each set of boxes. It is then helpful to let four children perform alone before giving them unpitched instruments. I like to use timbres to designate each box and to give tonal interest, such as drums for questions, triangles for first answers and wood blocks for second answers. By exchanging instruments with a neighbor each child can practice another role in phrase building.

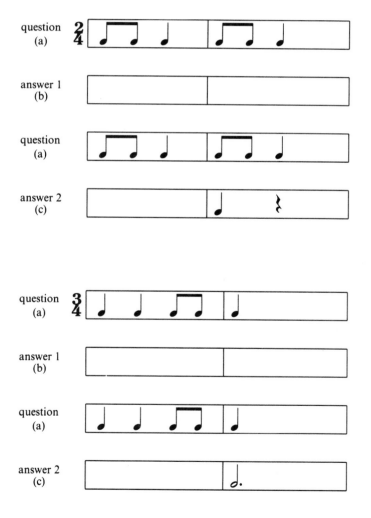

227

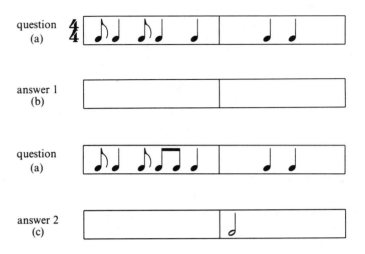

Exploration of rhythms, such as the activity described above, is even richer when it is used to add a contrasting section to a song or instrument piece just presented. Consider using this activity in meters of 2, 3 and 4, for it challenges the students to think of motives within phrase lengths. In every case, your children are improvising and performing the music they know and express as their own.

2 *Improvise melodies, using texts and question-and-answer phrases in* $\frac{2}{4}$*,* $\frac{3}{4}$*, and* $\frac{4}{4}$ *meters, in pentatonic scales on* do *and* la.

This may be integrated with the improvisation objective of melody 6.

I find it helpful to review rhythm question-and-answer improvisation activities as preparation for melodic improvisation. Then the children can respond with more confidence, for both rhythm and phrase length have been explored and established. Only pitch movement is added as a new dimensions of their improvisations.

As before, I may begin by echo singing with the class, following the outline given below. I also use the syllable ladder or an alto xylophone when giving my students examples of melodic ideas to help those who need to see as well as hear. In each case, the students echo by singing in syllables. Then you take the second step by singing the question, and ask the class to sing an answer. Then smaller groups respond, one with your question, and the other with improvised answers. Help the children to recognize that the melodic question avoids the tonic, while the answer comes to rest when it ends on the tonic.

When the children have the outline in mind the instruments are introduced, using a scale they know. I have found it helpful to use four alto or soprano xylophones, arranged in a square. A child is chosen for each instrument and task. The first states the question, the second answers, the third repeats the question, and the fourth answers, ending on the tonic.

Q

In pentatonic

A

Q

A

Q

(Student finishes question.)

A

Q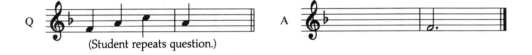

(Student repeats question.)

A

Q

A

Q

A

3   Improvise or compose sections to extend known materials to include rondo form.

The rondo is an extension of ABA or ternary form, with a theme alternating with two contrasting sections, ABABA or ABACA. Some singing games with a refrain and contrasting sections parallel the rondo in form, for the movement often alternates between larger group movement and small group or solo movement. When I introduce rondo form, I often use 'Going Down To Cairo,' for it is based on only four melodic ideas, yet has two distinct sections. Its organization is familiar to the children, and it is a good model for melodic improvisation.

Going Down to Cairo: melodic ideas

The children will see how the melodic ideas build to make a section through your introduction of the song. Place the first three short melodies on the board. Sing the melody on a neutral syllable or play it as the students watch the notation. When they have ordered the melodies, (2 3 2 1), label them as a b a c. (We used this form for our question–answer improvisations.) Teach the words and then the movement, first stepping to the right, adding a wave on 'Good-by and a By-by.' Then step to the right, adding a wave again on 'Good-by Liza Jane,' These two phrases become the A section.

Going Down to Cairo

230

Black your boots and make them shine! Good-by and a by-by.   Good-by Li-za Jane.

Next, review a selection of four-note melodic ideas, writing down the suggestions of students as well as your own. Then chant the words of the first verse on a single pitch, such as *do, sol,* or *mi* before singing it on one or more of the melodic ideas you have written on the board. The response of the 'goody-bys' helps to keep the tonality secure. Ask the students to share their ideas about other activities which happen aboard a ship. Chant each in four-beat phrases. (Some examples from my students were, 'All aboard, we're out to sea!' and 'Raise the sail to catch the wind!') Then divide the class into small groups and ask each group to provide a contrasting section which describes one of these activities, sung to their own melody and including the 'good-by' responses. They may also provide movement to fit their lyrics.

When you perform the song with movement and instruments, begin with the refrain as A, followed by one group, B, followed by the refrain, and then a second group, alternating until each group has performed, ending with the refrain.

Mozart's Rondo, from the often-played Sonata K545, has five sections and a theme which is easy to recognize. I find that an outline helps to guide the children as they listen. They can also visualize the movement of their rondo quietly, in place, as they follow the outline. Mozart gives the listener some surprises which the children will enjoy finding and describing in order to correct the outline you have provided.

A.

C.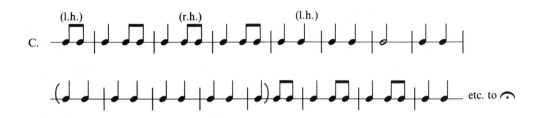

etc. to ⌢

A.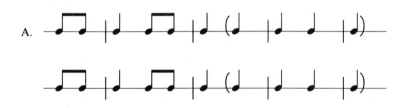

Coda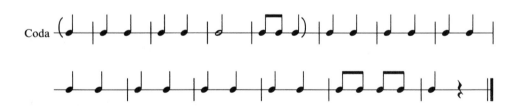

The first surprise is that A is played twice in the beginning, a practice, it is thought, meant to help the listener remember it as the form unfolds. The second surprise is that Mozart uses twelve measures for the second theme, the last four providing a transition to the A section. The return to A is exact, but played only once. The C section is lengthy, 24 measures and developmental in character. Mozart saves one surprise for the ending, a coda of 13 measures. After listening to this sonata several times, the children may wish to go back and alter their rondo to reflect what they have learned.

Rondo

Wolfgang Mozart (1756–1791)

234

Examples of rhythmic and melodic rondos are provided in all editions of Volume 1 of *Music for Children*. Orff used this form as a structure to encourage improvisation. The model was the A section and the contrasting sections were improvised. Your children will enjoy exploring these pieces as well.

As we move through the grades it becomes increasingly important to review the skills and knowledge the students have acquired during the year so that we can plan what will need review next fall. Also review the new skills and knowledge that may have been purposefully left for next year and determine where in the order of fourth grade objectives you wish to place them. You may also want to record or make a file of the lessons, songs and games which you felt were most successful. Finally, you will find it helpful to answer some questions concerning broader goals. First, did the children in this grade enjoy music? What did they enjoy most? Second, was there growth of musical skills, when playing, singing and moving, to support their enjoyment? And third, did the students have many opportunities to contribute to their own musical performances by solving problems and by improvising and composing? Answers to these questions help us to renew our interest in meeting the challenge to improve our own performances as teachers-musicians.

7 · Fourth Grade

We can anticipate making quite sophisticated music with fourth graders. They are physically able to perform some of the literature composed for Orff instruments in *Music for Children*. Many have sufficient reading ability and social skills to work with others in a variety of classroom settings. Because they are capable of performing more demanding literature we need to remember they are also young children with lively imaginations which can be tapped to interpret words and sounds in wonderful, spontaneous ways.

We expect independent, responsible behavior from fourth graders, and, usually, supported by our encouragement, they strive to meet our expectations. For example, classroom teachers in my school give long-term assignments, such as reports and book reviews. If you begin recorder instruction at this level you expect your students to practice daily in order to prepare for the next lesson. Our fourth graders want opportunities to prove their independence. Learning on their own gives evidence that they are maturing and becoming capable of caring for themselves. Yet, as they practice their independence, they feel the loss of the more obvious adult nurturing they received in the primary grades.

Maturation also accounts for some characteristics of fourth grade learning behaviors. There will be a narrowing of the differences between the attention spans of students. They will spend longer periods of time on a single task alone as well as when working with others. Their dexterity and ability to perform at various tempos will be greater, which explains in part, perhaps, why informal surveys of students and my experience indicate that instrument playing is a favored activity.

Goals

During this year we will challenge the children to listen carefully for shorter durations and more complex rhythm patterns in their music. Their rhythm studies will include sixteenth notes and many combinations of patterns that add to their rhythmic vocabulary. They will also discover that the underlying beat is not always symbolized as a quarter note, but may be an eighth or half note. Reading and writing in compound meter will be presented during the second semester, completing their introduction to reading and writing common meters.

Just as their rhythmic understandings will be refined, their melodic skills in reading and writing will be extended to include *ti*, completing the Ionian (major) and Aeolian (minor) scales. This increases dramatically the number of intervals and melodic patterns to which they may be introduced. With the ability to analyze diatonic melodies, many children this age can also hear the need to change chords. Near the end of the second half of the year we will begin our formal study of tonic and dominant chordal harmony.

It is also important to be sure we have taught the basic notation skills needed to help our students become music learners on their own. It is an excellent time to introduce recorder, for by learning to play a new instrument basic notation skills are reviewed.

Recorder instruction also gives us an opportunity to provide experiences for those who need additional help to acquire fourth grade reading skills. We also need to challenge the children who have many skills by giving them opportunities to explore what they already know well through a variety of performance mediums. Each child's best way of learning music should be addressed through processes that are personally and musically rewarding.

Begin the year with adequate time to become reacquainted with your students and their musical abilities before moving ahead. Then, remember to begin your list of new objectives with those you may have postponed until this year. Good preparation saves time in the long run. When these issues have been addressed you are ready to move on with the following objectives.

Fourth Grade Objectives

Rhythm

1   Perform, read, and write ♫♫ as the double divisions of the beat.
2   Perform, read, and write ♫♩ as ♫♫♩, and ♩♫ as ♩♫♫.
3   Perform, read, and write rhythms with the eighth-note rest (𝄾).

> Consider reviewing the pentatonic scales and then exploring hexatonic scales while introducing sixteenth-note patterns. Then move to 'Melody,' 1 and 2 before continuing with 'Rhythm,' 4.

4   Identify, perform, read, and write ♪ ♩. , ♩. ♪, and other uneven or dotted rhythms.
5   Take rhythmic dictation of two to four measures, using syncopation, sixteenth notes and dotted rhythms in 2/4, 3/4, and 4/4 meters.

> Consider introducing diatonic scales ('Melody,' 3–6) before moving to a new meter.

6   Perform, read, and write rhythms in 6/8 or other meters where an eighth note is the beat unit.

Melody

1   Review the *do*-based pentachordal (*d r m f s*) and hexatonic (*d r mf s l d*) scales in C, F, and G.
2   Perform, read, and write melodies containing *ti* in a, d and e(f♯), and C, F and G(f♯).

> See 'Rhythm,' 3 for suggestions regarding curriculum order.

3   Define the major or Ionian scale as an inventory of seven pitches, ordered by whole and half steps, beginning on *do*.
4   Define the minor or Aeolian scale as an inventory of seven pitches, ordered by whole and half steps, beginning on *la*.
5   Improvise and compose Ionian and Aeolian melodies over a tonic drone or bordun accompaniment.

6   Identify melodies aurally and from analysis of notation as being *do*-based (*do* pentatonic, major, or Ionian) or *la*-based (*la* pentatonic, minor, or Aeolian).

Next move to 'Harmony,' 1–4.

Harmony

1   Define 'chord,' and demonstrate chords on barred instruments.

These goals may be delayed until the fifth grade in order to give more time to develop the 'Melody' and 'Rhythm' goals.

2   Explore the function of harmony by changing chords.
3   Find chords outlined in melodies. Accompany these melodies with the roots of the tonic and dominant chords and the common tone between the two chords.

Texture

1   Perform alone, and individually in textures of up to four parts.
2   Perform canons in two to four parts vocally and on instruments.
3   Sing a melodic descant to harmonize a melody.

Timbre

1   Continue to develop playing techniques capable of expressing accurately the concepts presented and the ideas of the students.

Form

1   Identify the chaconne as a bass ostinato or ground bass over which melodic variations can be made.
2   Improvise over a bass ostinato.

Rhythm

1   *Perform, read, and write* ♩♫♫♩ *as the double division of the beat.*

Our children have recognized aurally and in notation that an eighth note is half the length or duration of the quarter note. Through past performances using speech, singing, movement and, perhaps, playing, they have experienced further division of the quarter note, or sixteenth notes. The next step is to present the symbol for sixteenth notes, defining it first through speech, movement, song and instrument playing.

I like to begin rhythm studies with speech because it is easy to perform accurately. When speech rhythms are then played on instruments the performance takes on the natural inflection of the voice. 'One Potato' is an elimination game used on the playground to select a leader or a player who becomes 'It.' The players stand in a line, holding their fists in front of them. One person moves down the line, tapping each fist in turn on the numbers as the group chants:

> One potato, two potato, three potato, four,
> Five potato, six potato, sev'n potato, more.

The fist that is tapped on 'more' is placed behind the player's back and the tapping resumes. The chant is repeated until all but the last fist are eliminated. (For the purpose of this lesson ask the children to chant the syllables in even durations.)

Begin the lesson by playing the game with some students as the class chants together. Then ask 'It' to choose a colored chalk to draw a quarter note for each fist she tapped as the class chanted the poem. It is easy for the children to see the relationship of the numbers in the chant to the beat they see on the board.

One two three four five six sev'n more

However, there are more sounds than one on each beat. Ask a second child to choose another color to draw the division of the beat, or eighth notes, which is familiar to them, over the first notation.

One ti two ti three ti four five ti six ti sev'n ti more

Now, as half the class pats this rhythm and half claps the rhythm of the words, the relationship between the two becomes clear. Continue the exploration by first patting the quarter note on one knee while patting the rhythm of the words on the other. Repeat the experience, only pat eighth notes on one knee and word rhythms on the other. Then it is an easy step to show the relationship of sixteenths to quarter and eighth notes. Using a third color, add a stem between each eighth note, topped with a second flag joining each group of four sixteenths. Be sure to label these notes as sixteenths and apply the rhythm syllables appropriate to your system.

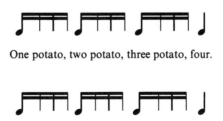

One potato, two potato, three potato, four.

Five potato, six potato, sev'n potato, more.

The following exercise I have experienced with several Dalcroze Eurhythmics teachers has been a useful way for my students to compare relative rhythm durations. Ask them to move in place to your tempo and echo the following sequence.

Most fourth graders have no difficulty clapping it correctly the first time. Then ask them to step the beat and clap the sequence as you regulate the tempo on a hand drum. It is important to keep the clapping light, giving attention to the up and down beats of each group of four. Tension turns to laughter when my students have attempted to clap the beat while stepping the rhythm sequence. An easier challenging variation that tests accuracy and understanding is to walk randomly, clapping the sequence in canon.

The next step is to recognize and use sixteenth notes to read and record melodies and accompaniments. Introduce 'Hey, Ho, Anybody Home?' by having the fourth graders read the rhythm with syllables and then with body percussion. It may be fun to read the rhythmic theme by patting sixteenths, clapping eight and snapping quarter notes. As they perform the rhythmic theme, you may perform the soprano xylophone rhythm. Ask your students to write this ostinato before assigning it to players. Continue in this manner to prepare all parts through body percussion. Then introduce the words and melody and apply the body percussion preparation to barred and unpitched instruments.

Hey, Ho, Anybody Home?

adapted AS

mo-ney have I none.   Put a pen-ny in,   please   mis - ter!____

Your students may enjoy playing the word rhythms from notation on hand drums, using their suggestions for dynamic markings to make the theme more exciting. They can test their accuracy by playing it in canon at the interval of two beats. This may become a B section for your final performance.

'Swapping Song' provides another opportunity to practice reading and playing sixteenth notes accurately. First, teach the song by rote. Then assign students to small groups to interpret the rhythm of the bass xylophone ostinato in movement that uses direction and space to contrast the verse with the refrain. Prepare other instrumental ostinatos by asking your students to read the rhythms through body percussion before they use instruments. As a culminating evaluation, ask the students to write the four-beat rhythmic theme of the refrain. Your class can use material from the song and setting to add an introduction and coda, or they may wish to create their own rhythms for these extensions.

Swapping Song

'Some Love Coffee' can be learned from sight-reading for the song is pentatonic and the rhythms are easy to read. The setting includes a melodic descant for voices and another for recorders. Some classes have found it effective to whistle the recorder part. Ask the students for ways to double the length of this song and its setting.

Some Love Coffee

arr. AS

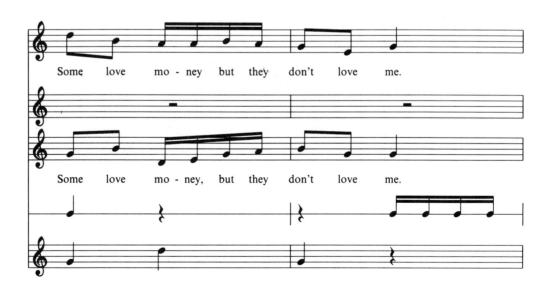

V1: Sing-ing in the lone-some cow-boy-ee, sing-ing in the lone-some sea.

R, AG or V2: 'Lone - some sea,' 'Lone - some sea.'

Additional resources

Boshkoff *All Around the Buttercup*
  'Chicken on the Fence Post' (p. 22)
Frazee with Kreuter *Discovering Orff*,
  pp. 152–5
Fuoco-Lawson *Street Games*
  'Do the Jive' (p. 2)
'Gill *Have You Any Wool?*
  'Doctor Foster' (p. 13)
  'Peter, Peter, Pumpkin Eater' (p. 16)
  'Diddle Diddle Dumpling' (p. 36)
  These scores serve as models for your own
  speech exploration and practice of rhythm.
  Fourth graders find this kind of work fun
  and humorous, particularly when they help
  create the ostinatos and determine the
  tongue-in-cheek interpretations.
Goetze *Simply Sung*
  'There's a Little Wheel A-turning in My
    Heart' (p. 10)
  'The Boll Weevil' (p. 20)

2 *Perform, read, and write ♩♫♩ as ♩♬♩, and ♩♫♩ as ♩♬♩.*

We can introduce combinations of sixteenth and eighth notes in notation by recalling the chant we used to introduce sixteenths. Have the children chant 'One Potato' (p. 239) and then ask them to write the rhythmic notation again. Here is a new version to chant and then clap.

> One tater, two tater, three tater, four,
> Five tater, six tater, sev'n tater, more.

Ask the children if our notation of the first chant is still accurate. They will see that the first two sixteenths in each group of four should be tied together to represent the new words accurately.

244

To hear the difference between sixteenth-note patterns they may chant and then clap the word rhythms this way:

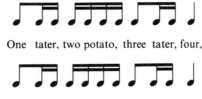

One tater, two potato, three tater, four,

Five tater, six potato, sev'n tater, more.

Ask your students to devise another version to chant and play which ties the last two sixteenths of each group of four. For example:

One pota-,   two pota-,   three pota-,   four.

Five pota-,   six pota-,   sev'n pota-,   more.

Practice in listening and performing these patterns is in order next. First, ask the class to assist you in writing a new eight-beat rhythmic phrase, using sixteenth-note patterns on no more than four beats. For example:

Using the same model, divide the class into small groups and ask each one to compose a new phrase using sixteenth notes. Give them standard-size sheets of paper with beats outlined as they were on the board and felt pens with which to notate their rhythm. Remind them that the rhythm will end with a quarter note. Ask them to practice their rhythm, checking each other for accuracy, returning to the use of word rhythms to help them. Finally, post their compositions on the board asking each group to perform their rhythms in order. Then play a game of 'Rhythm Scramble' by changing the order of the rhythm sheets but not the order of performing groups. The children enjoy the surprises in the new order and the challenge of reading their classmates' rhythms.

Continue to apply their new reading and writing skills by learning new songs with settings and instrumental pieces. 'Hop Up And Jump Up,' a Shaker melody, has sixteenth notes in the three patterns just presented. Because each phrase has different words you may wish to write them where all can see, and then place the rhythm above. After you have added the ostinato accompaniment your students may enjoy performing the rhythm of the melody with body percussion or on instruments as a canon at the interval of one measure. The Shakers danced this song and your students may wish to interpret the song through the movement the words suggest.

Hop Up and Jump Up

Shaker melody arr. AS

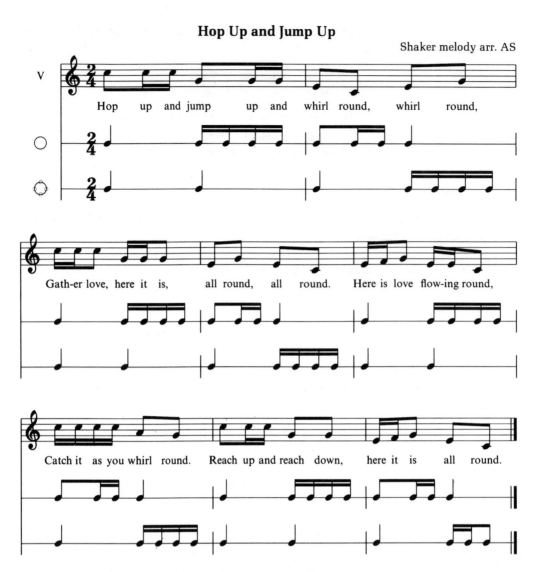

Hop up and jump up and whirl round, whirl round,

Gath-er love, here it is, all round, all round. Here is love flow-ing round,

Catch it as you whirl round. Reach up and reach down, here it is all round.

'Zum Gali' may be taught by rote or from solfege. Be sure to notate the melodic ostinato for dictation practice and compare sixteenth-note patterns they see with those they hear in the melody. The melody begins with an eighth-note rest which is the subject of our next objective. Consequently we will learn the melody by rote and save our analysis for another lesson.

Movement will help the students become aware of sixteenth notes as well as the rest, for they will begin the phrase with a step that fills the silence. While the style of the song dictates a grapevine step on eighth notes, I find that my fourth graders manage this step best by moving first with quarter notes. When they sing 'Zum Gali' have them cross the right foot with the left foot in front, step to the right, then cross with the left foot behind, repeating the pattern as often as they repeat the melodic ostinato. As they sing 'Hecha lutz le'man avodah' they make a small leap forward on the left foot as they clap their hands, then place the right foot beside the left, step back on the left foot, and bring the right foot beside. Repeat the pattern to finish the phrase.

Zum Gali

Hebrew work song

1. He - cha - lutz   le   'man   a - vo - da;_____
2. A - vo - da   le   'man   he - cha - lutz;_____

Zum   ga - li,   ga - li,   ga - li,   Zum   ga - li,   ga - li,

___   A - vo - da   le   'man   he - cha - lutz.
___   He - cha - lutz   le   'man   a - vo - da.

Zum   ga - li,   ga - li,   ga - li,   Zum   ga - li,   ga - li.

Now experiment with formations for movement, for it may be performed in several ways. You may sing 'Zum Gali' first, moving in a circle, followed by 'Hecha lutz,' (aba or ababa). Or, leaders may lead short lines around the room singing in a predetermined form. One group may perform and dance only the 'Zum gali' ostinato while the second group alternates between a and b. You may alternate singing with playing the word rhythms on drums and tambourines.

Additional resources

Earley *Something Told the Wild Geese*
  'This Little Gospel Light of Mine' (p. 10)
Frazee with Kreuter *Discovering Orff*,
  pp. 155–8
Steen *Orff Activities*, Grade 4
  'Happiness Runs' (p. 16)
Steen *Orff Activities*, Grade 5
  'There's a Hole in the Middle of the Sea.
    (pp. 5–9)

3   Perform, read and write rhythms with the eighth-note rest (𝄾).

It is easiest for children to hear this short silence when it begins the phrase. Begin your class with echo practice, but ask them to walk behind you, stepping the beat. After several rhythmic phrases of patterns that are familiar, clap this one:

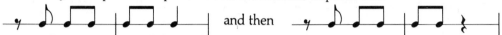

and then

Repeat these patterns until the students can clap them from memory. When they return to their seats, ask them to notate the pattern of their feet, and then the last two patterns of their hands. This leads them to discover the need for an eighth rest. When I present this symbol my students seem to be helped by comparing the flag of the eighth note (on the right) with the flag of eighth rest (on the left).

'Mama Paquita' is a delightful Brazilian song that begins with an eighth rest, and includes a generous number of quarter and eighth rests. Ask the children to notate this pattern: (♫ ♫ ♫ 𝄽) and listen for it as you sing the song. Point to it each time you sing (𝄾 ♪♫ ♫ 𝄽). Ask them to correct the notation. Then I like to give each student a copy of the song or place it on an overhead projector for them to follow, so they can circle the eighth rests and underline quarter rests as we learn it. The children can illustrate hearing the two rest durations by snapping the eighth rest and stamping the quarter rests.

Mama Paquita

Brazil arr. AS

Ma-ma Pa - qui - ta, buy your child-ren a pa - pa - ya. A ripe pa -

- pa - ya, and a ba - na - na, a ripe ba - na - na that your

child - ren would en - joy. Ma-ma, Ma - ma, Ma-ma Pa - -joy.

At the end of the lesson, put (♫ ♫ ♫ ♩) before them again and sing 'Zum gali.' They will find it easy to change the notes to represent 'Hecha lutz le'man avodah.'

Additional resources

Consider reviewing the pentatonic scales and then exploring hexatonic scales while introducing sixteenth-note patterns. Then move to 'Melody,' 1 and 2 before continuing with 'Rhythm,' 4.

4 *Identify, perform, read and write* ♪♩. , ♩. ♪, *and other uneven or dotted rhythms.*

Uneven rhythm patterns are often best understood and, consequently, are most accurately performed when we compare the longer sound with shorter sounds. This is the objective for the following experiment. Sit with your students in a circle, knees close together, either cross-legged on the floor or in chairs, and number off by twos. The ones are to gently pat eighth notes on the knees of both neighbors (twos), and the twos are to lightly clap quarter notes. Then reverse the responsibilities. As they are doing this, ask them to listen to be sure the quarter note sounds precisely with every other eighth note. Then write the following pattern for ones to pat on their neighbors' knees: ♫ ♫ ♩ ♩. The twos will echo you and all are to try to remember your sequence of patterns.

250

After they have an opportunity to recall your patterns, ask them to check their observations as ones echo your sequence and twos pat ♫♫♩♩ on their neighbors' knees. Now it is time to record the patterns they echoed. First write the pattern they patted on their knees and compare each clapped pattern to it. By using ties they will soon see that the short sound is only one eighth note long, while the long sound is as long as three eighth notes. Fourth graders usually understand the relationship of two eighths to a quarter note and that the third eighth note is represented by a dot, or half the value of the quarter note, just as the dot after the half note represented half its value.

While the fourth graders usually understand the reasoning behind the notation of dotted rhythms, it takes considerable practice to be accurate when performing them while reading. When you introduce 'Ama-Lama' ask your children to write the rhythm of each melodic phrase, discovering the need for ♩. ♪. Then introduce the accompaniment patterns in the order indicated in the score. The song is often accompanied by a hand clapping game. From hand jives they already know, have pairs or small groups make a hand clapping game to fit the song. You can create a B section by having some clap the word rhythms of the song while others continue their hand jive. One group may find a way to use eighth notes in their pattern. As they perform encourage your students to listen for the matching of longer durations to the shorter ones they felt in the circle exercise. This lively song is often more interesting and accurate when phrases are played softly when they are repeated.

Ama-Lama

Cincinnati playground

A - ma - la - ma coo - ma la - ma, coo - ma la - ma vee - stay.

Hard mallets

Oh, no, no, no, no, no, vee - stay.

252

Ee - nie mee-nie gyp - si - lee - nie, Oo - ah - oo, gyp - si - lee - nie,

At - chy pat - chy coo - mi - lat - chy, I mean you.

When you teach 'Old House,' begin by writing 'Tear it down,' as the eighth followed by dotted quarter note, and then ask your students to determine how many times it is sung as you introduce the song. Next, decide how many different solos precede this response. By the time they have listened for all the calls they will know the song and you can add the accompaniment. The additive orchestration will help to create a growing crescendo which suggests the noise of wrecking a building. Notice that the moving bordun is written for one player. If that is difficult, have one child play the tonic or lowest note, while another child plays the 'decorated' or moving fifth on the same instrument.

Old House

American Work Song/arr. AS

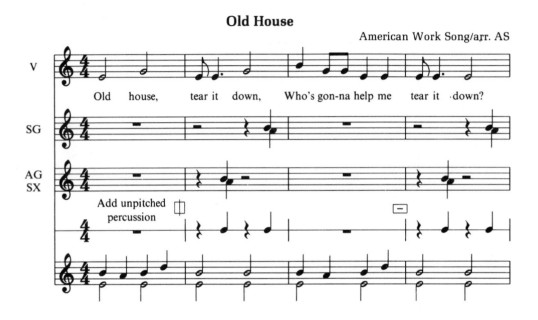

Old house, tear it down, Who's gon-na help me tear it down?

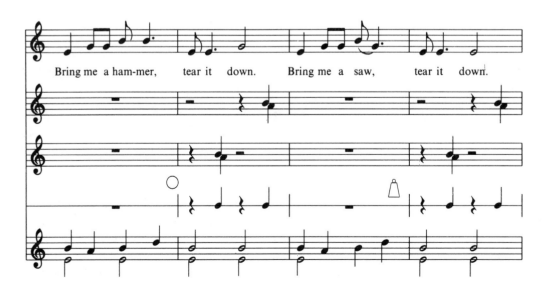

Bring me a ham-mer, tear it down. Bring me a saw, tear it down.

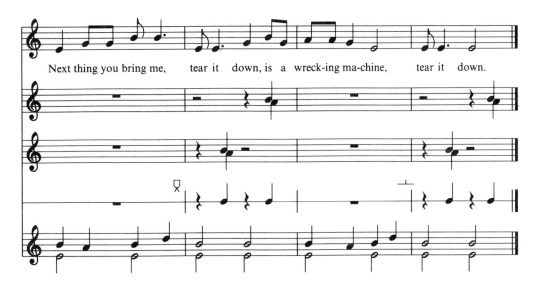

Next thing you bring me, tear it down, is a wreck-ing ma-chine, tear it down.

2. New house, build it up! . . .

Additional resources

Frazee with Kreuter *Discovering Orff*,
　pp. 161–8
Goetze *The Cat Came Back*
　'Goodbye, Old Paint' (p. 4)
　'John Kanaka' (p. 7)
　'The Cat Came Back' (p. 9)
　'Fourth Day of July' (p. 23)
Ladendecker *Holidays and Holy Days*, Vol. 1
　'Rubbleton' (p. 4)
　'The Singing Bird' (p. 11)
McRae *American Sampler*
　'At the Gate of Heaven' (p. 1)
　'The Old Ark' (p. 28)
Orff and Keetman *Music for Children*, adpt.
　Murray, Vol. II
　'Dance' (p. 25)

*5   Take rhythmic dictation of two to four measures, using syncopation, sixteenth and dotted
rhythms in 2/4, 3/4, and 4/4 meters.*

With the addition of sixteenth notes and dotted rhythms with half, quarter and eighth
notes the children now read seventeen or more specific durations in potentially endless
combinations in three meters. Our students are rarely fluent readers and, even less
frequently, writers of music, for most of them use their skills only when they are in the
music room. Dictation exercises, however, will help us evaluate what the students know
and understand, especially when the examples are drawn from their classroom music.
The exercise (or quiz) should be designed to help our students learn the usefulness of
notation and to celebrate how much they know. If eighty per cent of the class responds
correctly to eighty per cent or more of the examples, the students will feel successful and
I will know what they can identify, write and apply on their own. The ability to read and

write music should enhance their enjoyment of music, not threaten it. We must have that in mind when we give dictation exercises and quizzes.

I like to give my students some practice in using notation in less teacher-directed settings, such as a composition project, before I give a dictation quiz. This allows them time to use symbols in a personal, meaningful way. It also gives me a chance to work with them alone or in small groups where I can observe how comfortable individuals are with using rhythmic notation.

This is an example of a composition project I have used frequently. I assign the meter and the length of the phrase with a first and second ending (question and answer). We then work out one example together, before each student is assigned a partner. I find it best to match a stronger student with one needing more assistance. The partners then proceed, using the following steps.

1 Compose your rhythm together, then write it down.
2 Practice your composition, using body percussion, until it feels comfortable to perform.
3 A simple four-beat ostinato may be added as an accompaniment. (This is an optional step for those who work quickly.)
4 Perform it for your music teacher (or for the class if this is the final step).
5 Practice your composition on instruments and then play it for the class. (This step follows if you have the time, space and instruments.)

Composition Form

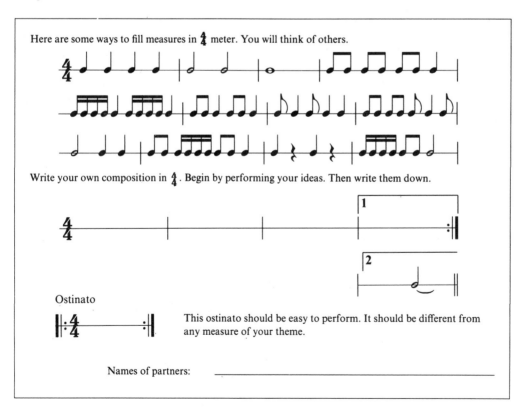

Fourth-grade composition projects

Paul and Ben

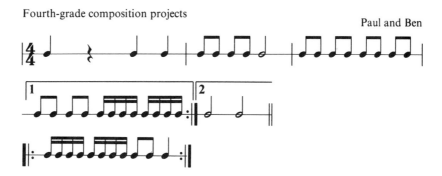

Dana and Elizabeth

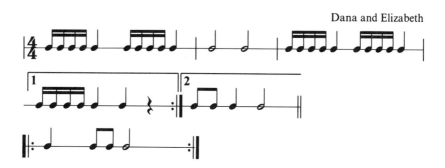

In the week preceding the time you plan to evaluate the children leave out beats or measures in the notated examples you present in your lessons and ask them to complete your examples. This is another easy way to give your students writing practice.

Now a dictation evaluation should be a comfortable exercise. The following examples use rhythms that are the same or very similar to music examples they have performed in class. A dictation quiz should take only a small portion of the class so there is time to make music also.

Place an X in the correct box

257

3. □

□

Fill in the measures.

4.

5.

6.

Put in the bar-lines.

7.

8.

Write what you hear.

9.

10.

*( ): to appear blank, but here are filled with possible answers.

Consider introducing diatonic scales ('Melody,' 3–6) before moving to a new meter.

6 Perform, read and write rhythms in 6/8 or other meters where an eighth note is the beat unit.

In several lessons preceding this one, use 6/8 patterns in your rhythm and movement warm-ups. I like to include 6/8 patterns in quick echo imitation exercises in body percussion when we review a familiar singing game like 'Pop Goes the Weasel' or 'Alley, Alley Oh' at the end of a class. These activities prepare our children to respond in a natural way to rhythms in this meter and provide a context for introducing new symbols.

After some exploration activities, your children are ready to compare the movements they use with familiar songs and singing games. Review 'Shoo Fly,' and as you sing, pat the eighth note pulse. If they don't know 'Charlie's Neat' you should teach it by rote at this point, for you want to get to the movement activity. Since the chorus and verse have the same melody, teach the chorus with repetitive words first, and then the verse. Ask your students to sing this song, patting the eighth note pulse. When both songs are learned, ask the students to make up movements to fit each one, assigning half the group to each song. For 'Shoo Fly' they are to use walking and running, while for 'Charlie's Neat' they are to use walking, but will find themselves skipping. Each group may determine the formation for each song, such as a line following a leader, or a circle, or two lines facing each other. When the groups perform for one another, ask them to describe and then clap the rhythm of the types of footwork each group used for each song. Guide them to see that it is easy to walk to both songs, but we run to 'Shoo Fly' while we can skip or gallop to 'Charlie's Neat.'

Shoo Fly

American singing game

Shoo fly don't bo-ther me, Shoo fly don't bo-ther me. Shoo fly don't

bo-ther me, for I be-long to some-bo-dy. I feel, I feel, I feel, I

feel like a morn-ing star. I feel, I feel, I feel, I feel like a morn-ing star!

Charlie's Neat

English-American singing game

Verse

Char-lie's neat and Char-lie's sweet and Char-lie, he's a dan-dy. Char-lie he's the

Chorus

ve-ry lad that stole my stri-ped can-dy. O-ver the ri-ver to feed my sheep, O-ver the ri-ver

Char - lie. O-ver the ri-ver to feed my sheep and mea-sure up my bar - ley.

The notation of these two songs will reflect these rhythmic differences. First, have the students look at the word rhythms of the chorus of 'Shoo Fly.'

Ask your children to imitate you as you pat eighth notes. Then continue to pat as they sing the refrain and follow the notation. Ask the children if they patted half, quarter, or eighth notes. When they answer that the eighth note was the pulse, ask them how the time signature or meter could reflect this. After you have changed the four to eight in the meter signature, half the class performs the eighth note pulse while the others perform the rhythm of the words.

Now ask your children to chant and then clap the rhythm of 'Over the river to feed all my sheep.' They should be able to notate this phrase in quarter notes.

Next, help them to assign the meter, which they may decide is 3/4 or 6/4, depending where they place the metric accent. Write it both ways if the discussion calls for it. Again, recalling their experience with 'Shoo Fly,' change the lower 4 to 8. This time ask them if the notation continues to be correct, and guide them to change quarter notes to eighth notes. If they choose 3/8, as my class did, perform it in this way before you then remove every other bar-line, chanting it with less stress on the fourth beat. Be sure to ask the class to correct the meter signature.

When we chanted 'Over the river to feed all my sheep,' we added 'all' to make the phrase easy to analyze. The students will have no difficulty finding your 'error' and will be able to correct the notation by tying two eighths to make a quarter. You may need to help them decide the notation for the last sustained note, comparing its duration to the dotted quarter note in the chorus of 'Shoo Fly'. Now ask your students to help you notate the word rhythms of the chorus.

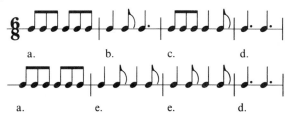

Then they can make an inventory list of all the one-measure patterns in the refrain of 'Charlie's Neat.' These patterns are lettered in the example above.

From these typical 6/8 patterns of the chorus the students can create new patterns. Divide your class into quartets. Each group is to perform a new rhythm of four measures, each person in the group performing one measure. Before they begin have them decide which measures make the best endings. When each group performs ask the others to guess what rhythms were used. To encourage a rhythmic flow and to simplify recognizing the patterns you may wish to limit each group to using two or three patterns, repeating to fill the four-measure phrase.

Your students can apply their skills by reading 6/8 patterns in another lesson while learning the setting of 'Charlie's Neat.' Write the three ostinatos for the verse above one another in one place and the three ostinatos for the chorus in another. Teach the setting by asking your fourth graders to read each ostinato as preparation for playing.

Charlie's Neat and Charlie's Sweet

Char - lie, he's the ve - ry lad that stole my stri - ped can - dy!
Take some more of your good old rye to bake a cake for Char - lie.

Chorus

O-ver the ri-ver to feed my sheep, O-ver the ri - ver, Char - lie,

O-ver the ri-ver to feed my sheep, and mea-sure up my bar - ley!

When I order my objectives for the year, I am often presenting 6/8 meter in the same month as I am introducing harmony and chord structures to the fourth graders. How you have ordered your objectives will determine how you will use each of the following settings. If you do not want to call attention to the chord changes, present the lesson through the rhythms only. If you are exploring or analyzing chord movement, call attention to these elements in the lesson process. In either case you can use these materials to practice and expand your students' awareness of the meter.

'Down the River' has a strong rhythmic feeling for compound meter which my children enjoy. The setting calls for contrasting timbres for verse and chorus to involve more children in playing parts from very simple to demanding, and to give variety when the song is sung repeatedly to accompany the play party. The cadence of the verse and the harmonic ostinato of the refrain also require different treatments.

To dance the play party, form two lines, partners facing one another. The game begins by the students skipping to the left, as though going around the circle, returning to their original place. For the refrain, directions most often call for the head couple to reel down the 'alley,' swinging first their partner, and then the next person in the opposite line for a half turn, returning to the center to 'swing your partner.' The couple continue moving down to the end of the line, and the second pair become the new head couple. Repeat the refrain as often as necessary to accommodate the reel. Another time have the children design a new singing game, outlining the two sections and using their favorite movements and formations.

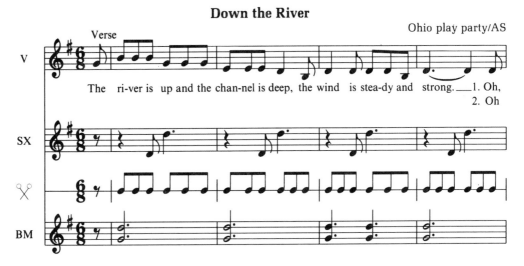

Down the River

Ohio play party/AS

263

won't we have a jol-ly good time as we go sail-ing a - long._____
Di - nah, put the hoe cakes on as we go sail-ing a - long._____

Refrain

V — Down the ri-ver, oh, down the ri-ver, oh, down the ri-ver we go._____

AX

BX

Down the ri-ver, oh, down the ri-ver, oh, down the O - hi - o._____

3. The waves do splash from shore to shore . . .

'Winter Song' was written to give children an opportunity to apply their skills in playing a simple instrumental piece in 6/8 meter. The ostinato accompaniments are easily played for only the soprano glockenspiel part requires crossing mallets. Measures one, three and five of the melody are the same, as are measures two and six. Be sure your children can sing the melody first; that will make learning to play it much easier.

This old nursery rhyme inspired this quiet piece.

> The North Wind will blow and we shall have snow.
> And what will the robin do then, poor thing?
> He'll sit in the barn and keep himself warm,
> And hide his head under his wing, poor thing.

Your students could interpret the poem by exploring timbres, first vocally and then on untuned instruments, providing a carpet of sound as one or several children read it. The instrumental piece which follows may become the conclusion or interlude for the poem's interpretive setting. I have also used the poem for improvisation, using the word rhythms as the basis for the melodies. To improvise, assign each student to one line of the poem and have them play or sing their new melodies as contrasting sections of a rondo.

Winter Song

AS

Additional resources

Carley *Recorders with Orff Ensemble*
  'Jig' (p. 28)
Frazee *Orff Handbook for World of Music – 3*
  'Night Herding Song' (p. 10)
Frazee with Kreuter *Discovering Orff*,
  pp. 189–194
Gill *Have You Any Wool?*
  'Humpty Dumpty' (p. 34)
  'Rub-a-dub-dub' (p. 44)
Hamm *Crocodile and Other Poems*
  'When Hannibal Crossed the Alps' (p. 2)
  'John Cook' (p. 8)
Ladendecker *Holidays and Holy Days*, Vol. 1
  'If' (p. 23)
McRae *American Sampler*
  'Shanty Boys' (p. 10)
Steen *Orff Activities*, Grade 4
  'Brethren in Peace Together' (p. 12)

Melody

1   Review the do-*based pentachordal (*d r mf s*) and hexatonic (*d r mf s l*) scales in C, F, and G.*

One of the challenges in teaching melodic reading is to help the children read intervals accurately. When melodies repeat pitches or move from step to step students have little difficulty in associating the direction of the notation with the direction of their voices or instruments. To read intervals of a third or more with fluency is considerably more difficult. Soon fourth graders will be learning melodies that outline chords other than *d–m–s*, the tonic chord, dictating more strongly than before the underlying harmony. Before moving on, then, I want my students to feel very familiar with the hexatonic scale and the most common intervals and patterns within that scale.

My children have enjoyed short dictation games which give them practice in identifying isolated intervals. The games are simple. For instance, I receive a point if I stump the class, but the class gets a point if I fail. The winner is the side which reaches ten points first. We warm up by singing the scale together, first from the syllable ladder, then the scale written on the staff, and from singing with an alto xylophone. This gives my students three ways to visualize intervals. The game begins when I play an interval, such as *do–sol* or *do–re*, on the xylophone. They sing it back, first on 'loo,' and then with the correct syllable. If most sing it correctly, the class gets the points. The next interval begins on the pitch of the last example. This is a first step, for I am only asking the children to learn the syllable names associated with the bars.

Another game involves dividing the class into two teams. I sing *do* and just point to another pitch on the ladder, staff or instrument. The first team is to respond together or designate a teammate to sing the correct interval and syllable. If they are inaccurate, the second team may have a chance to sing it. This game is more difficult, so at first I sing each example from *do*. As the children become more accurate I begin the dictation game on *do*, but begin subsequent intervals on the ending pitch of the last example.

In each of these games my purpose is to encourage my students to listen, analyze, and be successful, so I am careful to raise the challenge level very slowly. As the children soon discover, I want them to win. I like to have a repertory of these little games to play for warm-ups, for skill practice, and to play when a change of pace is needed.

Singing intervals in isolation does not make a melody. This little game of Melody Pass brings us one step closer. Give each student or pair of children a barred instrument with the b bar removed. The game is to pass patterns of four pitches from one person to another. Each pattern may include pitches that stay in place or move in seconds, but may include only one skip within the octave. At first the patterns must begin on *sol* or *do*, and later on either pitch. You begin by calling a child's name, and then play a pattern which he or she echoes. The child has three chances to play. When he or she responds correctly she may call another child's name and then play the same pattern again, only this time she may change one note. If this echo doesn't answer correctly in three tries, ask for a volunteer to answer and who then continues the game.

The following melodies are chosen for sight reading because they are familiar to most of my children, and recognition is a reward for reading accurately. Within and between them the students will recognize similar melodic motives and structures. Make a game of sight reading these melodies by giving a small group of children or soloists just one measure to sing or play. Give them a short time to think and then sing the song in syllables, passing the melody without pause from group to group. The purpose is to read the pitches, so do not correct rhythm reading, but guide it by the way you lead, pointing to each note, or, if you prefer, eliminate the stems of the notes. Let groups join one another as they discover measures which are alike or nearly alike. When one group has difficulty singing or playing their assigned measure, ask others to help. Soon the whole class will be singing or playing the entire melody, and you can congratulate them for learning it from notation.

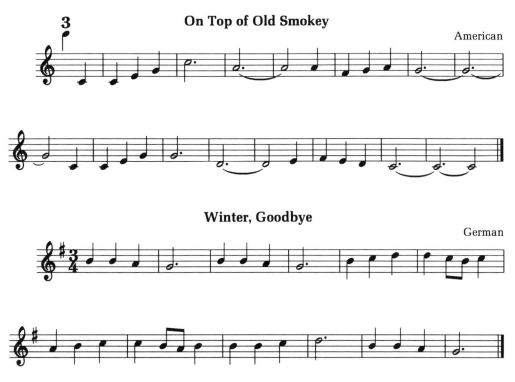

On Top of Old Smokey

American

Winter, Goodbye

German

Puppets

French

It Rained A Mist

American

This Old Man

Take some time to improvise new melodies over a tonic drone, or even without accompaniment. There are several structures your children have found in their songs and one may serve as a model: a a b b', or a b a c, or a a b a, for instance. Begin by demonstrating how the small groups are to work. First, establish the key (C, F or G), meter (2, 3 or 4), and length of each small section or motive. Then select the form. Give your children instruments, one for each motive. Ask the first child to improvise a motive to be followed by the next child who must follow the selected form, either repeating or composing a new motive. The third person must follow the form, as does the fourth person. If the class demonstrates a good understanding of the process, assign groups of four a form, meter and length of motive and send them off to work independently. Sometimes my children prefer to work alone, and this format works well for individual improvisation. Be sure to have a 'concert' at the end of their practice time.

268

In the settings which follow encourage the children to compose melodic introductions, bridges and codas. Even though the presence of *fa*, along with *re* on metric strong beats requires harmonic changes, these settings can be taught as having a bass ostinato or a rhythmic ostinato with pitch changes. Such patterns give the children aural experiences that prepare them for the introduction of harmony later in the year.

Additional resources
(This list contains both pentatonic and
   hexatonic melodies appropriate for the
   fourth grade.)
Boskhoff *Ring Around, Sing Around*
   'Grandma Grunts' (p. 12)
Earley *Something Told the Wild Geese*
   'Whistle, Daughter, Whistle' (p. 9)
Frazee *Orff Handbook for World of Music* – 4
   'Harvest Time' (p. 7)
   'Cindy' (p. 13)
Staton *Music and You*, Grade 4
   'He's Got the Whole World in His Hands'
      (p. 6)
   'Oh, Won't You Sit Down?' (p. 9)
Orff and Keetman *Music for Children*, adpt.
   Murray, Vol. II
   'Girls and Boys Come Out to Play' (p. 74)
Steen *Orff Activities*, Grade 3
   'Sarasponda' (p. 17)
Steen *Orff Activities*, Grade 4
   'Happiness Runs' (p. 16)
   'My Home's in Montana' (p. 26)

2   *Perform, read, and write melodies containing* ti *in a, d and e (f♯), and C, F and G (f♯).*

My students have watched the space below *do*, taken out the bar and queried 'When will we use *ti*?', and arrival at this point is a day to celebrate. Little do they know that being able consciously to sing intervals from and to *ti* leads them into the wider world of harmony, leaving the relative safety of borduns and drones behind. Much of our folk and popular music is harmonically based, and when we take this step I know the music will soon lead us to an introduction of basic chordal harmony.

Once we introduce *ti* we must consider how it functions in melodies. First, we find it as a passing tone in minor melodies, since it is a part of the pentachord. In this position I can continue to use tonic and bordun accompaniments and give the children opportunities to improvise without harmonic implications. (You will remember that *fa* was introduced first as a passing tone in the *do* pentachord.) There are very few major, or *do*-based, one-chord melodies that include *ti*, but this step follows so that *ti* is placed not only in notation but in the ears of the children in both *la* and *do* scales. Then I can move on to melodies where *ti* is approached by steps and skips which often imply the use of harmony. The function of *fa* and *ti*, along with familiar *re*, which dictate harmony, are experienced by my children throughout their elementary years. However, guiding them to analyze melodic chord patterns aurally and through notation unfolds slowly. Do not be in a hurry, for some children will grasp these concepts easily, but others will find the relationship of melody to harmony confusing.

I like to introduce *ti* through this simple, lovely round, 'Ah, Poor Bird,' because it can be played as well as sung, giving the children several opportunities to place it in the melody. Teach the melody first by rote. (I find that when I ask the children to explain what the song might mean the interpretation and tempo are more easily managed by them.) Because the melody is simple, I ask several children to play the first two measures on barred instruments set in d pentatonic. They quickly find that a bar is missing. It is an old trick, but it works well!

Ask several students to finish the melodic outline you place before them, and read it with syllables. All the children will enjoy an opportunity to play as well as sing this round at the interval of four or two beats. You may choose to use the setting as well.

Ah, Poor Bird

arr. AS

Up a-bove the sor - row of this dark night.

In 'Ghost of Tom,' *ti* is approached in stepwise motion as it was in 'Ah, Poor Bird.' The difference, the students soon discover, is that f♯ is required. This is the time to review the placement of sharps in the key signature and perhaps to check your notation, circling all the *tis* found in the melody. The setting uses augmentation and diminution of the rhythm of words to provide contrast in the ostinatos. My students have enjoyed making movements for each phrase of the melody and performing them in canon over the accompaniment.

The Ghost of Tom

American arr. AS

V: Have you seen the___ ghost of Tom?

AG: (Ghost of

AM: (Ghost of Tom)

BX: (Ghost of Tom, ghost of Tom,   have you seen the ghost of Tom?)

271

Long white bones with the skin all gone.____ Oooh____

Tom)

(Have you

____ Would-n't it be chil-ly with no skin on?

seen the ghost of Tom)

In 'Artza Alenu,' *ti* appears only in full cadences at the end of the first and last phrases, *do–ti–la*. Your children will recognize this as parallel to a common cadence in *do* scales, *mi–re–do*. I like to teach this song from notation in the following manner. I sing the song on 'loo,' but ask them to finish by singing the last phrase with syllables. The next time they sing the last two phrases, and so on, until they have practiced singing syllables and have learned the song.

This energetic song will inspire movement suggestions from your students, or you can teach the grapevine step that you presented in 'Zum Gali.'

Artza Alenu (Come to the Land)

Hebrew song arr. AS

Ar - tza a - le - nu,   Ar - tza a - le - nu,   Ar - tza a - le - nu.
Come to the land with   joy and with spi-rit,   Come to our na-tive land.

K'var chat - ash - nu,   V'gam a - zar - a - nu,   A' - val   od lo   katz -
We have plowed the   fields and have plan-ted grain.   We'll reap   a migh - ty

ar' - nu.   A' - val   od lo   katz - ar' - nu.
har - vest.   Come to   our na - tive   land.

273

The next step in practicing *ti* is to hear and place it in the major or Ionian scale. The form of the song, a Jamaican melody which describes playing ball, is easy to understand when the students can see the notation this way.

They will have no difficulty reading the answering refrain. Ask them to find the phrase or phrases with *ti*.

The music provides our students with an opportunity to practice alternating mallets to play a smooth-sounding melody. This may be the focus of a lesson following its presentation. After my students learned the song and setting they enjoyed trading parts, creating new variations just by changing the timbres of the phrases numbered in the score.

274

Round and Round

Jamaican folksong arr. AS

Additional resources

Staton *Music and You*, Grade 4
    'Old Abram Brown' (p. 21)
Frazee *Orff Handbook for World of Music − 4*
    'Watch Out!' (p. 17)
Frazee with Kreuter *Discovering Orff*,
    pp. 174–5
Orff *Music for Children*, American edn., Vol. 3
    'Týnom, Tánom' (p. 43)
    'Two Canons', no. 1 (p. 70)
Orff and Keetman *Music for Children*, adpt.
    Murray, Vol. II
    'Simple Simon' (p. 42)

See 'Rhythm,' 3 for suggestions regarding curriculum order.

3   *Define the major or Ionian scale as an inventory of seven pitches, ordered in whole and half steps, beginning on* do.

(W   W   H   W   W   W   H)

(d   r   m   f   s   l   t   d)

4   *Define the minor or Aeolian scale as an inventory of seven pitches, ordered by whole and half steps, beginning on* la.

(W   H   W   W   H   W   W)

(l   t   d   r   m   f   s   l)

Because your students have sung and played songs using all seven notes of the diatonic scale, it is time to introduce scales and review the need for key signatures.

Ask your students to recall 'Round and Round.' Explain that a scale is a shopping list of ingredients or an inventory of all the notes they need. Begin with an empty xylophone box and ask the students to put on only the bars needed to play the melody. As each bar is placed on the instrument, have another student place the note on the staff with the letter and syllable written below it. This is not the melody, but the notes from which the melody is made. You may ask a student to play the same scale on the piano as they watch him or play on cards picturing the keyboard. Ask them to identify the places where no black keys fell betwen white keys, for these are half steps. Strips of construction paper can be taped on the board to show the order of whole and half steps, like this:

■　■　■■　■　■　■■
d　　r　　mf　　s　　l　　td

Ask other students to play 'Round and Round,' but begin on g. Again, make an inventory of pitches, exchanging the f bar for f♯. Ask a student to check their inventory by playing the song and/or scale on the piano while another student watches to see and hear if the order of whole and half steps is correct. The same process can be used, of course, to build the scale of F.

Next, look at the notation of 'Artza Alenu' and ask the students to tell you what pitches and/or syllables they find. You or one of the students can place these pitches on the staff, as before, placing the song's beginning and ending pitch first. Using the keyboard again, ask the students to order the whole and half step. When this is finished ask them to place a different set of colored strips below those that illustrated the Ionian scale. Help them to see that at first this appears to be a different order, but that when they begin on *la–ti* of the *do* scale the intervals remain the same.

d r mf s l td
l td r mf s l

Because I want the children to see how these scales are related, I always set the instruments in the pentatonic. Then the place of *do* is always clear and the tonal center of the scale is established in relationship to it. This will provide the basis for the way I introduce modes in fifth and sixth grades.

Children find discovering scales more interesting when the challenge is related to a familiar song. Be sure that lessons exploring and understanding this objective include some lively singing and playing, for performing the scale without attaching it to the music it inventories is not a satisfying musical experience.

5　Improvise and/or compose Ionian and Aeolian melodies over a tonic drone or bordun accompaniment.

As notes are added to the scale the student has increasing numbers of choices when improvising and composing melodies. So many choices can lead to unmusical results and discouragement. We can help fourth graders develop an ear for tonality and assure them of musical results if we build each experience with increasing numbers of choices on familiar structures.

'Ah, Poor Bird' is an ideal model for improvisation for it is short and uses pitch material economically. After the class has reviewed the canon (p. 270) place the melodic outline on the board again. Guide your students to observe that each measure began on *la, do,* or *mi,* notes of a chord based on *la.* With their assistance, fill in the melody again, and ask them to compare measures one, two and four. Measures two and four are related to the first, for the second measure repeats the first, beginning on a higher note, while the last measure is the first in reverse. The melody holds our interest because the third measure has contrasts in rhythm and pitch range.

Now it is the students' turn to use this information to construct their own Aeolian melodies. I like to place four alto xylophones in the center in a square with the class sitting in a circle around the instruments. The first child plays a simple four-beat idea, beginning on *la, do,* or *mi.* The second child repeats the idea from another of the remaining three starting points. The third child is to play a contrasting idea, while the fourth child uses what he can of the first idea, while ending on *la.* Ask the children to repeat their melody while another child accompanies them on a bass instrument by playing a tremelo on the tonic, or composing a four-beat ostinato on bordun pitches.

Here is one way I have found to give every child a chance to explore and improvise before playing alone in front of others. I give each child an instrument but I allow them to experiment, using only their fingertips. I usually establish the tempo and guide the practice by lightly tapping the beat on a hand drum. When they share their melodies they use mallets, of course.

Another model for improvisation can be drawn from 'Round and Round,' an Ionian melody. The students will recall that each phrase was answered with the same melody. Again, form a circle so that all children can see and hear their classmates perform. Place a bass xylophone, four alto xylophones and four glockenspiels inside the circle. Ask the bass xylophone player to be responsible for providing a bordun accompaniment of four beats, beginning on *do.* The first alto xylophone player makes up a question phrase of eight beats. The four glockenspiel players then play the response from 'Round and Round.' Each of the three remaining alto xylophone players then in turn play question phrases of two measures, beginning on *do, mi,* or *sol,* and each is answered by the glockenspiels. The roles may be reversed, with glockenspiels improvising the question phrases. Remind your class that very pleasant melodies can be improvised by repeating single notes before stepping off to other bars. Short ideas can be repeated at several levels. I find that children are intensely interested in the experimenting of their classmates and are eager to try out melodies based on what they have seen others do. Another time use the same structure, but have the class compose the question phrase and improvise the answer, ending on *do,* or the tonic.

6   *Identify melodies aurally and from analysis of notation as being* do-*based (*do *pentatonic, major, or Ionian) or* la-*based (*la *pentatonic, minor, or Aeolian).*

This objective reminds us that even after we have guided our students through an analysis of scales and keys, tonality has no meaning unless we continue to apply our knowledge to the music we hear and perform. It isn't necessary to spend a lesson on this goal, but rather choose, for the remainder of the year, to ask your children to identify the tonality of each song they perform. My goal is to have my students identify the tonal center as easily as they identify meter.

The terms Ionian and Aeolian are not important unless you intend to link them with an introduction to other modes later. The terms, major and minor, however, have common usage. I use the modal names in addition to the terms major and minor because my students are exposed to Dorian and Mixolydian modes and my approach links Ionian with Mixolydian as sharing the same major pentachord, and Aeolian with Dorian sharing the same minor pentachord. (I am indebted to Mary Goetze of Indiana University for this approach to modes.)

Your children may be surprised to know how many major and minor songs they already know. They may wish to keep a list, and begin each lesson with one of these songs as part of their warm-up. Here is a list of songs presented in this chapter.

Do-centered songs	*La*-centered songs
Swapping Song	Hey, Ho, Anybody Home?
Some Love Coffee	Zum Gali
Hop Up and Jump Up	Ama-Lama
Mama Paquita	Old House
Shoo Fly	Charlie's Neat
Down the River	Ah, Poor Bird
On Top Of Old Smoky	Artza Alenu
It Rained a Mist	Ghost of Tom
This Old Man	
Round and Round	
Winter Song	

There are several ways you can help children listen for the tonality of a melody. You can introduce a familiar song by singing the tonic note followed by a major and then a minor triad from that note. Many children will be able to remember and compare the tones to the melody. Another way is to sing the ending phrase several times. The ending cadence usually clearly states the tonality. Make it a game to listen to and analyze songs by giving the class 'detective work' or specific listening tasks. Then reward them with high praise when they answer correctly, for I find careful listening is rarely my fourth graders' best skill unless I help them be conscious of its value.

We can also use what we know about tonality to help us sight-read better. Here are some melodies which the children can sing at sight. Before they begin ask them to guess whether the song is major or minor by looking at the key signature and the beginning and ending notes. Then sing the scale they have chosen in syllables before they begin to sight-sing. Notice that these examples are fairly short. If you are learning a longer song, choose only a portion to sing at sight, and teach the remainder by rote as they watch. Learning should not be laborious, especially because we know most of our students learn music by rote more quickly.

The comments which follow suggest how each song may be used by you and your students to apply previously learned skills. Some songs can be used now for reading practice and then used later for harmonic analysis. Remember to guide your fourth graders to discover the tonal center of each example first as they read and analyze.

Moon Magic

This melody lends itself to a bordun or tonic setting. If you wish to develop a setting, your students can use e's and b's in various ostinatos, establishing the *la*-based or minor tonality. Add glissandos and unpitched percussion color to create a mysterious background. Alternate their setting of the song with a Halloween chant, add their movement, and you have an exciting performance that may produce some music magic.

To Stop the Train

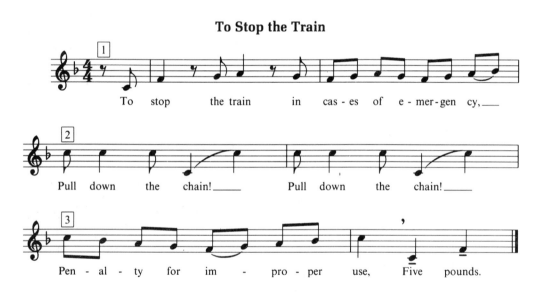

'To Stop The Train' is a round which my fourth graders teach to their sisters and brothers so that it is passed from grade to grade before I teach it each year. After they have learned the melody ask your students which phrase tells them most clearly whether the song is *la* or *do* centered. My children have created movement to accompany each line. They have performed the song by singing and moving, followed by moving only, followed by singing only. Then when they sing in a three-part round the entrances and endings are visual as well as aural. They have also learned to play this melody on instruments, and have experimented with several borduns to accompany their performance.

Oh Music, Sweet Music

from *The Hallelujah* (1860), Lowell Mason

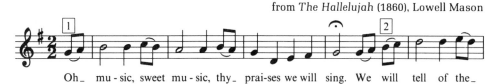

Oh_ mu - sic, sweet mu - sic, thy_ prai - ses we will sing. We will tell of the_

plea - sures and hap - pi - ness you bring. Mu - sic, mu - sic, let the cho - rus sing.

Lowell Mason's canon is more demanding to read because of the skips of a fourth and sixth in the last line. Learn this phrase first by isolating these intervals. Ask the children to sing the first note, followed by all the steps to the next note. Then sing the interval without the intermediate steps. Practice each wider skip this way. It should be much easier now to sing the phrase accurately, in tempo.

The canon is based on tonic–dominant harmony which the children can hear as they pile up the phrases. You may want to record their performance of 'Oh Music, Sweet Music' and then play it for them, this time to hear if each line is independently clear and in tune. Later, when chords are introduced, you can play the tape and ask your students to identify the chord changes. One student can play a g chord on the piano or an instrument. The class can raise hands for measures they think the chord built on *do* will harmonize.

Rise Up, O Flame

Christoph Praetorius (1535–1609)

Rise up, O flame,_____ By_ thy_ light glow - ing,

Show to us beau - ty,_ vi - sion_ and joy.

'Rise Up, O Flame' may also be accompanied with a tonic or bordun setting, composed by your class. Guide them to decide the tonality and then use the tonic and fifth to create their setting. If the students are going to perform it in a round keep the instrumentation very simple. Children find this melody easy to play on barred instruments, and some may be able to play it on soprano recorders.

Alleluia

German

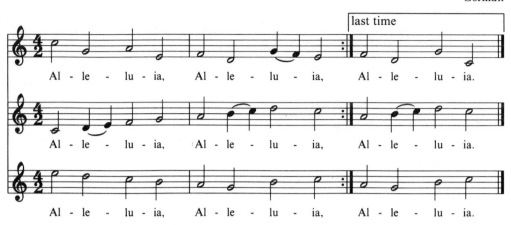

After you have sung 'Alleluia' for your class ask them to sing the note they remember as most important, for it defines what they hear as the tontal center. Then, after you sing the second and third phrases again ask them to repeat them in syllables. They may need guidance in singing the first phrase accurately.

The first line is familiar across centuries of music composition. Notice the time signature. The half note beat gives fourth graders the clear message that a slow tempo is desirable. If you have not presented 6/8 meter, preparing to read this song will be a good introduction to the significance of the note value which indicates the beat in the time signature. We will end the year with a study of chaconnes, and Pachelbel's Canon in D is based on a nearly identical theme. This canon may become your starting point for that lesson.

> These goals may be delayed until the fifth grade in order to give more time to develop the 'Melody' and 'Rhythm' goals.

> Next, move to 'Harmony,' 1–4.

Harmony

1   Define 'chord,' and demonstrate chords on barred instruments.

I can soon learn how much my students already know about chords and harmony by asking them to define a chord in words and on an instrument. From this lively discussion we come to the conclusion that a chord is two or more intervals of thirds which sound together. At this point I like to give each student an opportunity to build and play a chord on an instrument, beginning on a pitch which I name. As the child plays the chord I draw it on the board. When a child plays chords on Orff instruments he can use three mallets or ask for another person to play the third note. Then ask them to play a chord, each using two mallets. Let them find different ways to order the notes, always doubling one of the notes, then return to the triad with the root note being lowest. Sing several one chord melodies, such as 'Ama-Lama,' or 'Crawdad Hole' as the students play the tonic chord on strong beats.

2 *Explore the function of harmony by changing chords.*

The students have found that chords can be built by thirds from any note, called the root. The next step, then, is to find out how they are named and used. I like to begin by building the scale, using eight cards as illustrated here:

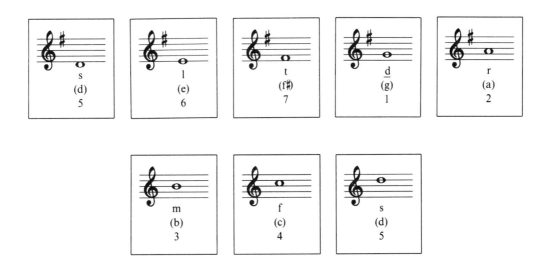

I use *sol* to *sol* because the root of the dominant will sound most clearly when the root falls below the tonic.

A volunteer holds each card, forming the scale in front of the class. Several children are chosen to sing and play the note each card represents on a barred instrument. Be sure to assign d and g to bass instruments. Begin by asking the students to build a chord on *do*, or *do–mi–sol* (g–b–d). The card holders direct classmates to play the chord at the tempo you establish by stepping forward and raising their cards. I also give the chord three names at this point; the tonic chord, the I chord, or g chord, and explain that each name refers to the root note and its position in the scale.

Next, ask them to build a chord on *sol*, the last note of the tonic chord. I ask my students to add another third to make the dominant seventh chord, or *sol* (d), *ti* (f♯), *re* (a), and *fa* (c), because the seventh is often present in diatonic melodies, outlining the dominant chord. As these students step forward their partners play the chord. Perhaps your students will notice that while most people were able to move, one always had to stay in front as a member of both chords and one person never moved because *la* was not in either chord.

Now you can play a little game of 'Chord Sharks.' You, and later a student, can signal the chord changes by raising your hand to indicate I or V. As soon as one child can identify the pattern or harmonic ostinato, write the child's name and the ostinato on the board. Then ask a student to direct the playing by pointing to the numerals while you play or improvise a melody. Here are some common harmonic ostinatos, changing on the metric accent. Use familiar songs as much as possible to encourage the children to sing as they play.

```
I—I— V— V—        Here We Go Round the Mulberry Bush
I—I— V— I         Skip to My Lou
                  Paw Paw Patch

I—V— I— V— (etc.)  Streets of Laredo
I——— V— I—

I—I— V— I—        London Bridge is Falling Down
                  Kansas Girls
                  Rig-a-jig-jig
```

3   Find chords outlined in melodies. Accompany these melodies with the roots of the tonic and dominanat chords and the common tone.

I like to teach 'Springfield Mountain' by rote, for the story motivates my students to learn it and we will be using our reading skills to find chords later. The story, as told in a tragic 1761 New England ballad version, is thought to have some basis in fact. The more humorous version from a later era always prompts a discussion of first aid techniques for snake bite. I owe the last verse, which invariably sells the song to my fourth graders, to Tossi Aaron.

On Springfield Mountain

Comic ballad (1761)

On Spring-field Moun-tain there did dwell   A love-li youth, I knowed him

well.___ Too-loo-re - ay, too-loo-re - oo, Too-loo-re - ay, too-loo-re - oo.

2   This lovely youth one day did go
    Down to the meadow for to mow. (Refrain)

3   He scarce had moved quite round the field
    When a cruel serpent bit his heel. (Refrain)

4   They took him home to Molli dear
    Which made him feel so very queer. (Refrain)

5   Now Molli had two ruby lips
    With which the poison she did sip. (Refrain)

6   Now Molli had a rotten tooth
    And so the poison killed them both. (Refrain)

7   The moral, friend, is very clear,
    Please see your dentist twice a year. (Refrain)

Call your children's attention to the 1½-beat anacrusis of the first phrase, for the focus of our lesson is these pitches. Have them circle the notes which outline the tonic chord as it appears in the melody. Then ask them to circle the outline of the dominant chord, which they will find in the second full measure. Measure four again outlines the tonic chord, and the sixth returns to the dominant. Now have them write the roman numeral for the tonic or dominant chord above the first beat of each measure. We have identified the need for each chord by reading and identifying the chord outlines in the melody. Next we will identify the need for changing chords through aural analysis.

Now ask the children to turn away from the notation of the song and sing the first verse and refrain while you accompany them. Play only the tonic chord. It is always fun to see the faces of many children grimace at my 'mistake.' Ask them to tell you what is wrong and ask for their help. Tell them that when they sit you will play the tonic chord and when they stand you will play the dominant chord. After they have dictated your harmonization by sitting and standing ask them to check their aural analysis with their written analysis.

Teaching the setting through notation should take little time because they have been reading as they analyzed the song. The setting places the chord root note in the bass, while the common tone, or fifth degree of the scale is found in the alto voice. Seeing the chords on a staff as illustrated below will help your students understand how their instrument parts work together to make harmony. There is a finger-cymbal part for the refrain. Your students will have good ideas for unpitched percussion ostinatos to illustrate the story line of each verse. An introduction and bridges between the refrain and the next verse, using material from the setting and ideas of the students, can give other children an opportunity to play and sing.

On Springfield Mountain

arr. AS

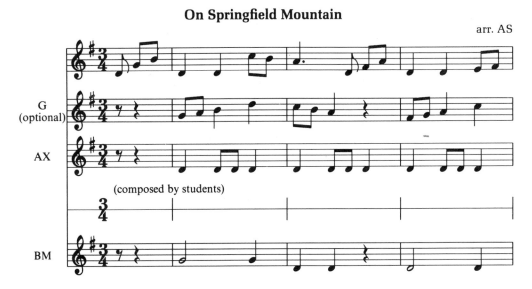

Pentatonic songs contain only two pitches of the dominant chord, *re* and *sol*. Yet, when one note of the dominant chord becomes important by occurring predominantly in the measure, sounding next to another dominant chord note, or falling on the metric accent, dominant harmony is indicated. 'Perry Merry Dictum Dominee' is a beautiful example of this, and our approach to teaching the song will make movement of tonic to dominant harmony the focus of the lesson.

Begin by asking your students to sight-sing the melody silently, then audibly sing only *do* as it occurs. Repeat, singing only *mi*, and then *sol*. Finally, sing only *re*. The children will want to resolve to *do*, which leads the class to singing the entire melody in solfege.

The harmonic change which is indicated by *re* in the melody can be anticipated through movement. After the students form a circle, have them step quarternotes to the right unless *re* is in the measure. They can show that they know where *re* is by stepping toward the center as they sing it, bring their feet together to balance on the next step, and then step back again. They will find that *re* is present in all phrases but the fourth. The resulting movement pattern will be:

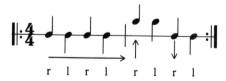

For movement for the fourth phrase, ask your students to turn to a partner. First bow to their partners, and then bow to the person at their back. Return to the first movement pattern for the fifth phrase.

Their movement demonstrates the bass ostinato. Tell them to sing *do* for each step going to the right, and low *sol* for each step toward the center. Then play that pattern.

I like to teach the instrument parts for the fourth phrase next. Then teach remaining parts for phrases 1, 2, 3 and 5 from body percussion preparation and notation.

Perry Merry Dictum Dominee

Ohio

Par - tum guar - tum per - ry dic - cen - tum,

Per - ry mer - ry dic - tum Do - mi - nee.

Additional resources

Boshkoff *Ring Around, Sing Around*
   'I Married My Wife in the Month of June'
   (p. 23)
Ladendecker *Tunes for Young Troubadours*
   'Song of Spring' (p. 8)
Orff *Music for Children*, American edn., Vol. 3
   'Liebe ist ein Ring' (p. 37)
   'All 'Round the Ring' (p. 143)
Staton et al. *Music and You*, Grade 4
   'Sheep Shearing' (p. 24)
   'Tap on Your Drum' (p. 37)
   'Let Us Sing Together' (p. 43)

Steen *Orff Activities*, Grade 4
  'Lady from Baltimore' (p. 19)
  Verse in minor, refrain in major.
  'Who Did?' (p. 22)
  'Polly Wolly Doodle' (p. 23)
  'I Ride an Old Paint' (p. 29)

Texture

1   Perform alone, and individualy in textures of up to four parts.

This objective reminds us that we need to give each child the opportunity to perform as a soloist and as the one person responsible for a part in the classroom ensemble. One of the strengths of Orff music is that the philosophy encourages the special contributions of individuals by having them perform alone. At the same time, the performance of each child is valued for its contribution to the musicality of the total class performance. This demands both individual musical skill and cooperative effort between the student and the performance objectives of the class.

I am always looking for ways to solve the practical problems that accompany this objective so that individuals are given opportunities to contribute while the class addresses its objectives. One way is to plan the lesson so that each child has an opportunity to play a part alone. You can determine how many instrument parts you can offer in your lesson and divide the number of students you have by that number. Then write into your plan that many opportunities to exchange parts. You can also keep a class book with you and check each time a child performs independently. A simple code will make your record keeping clear. Enter the abbreviation used in scores for instrument playing, an S for singing, an M for solo or small-group movement, an I for individual improvisation, and an ! for an unusually good musical contribution. Refer to your book when you assign students parts to help you distribute responsibilities equally. When the class is practicing a barred instrument piece I sometimes divide the class into small ensembles, assigning one or two children to each part. They are to help each other play accurately and together. Then, when all the groups play together again, the results are more musical and expressive.

We need to remember that in song settings it is more rewarding musically for the group and the student to use only one or two children on each part, exchanging parts frequently.

2   Perform canons in two to four parts vocally and on instruments.

This goal may be combined with practicing sight-reading skills. The canons listed below provide our children with additional opportunities to improve their technique. They especially enjoy 'Ding, Dong, Diggidiggidong' and 'No. 40, Canon.' When working on these pieces be playful and encourage experimenting with timbres, accompaniments, and extensions of introductions and codas.

Additional resources
Orff *Music for Children*, American edn., Vol. 3
  'Two Canons' (p. 70–71)

Orff and Keetman *Music for Children*, adpt.
   Murray, Vol. I
   'I Love Sixpence' (p. 24)
   'Ding, Dong, Diggidiggidong' (p. 24)
   'Ding, Dong, the Bells Do Ring' (p. 24)
   'No. 40, Canon' (p. 131)
   'Canon Exercises' (pp. 91–2)

3   Sing a melodic descant to harmonize a melody.

In 'Springfield Mountain' one descant is written for the verse, on glockenspiels or, perhaps, voices, and another descant is written for the refrain with a more sustained sound for recorders or voices. I find that I prepare descants for instruments like those found in the settings cited below by singing them. The class and I enjoy adding words or neutral syllables to an instrumental descant to make pleasing harmony with the melody. The instruments can also play with descant voices to support tuneful singing or can play in place of voices when sections repeat, making more interesting settings by contrasting timbres.

Additional resources
Frazee *Orff Handbook for World of Music – 3*
   'I'se the B'y' (p. 12)
   'Oranges and Lemons' (p. 14 only)
   Both settings include instrumental descants.
   However, both descants are in the vocal
   range of fourth graders. Use words,
   nonsense syllables or 'loo' to make vocal
   descants.
Goetze *The Cat Came Back*
   'Goodbye, Old Paint' (p. 4)
Goetze *Simply Sung*
   This is a collection of ten folk-songs
   arranged in three parts and sequenced from
   'polyphonic toward homophonic' textures.
   These settings are appropriate for school
   choirs, but if your fourth grade can sing a
   three-part canon clearly these arrangements
   are very satisfying early part-singing
   experiences.
Steen *Orff Activities*, Grade 3
   'Debka Hora' (p. 22)
Steen *Orff Activities*, Grade 4
   'I Ride an Old Paint' (p. 29)

Timbre

1   Continue to develop playing techiques capable of expressing accurately the concepts presented and the ideas of the students.

We should give attention to this objective each time a new rhythmic duration is presented. Students should be able to choose and properly use appropriate instruments for each playing assignment. For example, when sixteenth notes are being studied give students practice opportunities to play untuned pieces so they can listen and evaluate their playing of evenly divided beats. One easy way to do this is to expand the usefulness of songs containing interesting melodic rhythms. Use the word rhythms of songs on hand drums, for example, as the theme of a B section with accompanying ostinatos on woodblocks or play the theme in canon, using one timbre for each part. After the rhythms have been mastered they may become the basis of improvised variations. In this way songs may be extended into larger forms, such as a three-part (A B A) or rondo (A B A B A or A B A C A) form.

When melodic objectives are presented songs may be explored by playing as well as singing them. When I ask my students to play the way they want to sing the song I find that they perform with better phrasing and expressiveness. We often work out several solutions for malleting so that the children can play their instruments smoothly. This gives me the chance to guide them through mallet exercises which relate to specific problems in the music. To play a melody well is always rewarding to children, for it is concrete evidence that they are musicians.

Form

1 Identify the chaconne as a bass ostinato or ground bass over which melodic variations can be made.

Pachelbel's Canon in D usually sounds familiar to many of my students and, because of this, it is a good place to begin our studies of variation techniques. There are numerous recordings available for this popular work. To guide their listening of this or other chaconnes I have used the following process. First, I ask the students to sing the bass line theme from notation. Below the theme I list various ways the music may change above the bass theme. The list may include descriptions such as: mostly half notes, mostly eighth notes, thick texture, solo instrument, thin texture, scale-like theme, change of range, change of timbre, and so on. Then I give each child a number. As they listen, I call a number at the beginning of each variation. During that time the person with the corresponding number looks for the words that describe that variation. After they have listened, we review the composition by asking each child to report what was heard. You can list these descriptors for each variation so that when your class listens to the music again they can compare what they heard the first time to what they are able to hear when the music is a little more familiar. When my students are asked to listen in this way, I find they not only analyze their assigned sections, but they describe by comparing sections, becoming familiar with more than the music assigned them.

A chaconne for keyboard is included here to give your children another opportunity to hear this composition technique. Put the bass ostinato or theme on the board to follow as they listen.

Bass theme

After you have played the score once, ask them to follow the notation of the bass theme and the first melody. They will soon discover that the theme, while always present, is sometimes disguised or becomes a variation as well. The students will enjoy playing these parts before and after the Chaconne is played for them.

Chaconne

G. Böhm (1661–1733)

293

2 *Improvise over a bass ostinato.*

After your students have heard several chaconnes they will enjoy exploring the possibilities of creating their own based on their observations. First put the bass ostinato or theme on a visual and have the class sing it until it becomes familiar. When they observe that the theme is a sequence which skips down a fourth and then up a second it becomes easy to play.

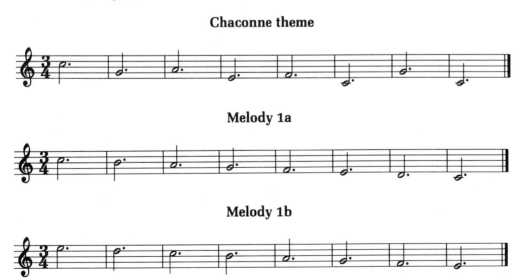

Chaconne theme

Melody 1a

Melody 1b

Melody 2

Melody 3

The beauty of the Purcell theme is that the scale moving up or down makes a beautiful complementary line. Begin by asking a soloist to play the bass ostinato. Then double the bass ostinato before adding an alto metallophone to play a descending scale in dotted half notes. Then ask your students to compose a rhythmic ostinato to play on each scale step to vary the way the scale melody is played. Assign this variation to a higher instrument or to the same timbre a third higher. Next, add a second melody, an ascending scale, guiding them to put *mi* and *fa* in the second measure, and *la–ti* in the fifth measure. This melody may also be played with rhythmic variations. The third melody is based on our students' understanding of chords. Once they have learned the sequence of chords this theme may be altered in several ways. One way is to vary the rhythm on the fifth of each chord in the second measure of each pattern. Another is to begin on the third, fifth or root of the chord and add passing tones to the chord outline.

However, the texture becomes thick when all these variations happen at once. The class needs to decide how to group their variations of the melodies into alternating duets, trios, or quartets over the continuing bass theme. My students enjoy recording the results of this lesson and comparing their chaconne with others.

Additional resources

Bisgaard with Aaron *In Canon*
  'Purcell Canon for Instruments' (p. 25)
Frazee with Kreuter *Discovering Orff*, p. 178
Frazee and Kreuter *Sound Ideas*
  'Chaconne in F' by Henry Purcell (p. 13)

During the fourth grade our students have matured to reach a higher level of independent musicianship. They are able to learn pentatonic and diatonic music through reading and aural analysis. They are familiar with major and minor scales, and the need for harmony has been introduced. Their rhythmic vocabulary has been more than doubled by the addition of sixteenth-note patterns and new meters, especially 6/8. The year's experiences have added new layers of knowledge about rhythm, melody, texture and form. The music to which they are introduced in fifth grade will contain these concepts, only at a more challenging level. Because our students need many experiences and applications of knowledge to be comfortable with what they know, record your assessment of what concepts and skills should be reviewed and what you can assume most students know well. This will help you determine where and how you should begin your fifth grade year.

8 · Fifth Grade

From fourth grade on through the middle years your children's social development has a profound effect on their ability to learn in school. For example, we are aware that the typical fifth grader highly values the opinions and approval of peers, sometimes in competition with their need for the approval and instruction of parents and teachers. These children also build strong loyalties to each other and this can affect their ability to work in smaller groups. These factors alter the child's perception of our role as teachers, for fifth graders want to be independent of us while, at the same time, they need our guidance, support, patience and knowledge.

Performing before others becomes a way for fifth graders to be recognized by others important to them. Most of them, I have found, value an opportunity to demonstrate what they know and can do. We can use performing opportunities as teaching tools to summarize and symbolize the attainment of goals we set with our students. I have found this can give them the motivation and energy to exceed the boundaries they may otherwise set for themselves.

There may be program factors that influence your curriculum objectives. Recorder instruction may be an important part of your program, and you will want to allow time to build playing skills. If you have a choir, either as enrichment for those who choose it, or for everyone at the same grade level, consider how its objectives enhance and support your classroom curriculum.

Finally, the organization of the school influences how fifth graders function socially. They may be the youngest in a middle school, in awe and influenced by the pressures of comparing themselves to students older than they are. If they are the oldest in an elementary school they may view themselves as leaders of the younger students, and the differences between their abilities and those of primary students dramatically supports this positive view of themselves. There may be a sixth grade above them, which places them in the role of heirs to leadership, while being influenced by the nature of their relationships to sixth graders. Because their placement in the school system affects their view of themselves and their relationships to those in grades below and above them, it becomes a factor, not so much in what we teach them but in how we teach them.

Fifth graders' ability to make music parallels their evolving social and academic independence. Their interest and taste in music includes that which they choose outside of school, increasingly a symbol of their desire for their own manner of expression. Our goal is to teach a broad repertoire of literature which expands their skills and abilities to understand many kinds of music beyond what they know best. We should explain this as a value and function of their musical education while accepting the legitimacy of their own varied explorations of music beyond our classrooms.

Fifth graders are generally well coordinated, making it possible to perform more Orff instrumental literature. For many of my students playing instruments is appealing, especially when the pieces require rhythmic accuracy and drive. They are vocally strong and enjoy the sophistication of singing melodic ostinatos, descants, and, this year, parallel harmonies. Those who have special talents and skills appreciate being given extra challenges and ways to use their abilities within the group without necessarily drawing attention to themselves.

I have found it helpful to begin the year by conducting an informal survey, asking the children to rank what they enjoy doing most in music; singing, moving, playing instruments or listening. I also ask them if they enjoy solving musical problems, such as improvising or composing, with the whole class or in small groups. By ranking all these as 1 (enjoy most), 2 (enjoy), or 3 (enjoy least), leaving none out, I demonstrate my interest in their views concerning music instruction. It also indicates my willingness to use their favorite ways of learning more frequently. On the same survey I usually ask the children to list their music activities outside of school.

Goals

Skill building to assure musical independence may be the most important work you and your fifth graders do this year. It will be more important to broaden their abilities to use what they already know than to teach them more complex music concepts. We will use augmentation and diminution to learn how to read familiar rhythms in new notations. We will then perform familiar rhythms in new meters. When the Ionian and Aeolian scales are familiar, Mixolydian and Dorian modes will be introduced as being related to them by sharing the same pentatonic core. Harmony and the introduction of new chords will be drawn from the analysis of melodies, and this understanding will lead to improvising new melodies over chord patterns.

Fifth Grade Objectives

Rhythm and Melody Review
1   Review known durations through performing, reading, writing, and improvising.
2   Review the pentatonic scales, based on *do* and *la*, and then the diatonic scales, Ionian (major) (*d r mf s l td*) and Aeolian (minor) (*l td r mf s l*).

Rhythm
1   Perform, identify, read, and write patterns using ♫ ♩, ♩. ♩, and ♫. as diminutions of ♪♩ ♪, ♩. ♪, and ♪ ♩. .
2   Use augmentation and diminution to change familiar patterns.
3   Review 6/8 meter and practice an inventory of patterns common to that meter (♫♩,♩ ♪,♩. , ♪♩, ♩.♫,♩. ♩ ♪, etc.).
4   Write, read, and perform short compositions in 6/8 meter.

> Consider covering melody objectives ('Melody,' 1–3) and harmony objectives ('Harmony,' 1, 2) first before focusing on a new meter.

5   Perform and identify 5/4 or 5/8 meter through movement, listening, and reading.

Melody
1   Explore Ionian and Aeolian modes (major and natural minor scales) through improvisation.
2   Imitate, then write down from dictation, two, three and four pitches in Ionian and Aeolian modalities.

Consider the study of 'Harmony,' 1 through 4, before an analysis of Mixolydian and Dorian modes.

3   Perform to identify Mixolydian mode by its characteristic flatted seventh, or *ta* instead of *ti* (*d r mf s lt d*).

4   Perform to identify Dorian mode by its characteristic raised sixth degree, or *fi* instead of *fa* (*l td r m fs l*).

Harmony

1   Review the tonic (I) and dominant (V) chords.
2   Identify the sub-dominant or IV chord, and then identify I–IV and I–IV–V patterns.
3   Identify the dominant and tonic chords in half and full cadences.
4   Identify and improvise over tonic–dominant patterns.
5   Play and sing in parallel thirds or sixths with a melody.

Timbre

1   Demonstrate an understanding of the characteristics of instrumental timbres when composing and improvising.

Texture

1   Perform alone or in pairs a single line in an ensemble.
2   Perform in canons of up to four voices.

Form

1   Analyze a theme and variation, and then compose a variation on a selected theme.

Rhythm and Melody Review

1   Review known durations through performing, reading, writing and improvising.

2   Review the pentatonic scales, based on do *and* la, *and then the diatonic scales, Ionian (major) (*d r mf s l td*) and Aeolian (minor) (*l td r mf s l*).*

As the children become more knowing and skillful in music there are more possibilities to integrate, compare and combine objectives. It is easiest to think of learning music as adding one new skill or objective at a time when, instead, it is more like building a pyramid. Each new skill or knowledge is at the peak, but as it is assimilated it sifts down and affects every part of the structure of previous knowledges and skills, multiplying, rather than adding, to the possibilities for application. This is the reason taking more time each year to review, using new, age-appropriate literature, is important. We will begin with a collection of pieces which demonstrate this point and will provide us with a basis for learning the new concepts and skills to be introduced this year.

We begin by introducing 'Fooba Wooba John,' focusing on the rhythms of the song and setting. First, ask your students to demonstrate each duration with its parallel rest in ostinatos against an established beat, and then label each of the following symbols.

Then ask them to perform these durations in body percussion, as found in the score below, and drawn from the 'Fooba Wooba John' setting.

Fooba Wooba John

Your students can experiment and practice these rhythms by stepping with the body percussion they created. Divide them into four groups and assign one line of the rhythm score to each group. As they explore, call attention to the variety of possible solutions they demonstrate. Finally, with their help, find a way to relate their movements to each other to create a movement composition using their combined space to add and stop each line of the score according to the class plan. Or you may wish to continue this exploration of relative note values by dividing the class into quartets with one person moving each rhythm, while relating to the others in the group.

It will be easy to pick which of the four rhythmic patterns matches most closely the rhythm of 'Fooba Wooba John.' Write the first rhythm four times and then ask the students to help you correct each line to match the words of each phrase. After the class has learned to sing the first verse, introduce the tonic bass line and then the alto xylophone and metallophone patterns.

Fooba Wooba John

American folk song

Saw a flea kick a tree,
Saw a crow fly-ing low,
foo-ba woo-ba John.
Saw a flea kick a tree
Saw a crow fly-in' low,

in the mid-dle of the sea!
sev-'ral miles be-neath the snow!
Whoa, John, oh, John
foo-ba woo-ba John.

AX/AM

3. Saw a whale chase a snail . . .
   all around the water pail.

4. Saw a louse push a mouse . . .
   down the chimney through the house.

In the next lesson focus on the melodic patterns in the song and setting. Begin by having the students echo sing pentatonic melody patterns on a neutral syllable which they then repeat, singing in solfege.

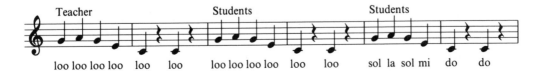

Teacher   Students   Students
loo loo loo loo loo loo   loo loo loo loo loo loo   sol la sol mi do do

The C-pentatonic scale, read from high to low, is the basis of the last phrase of this song (e.g. phrase 4, 'Fooba Wooba John'). After the children have read the scale and reviewed the song, ask them to add to the scale to notate the last phrase of the song. From this review of notation the students will be able to read the melody from score. Have them sing the recorder/soprano xylophone part in syllables and letter names before playing it on an instrument and adding it to the setting.

Using the word rhythms of measure 2 and 7, ask the class to compose an introductory melody which they then write on the board. This, along with rhythms and melodic motives from the song, can be selected to make bridges to be performed between verses.

Four improvised phrases of rhythm on bongo and conga drums, each interrupted by a phrase of John's fooba wooba motions could be developed in a third lesson, replacing the bridges and resulting in a rondo.

Very early in the year I like to give the children an opportunity to practice their rhythm and playing skills, for this is one of the ways they most frequently demonstrate what they know. If you have barred instruments for half your children you may consider teaching an instrumental piece from *Music for Children*, Vol. 1 (adpt. Murray). 'Hi-yah', (no. 38, p. 123) is a demanding, fast-moving piece which my children find challenging and enjoyable. While the individual parts are easy to read or learn from imitation of body percussion, they are demanding to play accurately in combination with other parts.

I begin by asking them to echo my greeting, 'hi!,' four times, each with a slight variation of dynamic level and accent. Without pause, I move on to 'Hi-yah' two times, and then I motion them to join me in the crescendo of eight beats of 'Hi-yah' on eighth notes. Divide the class into two groups and repeat the sequence, using their notation of each motive to help them perform accurately. Sometimes we have chosen percussion instruments to play the rhythmic chant a second time.

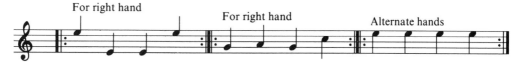

At this point I often play a recording of this piece.[1] As they listen we follow the main themes from notation. This invariably motivates them to continue with the next step, which is to learn the more demanding barred instrument section.

When I introduce the barred instrument parts I teach the theme without the eighth note, e, for left hand, adding it after the children have mastered the theme and most can play it with the right hand alone. The accompaniment is taught from their body percussion imitation of my demonstration on the instrument. I have learned that the parts are played most accurately when there are several students playing the theme, but only one player for each accompaniment line. The alto xylophone chords may be divided between two students. Their classmates chant the contrasting B section, and then trade responsibilities during the woodblock introduction. One class asked to demonstrate the chant with karate moves!

1   *Orff-Schulwerk, Music for Children*. London: Schott. Cassette 1, no. 20

'Don't Let Your Watch Run Down' is a work-song from the time when the Mississippi River was a primary thoroughfare for transporting goods. It gives us an opportunity to review F pentatonic and syncopation. After you have placed the notation of the following three melodic fragments before the children, sing or play each one on the recorder. Your students should be able to identify and then sing the notation which matches your performance. Then sing each motive, using these sayings about the value of time to provide the rhythm.

measures   1 & 2 ___   15 & 16   5   6   ___   9–10,   11–12 13–14

A stitch in time saves nine.

Better late than never.

All work, no play, makes John a dull boy.

Time is money.

Early to bed, early to rise,
    Makes one healthy, wealthy and wise.

Better late than never   Time is money

Early to bed, early to rise, Makes a man healthy, wealthy and wise.

Guide them to sing each adage by following your pointer across the melodic outlines.

Next ask the children to identify the melodic motives in your song, 'Don't Let Your Watch Run Down.' Help them to identify the A B A form of the song. This will be even more obvious when you introduce the bass parts first for each section. The remaining parts may be added in a future lesson focusing on syncopation.

Don't Let Your Watch Run Down

American work song

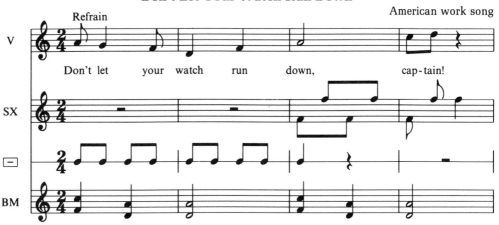

Don't let your watch run down, cap-tain!

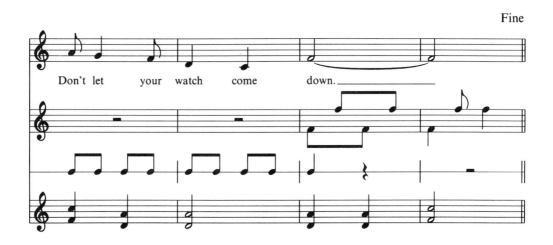

Don't let your watch come down.

Fine

Work-ing on the le - vee, fif - ty cents a day.

Work - ing for my Lu - lu, draw - ing my pay.

To explore the pitches of F pentatonic further, a song of contrasting sections may be created by using the word rhythms of 'Early to bed' and 'All work, no play' as the outline. You may guide your class through this exploration of F pentatonic or you may organize small groups, placing one instrument, set up in F pentatonic, with each one. First, chant each proverb until the class has agreed on the rhythmic phrasing of each one. Then assign the maxim 'Early to bed' to half the groups, and ask them to compose a melody on their instrument which has F and C as the most important pitches, ending on *do,* or f. The other groups will compose a melody for 'All work, no play,' with d and a as the most important pitches, ending on *la,* or d. Ask them to sing and play their group composed melodies, and compare their solutions by describing the melodies of each.

Introduce the second lesson by asking your students to echo you as you clap the word rhythms of the second phrase of 'Don't Let Your Watch Run Down.' Repeat it to make an ostinato, then a two-part canon and, finally, a four-part canon at the interval of two beats. They will recognize this rhythm from the previous lesson.

My children recognize syncopation from aural analysis quite easily, but how to write the value of each note needs frequent review. Ask the children to correct your notation of each phrase. Help them to solve the problem by dividing the eighth notes, placing one on each side of the quarter note. Remind them that each syncopation is two beats.

My notation:

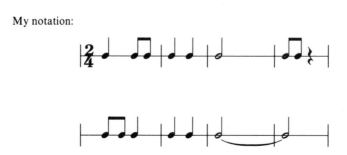

This time, review the bass accompaniment and teach the remaining parts from rhythmic notation. The rhythmic canon used to introduce this lesson, played on drums or wood blocks, in combination with one of the pitched ostinatos, may become the introduction, interlude and coda.

After we have reviewed our students' abilities to perform, improvise, read and write basic rhythms and pentatonic melodies, we should evaluate their skills before proceeding to the next step. 'Now Let Me Fly' serves that purpose. Challenge your students to learn this song and setting on their own, using their reading and performing skills. The objective is to demonstrate to themselves and you their ability to learn music independently. Your role is to be their consultant, first by guiding the process and second, by helping them to solve reading and performing problems. Your evaluation will be easier if you prepare the notation of the song and the setting on overhead transparencies, individual handouts or on newsprint visuals which can be saved from lesson to lesson.

Now Let Me Fly

*With triangle beater on bell.

an - gel work - ing at the cha - ri - ot wheel.
just want to see how the cha - ri - ot feel. Now

Refrain

Let me fly, _____ now, let me fly! _____ Now

Now let me fly, __ now let me fly, __

let me fly, __ way up high! Way in the mid-dle of the air.

way high, way high, O, let me fly, __ let me fly. __

Begin by looking at the melody, a verse and a refrain, and choose the easiest section to read. Many of the children will be able to read first the rhythm and then the melody of the verse from notation. After they have learned the nearly identical phrases, add the words. It is easy to add wheel motions. Groups of four or more students can form a Texas star by forming a circle, placing left hands in the center. On the fifteenth beat they raise their hands, and on the sixteenth beat they turn out and reverse directions. The accompaniments are easy to read for rhythm and pitch. Consider asking a student to teach each part and then choose a classmate to play it on the designated instrument.

The refrain is more challenging. Present the melody without words and tied notes first. When they have learned the melody, add the ties and then the words, which make the rhythm easy to perform accurately. Guide them to identify the upbeat to the first three phrases, and ask them to echo these on the upbeat to the next measure. Write out this descant for them and have them learn it from notation. The remaining parts are easy to analyze and learn from student leaders.

Let each movement group decide how to demonstrate a flying motion. After a short discussion to recall legends and stories of attempts to fly, give each group the assignment of creating movement to fit the refrain, singing as they move. They may choose to leave their circle, but they must return to the wheel to begin the verse.

This song and setting may take several lessons to finish, giving the children opportunities to review what they have learned by using their notation skills. Each time a student demonstrates ability to read or write a portion of the music by demonstrating as 'teacher' through body percussion, by singing or playing, or helps to solve problems in learning the music, write his or her name on the board and record the information for yourself.

Our last review example, 'The Bullgine Run,' a sea chantey about 19th-century clipper ships, provides students an opportunity to review sixteenth-note patterns with the reinforcement of the rhythm of the words. Make four sets of notecards, using the rhythmic notation illustrated below. To begin this review of sixteenth notes, show the students the blank side of the cards, each representing one beat. As you turn each one around to show the durations, have an individual or the class clap what they see four times. Place them in the order illustrated here so that the students can point out the special relationships of the notation as they name the notes and give the rhythmic syllables. I often use 'Mis-sis-sip-pi' as a basis for comparison.

Then make a line, illustrating four beats, and select four cards to place on it. Ask the class and individuals to perform the phrase with body percussion or rhythm syllables.

After several patterns have been performed the students will enjoy improvising first, and then placing the cards in the line in the correct order.

The students will be able to find words from the song 'The Bullgine Run' to match each two-measure pattern of the reading example. They can arrange the four-measure patterns in various ways; in a one-line sequence, as a four-bar, two-part rhythm piece, or as a rhythmic theme with ostinato accompaniment. Use these ideas as an introduction and coda.

The Bullgine Run

Tune: Shule Agrah

Oh, the smart-est clip-per you can find, ah hee, ah ho, are you most done? Is the

Mar-g'ret Ev-ans of the Blue Cross Line, So clear a-way the track, let the bull-gine run! To my

hey rig-a-jig in a low back car, ah hee, ah ho, are you most done? With

Li - za Lee all on my knee, So clear a-way the track, let the bull - gine run!

The second lesson can focus on the melody of the song. The melodic outline of the first eight bars is duplicated in the chorus. By comparing the melodic outline to the melody of the verse and then to the chorus, the students will be able to observe and read the subtle differences. You may write the verse melody in one color and ask your students to add the changes in the chorus in another color. The pitched accompaniment parts are composed to ouline the solo—response style of the song by adding and contrasting timbres for the responses. They should be easy to read in syllables and on pitch names. Ask the class to make a pitch inventory of the song and setting to determine the scale and tonal center. They will discover that the scale is e Aeolian and that they have used all pitches except c or *fa*.

As a way of knowing the musical thinking of my fifth graders better, I often end our review with a Theme and Variations project. Gunild Keetman presents a very simple theme in *Spielbuch für Xylophon*.[2]

We first sight-sing and then play the theme before we discuss ways it can be varied. We play it in octaves, then broken octaves, and then one phrase in the upper octave, the second in the lower to illustrate how easy it is to make a variation. Then I invite the children to create their own variations, giving them only a few minutes to work it out. (I

2   Gunild Keetman *Spielbuch für Xylophon, Music for Children,* Book 1. London: Schott, p. 7

find that if the time is short, they are less inhibited.) Because I have an instrument for each child, each can work this problem out alone. You may have several children work out a variation together, or you may invite children to work together as a class to create a set of variations. I am always amazed at the creative ways the students find to treat this theme. It also gives me an opportunity to observe the students' level of musical understanding, mallet technique, and skill in maintaining a tempo.

Additional resources

Frazee *Orff Handbook for World of Music – 5*
  'This Little Light of Mine' (p. 21)
  'Blow the Winds Southerly' (pp. 16–17)
Frazee with Kreuter *Discovering Orff*
  'Mama Don't 'Low' (p. 45)
  Add improvised four-bar introductions and
  bridges.
Fuoco-Lawson *Street Games*
  'Do the Jive' (p. 2)
  'Down, Down, Baby' (p. 8)
Steen *Orff Activities*, Grade 5
  'Turn the Glasses Over' (p. 3)
  'There's a Hole in the Middle of the Sea' (p. 6)

Rhythm

1 Perform, identify, read, and write patterns using ♫ ♩, ♩. ♩, and ♫ ♩. as diminutions of ♪♩ ♪, ♩. ♪ and ♪♩..

There are two factors to consider when approaching this step. One is that most rhythms can now be explained as either the diminution or the augmentation of a pattern they already know. Second, children frequently speak quick moving patterns easily so that the longer durations can be measured against shorter ones. The key to musically clear performances is feeling the shortest duration evenly.

Let us begin this study with an experiment similar to one the children had in fourth grade. Prepare the following patterns on visuals. Ask some students to pat the eighth notes, listening to evaluate how clearly they pat them as an ensemble. If their sound is not clear, ask a listening group to critique the performing group. Look at each of the following patterns written above the eighth notes. Chant the top line, using rhythm syllables or patterns which the students suggest, such as 'huckleberry pie,' or 'Mississippi state,' leaving off syllables as the notation indicates. Next think the syllables and clap the notation as others pat the underlying eighth notes.

Have the students turn to each other and perform the task again, one patting the constant eighth notes and the other performing the rhythm patterns. This should move smoothly and quickly as preparation for the next step.

Show the children new visuals which place sixteenth notes on the bottom line. Guide them to see the relative length of the top rhythms to the sixteenth notes below. Now sit in a circle and ask every other student to pat sixteenth notes on the knees of their neighbors. The other students will echo pat on their neighbor's shoulders your four-beat patterns drawn from the practice example. It helps students to close their eyes as they feel the rhythms fall into place. Be sure to trade responsibilities. Do not change the length of the lower note so that the notation is the only new adjustment.

312

Experiment to hear how accurately they perform at a quicker or a slower tempo. It is also important to improvise short rhythmic phrases using these new patterns on body percussion or on instruments.

'Buck-eyed Jim' may be introduced by comparing your performance of the song with the melodic rhythm of the song on a visual. The accompaniment is meant to be played very softly, but precisely, so that the new patterns may be measured against the underlying sixteenth notes. Encourage your students to make up new nonsense chants that could conjure up the same sort of dream magic, beautiful but mysterious.

Buck-eyed Jim

Appalachian nonsense song

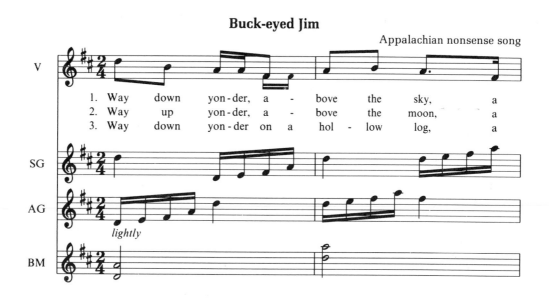

1. Way down yon - der, a - bove the sky, a
2. Way up yon - der, a - bove the moon, a
3. Way down yon - der on a hol - low log, a

lightly

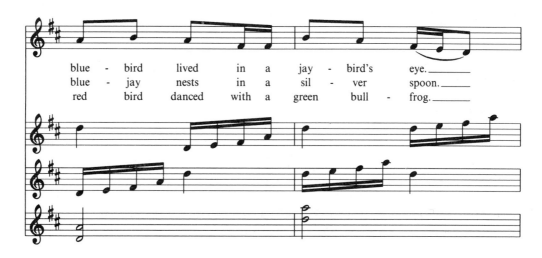

blue - bird lived in a jay - bird's eye.
blue - jay nests in a sil - ver spoon.
red bird danced with a green bull - frog.

'Sambalele' requires more energetic and demanding accompaniment, measured against the constantly moving alto xylophone chords. A contrasting section, using some South American sounds, such as maracas, claves, conga and bongo drums, cabasa and choked cowbell, should be planned by the students. They can use patterns taken from the song setting, or they may write new material. The section should be two eight-beat phrases to balance the length of the song.

Sambalele

Brazilian folk song

Sam - ba, sam - ba, sam - ba - la - le - le, Sam - ba, sam - ba, sam - ba - la - le - le.

Sam - ba, sam - ba, sam - ba - la - le - le, Sam - ba, sam - ba, sam - ba - la - le - le.

Additional resources

Frazee *Orff Handbook for World of Music – 5*
'Keep in the Middle of the Road' (p. 14–15)
Frazee with Kreuter *Discovering Orff*,
pp. 181–8
Frazee and Steen *A Baker's Dozen*
'La Raspa' (p. 29)

2 *Use augmentation and diminution to change familiar patterns.*

A simple way to begin is to review a familiar rhythm and movement exercise they have performed in previous grades. As the class walks the beat, ask them to clap durations twice as long (half notes), then twice as long again (whole notes). Then return to the beat and clap durations half as long (eighth notes), and half again as long (sixteenth notes). Fifth graders, however, have a new challenge. Give them a two-beat pattern, such as ♫ ♩, and ask them to repeat it several times as they walk. Then, when you give a signal they are to augment it or make the pattern twice as long (♩ ♩ ♩). If the students stop walking while they think have the group step the beat in place. Because the problem deals with the length of time, I want them to feel the relative durations as well as think them through. Some students may have suggestions for other two-beat patterns that can be augmented. To practice diminution, use four-beat patterns, such as ♩ ♫ ♩ ♩ to ♫ ♫ ♫ , or ♫ ♩ ♫ ♩ to ♫ ♫ . With this experience of feeling the differences they are ready to work with rhythm symbols.

Another way to practice the relative value of notes is to compose settings with all parts having the same rhythms, just twice as long or half as long. The first phrase of 'Ghost of Tom' may be spoken with accompanying chants, one augmented and one in diminution (this score is given on p. 271). Write 'Have you seen the Ghost of Tom?' on the board and ask several students to read the question until a rhythm is established. Then write the rhythm above the words and ask your students how it would be said if you doubled the value of each syllable. Your class should add this notation to the score on the board, writing the original theme a second time to equal the augmented statement. When they chant the phrase in diminution ask your fifth graders to consider whether to repeat it four times, or alternate speaking with rests.

'Don't Let The Wind,' as scored below, has a contrasting section composed in the manner we explored rhythms in movement. Encourage your students to observe and add dynamic markings to make the song and chant expressive of the dread of disaster which the song predicts the wind will bring.

Don't Let the Wind

West Indian shanty

Oh,_____ don't let the wind,

wind, The wind is blow - ing oh, don't let the wind,

decresc.

don't let the wind blow here no more.

pp

don't let the wind blow more.

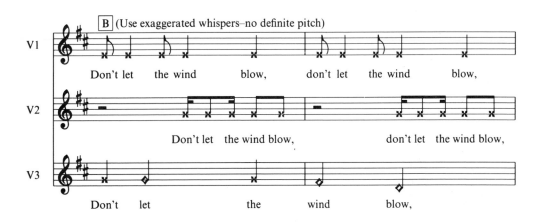

B (Use exaggerated whispers–no definite pitch)

V1

Don't let the wind blow, don't let the wind blow,

V2

Don't let the wind blow, don't let the wind blow,

V3

Don't let the wind blow,

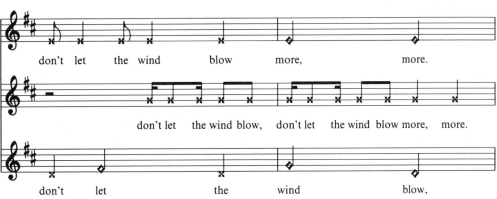

don't let the wind blow more, more.

don't let the wind blow, don't let the wind blow more, more.

don't let the wind blow,

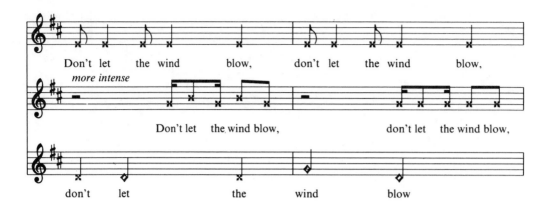

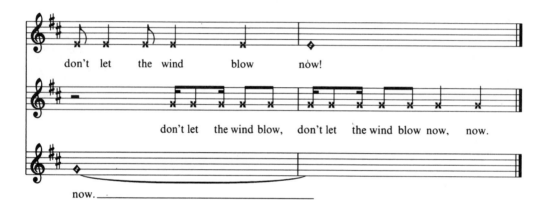

Benjamin Britten used these same contrapuntal techniques when he set 'Old Abram Brown' in his *Friday Afternoons*.[3] If you have this collection, this is a good time to introduce the song.

Not only are augmentation and diminution wonderful, easy ways to explore rhythms when improvising and composing, the skill to use these tools can be employed to unravel and practice difficult rhythms throughout the year.

3   Review 6/8 meter and practice an inventory of patterns common to that meter
(♩♪♪,♩ ♪,♩. , ♪♪, ♩.♪♪,♩. ♩ ♪, etc.).

Our objective is to make our students familiar with the feeling of the eighth note pulse in 6/8 meter and to build a repertoire of familiar patterns which can be read, written and used in improvisation and composition. Begin the lesson by asking your students to recite and then clap the word rhythms of familiar nursery rhymes, such as 'Hickory Dickory Dock,' 'Little Miss Muffet,' 'Rain, Rain, Go Away' and others. If your school

3   Benjamin Britten *Friday Afternoons*, op. 7. London: Boosey & Hawkes, 1936.

population is not familiar with these rhymes, prepare a list of some of their familiar chants and poems in meters of twos and threes. By clapping speech rhythms your students are imitating the phrasing and natural accents of the meter. They can determine the meter by finding the downbeat and patting the number of beats between.

Now ask them to determine the meter of a new song, 'Hineh Ma Tov.' After they have learned it by rote, ask them to clap the word rhythms and decide which of the following measures were present in the song. Because only four different patterns were used to make eight measures of melody, the students may want to add their own rhythms to the list. The setting will also contain patterns not found in the melody. Practice reading the rhythms in the list, moving down, up, skipping every other one, and so on.

Hineh Ma Tov

Hebrew

Hi - neh ma tov - u ma - nay - im, she - vet a - chim gam-yach - ad.
How good and how plea-sant it is for breth-ren to dwell to - ge - ther.

Hi - neh ma - tov, she - vet a - chim gam - yach - ad.
Good and plea - sant, breth - ren to dwell to - ge - ther.

When they perform the song, the students sit in a circle, accompaniment instruments in the center. Give tambourines to two students who are sitting opposite one another; their challenge is to develop a musical conversation using rhythms from the lesson. One student will fill two measures followed by the second student playing the same length. Both will pass their tambourines to the right so that the rhythm can continue uninterrupted around the circle. I have heard this song performed in slow and quick tempi. Let the class determine their interpretation. Perform it as ABA, or expand it by including the tambourine improvisation as a C, to make it a rondo, ABACA.

There are opportunities for the students to use their growing vocabulary of 6/8 patterns in 'An Old, Old Shack.' This song moves at a quick tempo with strong metric accents which may be a contrast from 'Hineh Ma Tov.' Have the students read the instrument parts from notation and prepare them with body percussion suggested by your students. With their help, prepare a selection of unpitched instruments, such as sandblocks, hand drum, cabasa, slide whistle, vibraslap and claves, and invite the children to add an unpitched ostinato and a sound effect for each repetition of the song.

An Old, Old Shack

American depression song

Down home we have an old, old shack. The bats fly in and they fly back out. Hi lee, hi low, hi lee, hi low, how we make a liv-ing I do not know.

At school we have disgusting food,
The spaghetti is raw and the pizza rude,
Hi lee, hi low, hi lee, hi low,
How we live through it I do not know.

4   Write, read, and perform short compositions in 6/8 meter.

Composition projects give us a wonderful opportunity to observe our students taking responsibility for creating and performing their own music. Some critics would say that this is an exercise in reasoning rather than musical feeling, and for most children that may be so. Our purpose is not to train composers, though this experience helps them understand that role better. Rather it is to give our students the opportunity to use their tools independently of us to express what they know.

This is an excellent opportunity for the teacher as well. As we watch our students discuss, write, read and practice we can observe their skills and knowledge intertwined in action. We can see what we have taught them, and we can learn what they need to practice and what they are ready to learn next.

To prepare the class to compose in 6/8, begin with a review of familiar material. Sing a familiar song in the meter, and then perform its word rhythms. Then you may ask the class to echo some additional patterns using body percussion. End the warm-up reading the patterns they may have collected from the past few lessons.

Give each student a work sheet like the sample below. The first sentence of each step is written on a visual and posted where all the students can see it. My students usually compose and practice using body percussion, but give their performance before the class on instruments.

1   Put the names of each person in your group on your worksheet. Also write down the names of the instruments you think you will want to use.
2   Read the patterns on your sheet together. Try out several combinations of measures.
3   Agree on your first measure and write it down. Perform it, followed by another pattern. Continue until you have completed your theme.
4   Together practice your theme.
5   Compose the accompaniment. It may be a one- or two-measure ostinato. Keep it simple. Each measure should be different from any in your theme above it.
6   Practice the accompaniment. Practice it while your partner performs the theme. Reverse parts.
7   Perform your composition for the teacher, and then for the class.

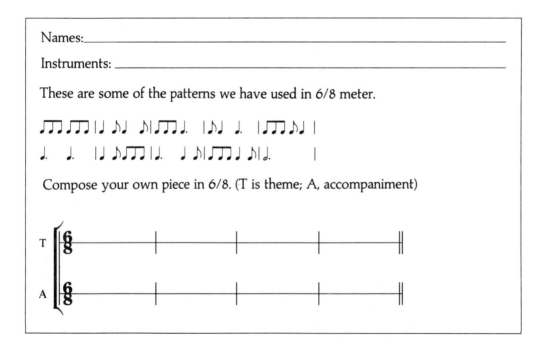

Consider covering melody objectives ('Melody,' 1–3) and harmony objectives ('Harmony,' 1, 2) first before focusing on a new meter.

322

5   *Perform and identify 5/4 or 5/8 meter through movement, listening, and reading.*

The difficulty in presenting the five-beat meter is often in the mind of the teacher. As with all we teach, the more confident we are in presenting new music to children the more they accept the proposition that they can master it as well. If performing in five is an unusual experience for you, take the time to practice your lesson before your present it. Then both you and your students will have an enjoyable experience.

We will begin with what we do most naturally: speak and move. Chant this poem, asking the students to remember four ideas contained in it.[4]

Walk straight ahead and, | | | | |
Stop, bend and turn now, | | | | |
Make a big circle, | | | | |
You're at the end now | | | | |

As they chant, ask them to move as the words suggest. Be patient, giving them time to work out their ideas individually.

The next step is to have each student combine ideas with a partner. When the partners are ready ask each half of the class to perform their solutions for the others.

Your students will enjoy performing their movement to music. You might try *Take Five* by Dave Brubeck or *Javanese*, from Suite for Flute and Jazz Piano by Claude Bolling.[5]

Before asking your students to read the following rhythm ask them to look for repetition and similarities between measures. Then have them read silently as you point to the first beat of each measure, indicating the tempo. They will discover that the parts are traded for the last four measures. Guide the children to suggest dynamic levels for each part and percussion instrument to perform the piece.

The ostinatos which accompany 'Count 5' are one measure long (the bass xylophone part becomes a two-measure ostinato by tying the last two beats in even measures). Teach these parts first, using both notation and body percussion imitation. Then you play the melody to their accompaniment as others watch. In this way they can use both hearing and seeing to assess the final product you expect.

4   I owe this idea to two fine Orff teachers, Richard Gill and Jay Broeker.
5   *Take Five* by Dave Brubeck, on The Dave Brubeck Quartet, *Time Out* (Columbia, 8192). *Javanese* by Claude Bolling, on Claude Bolling and Jean-Pierre Rampal *Suite for Flute and Jazz Piano* (Columbia Masterworks, M 33233).

The melody is based on an ostinato pattern as well. You can play for the class as they pat alternating hands as they learn to wait five beats in measures four and eight. All the melodic patterns move by steps. The melody begins each phrase on g, and the descant always begins on b. One only has to remember how far up and how far down each phrase goes. The Mixolydian melody gives your students an aural experience in this less familiar mode.

Count 5

AS

Melody

1   Explore Ionian and Aeolian modes (major and natural minor scales) through improvisation.

Learning the functions of harmony (chord changes which give vertical dimensions of pitch to music) makes sense when they are related to the student's ability to hear, read and analyze melodies. For that reason it seems helpful to explore diatonic melodies over the tonic chord only before introducing harmony.

It has been said that one of the most beautiful melodies in the world is the scale, and melodic sequencing is a way of embellishing it. As part of the children's vocal warm-up, lead them in singing the Ionian scale, either by pointing to the syllable ladder or to the scale written on the staff. When you use the syllable ladder, show the half step intervals by placing *fa* close to *mi*, and *ti* close to *do*. To review this relationship, place a model of a keyboard before them and review first the pentatonic scales from f, g and c, and then the diatonics, showing the half and whole steps.

Then lead them through a simple melodic sequence; when they have sung it, ask a student to lead the class, using the same sequence. Ask your students to suggest and lead the class in singing other sequence patterns. Notate the first three 'legs' of each one. Here are several patterns which the children can quickly recognize and sing on their own down or up the scale.

325

The melody of 'Old Roger Is Dead' outlines the tonic chord. Begin by singing the outline from notation. Then use one of the sequence patterns to fill out the melodic outline. After exploring several possibilities, sing or play the song and ask your students to add to the outline to accurately represent the melody.

Old Roger is Dead

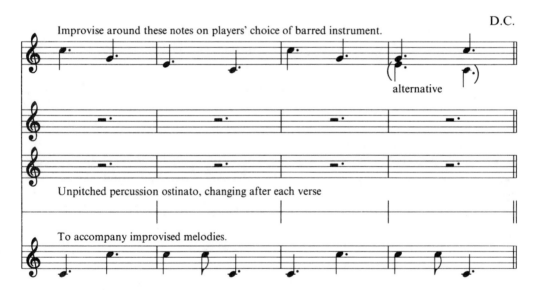

2   An apple tree grew right over his head.

3   The apples grew ripe and ready to fall.

4   Then came an east wind to blow them all off.

5   Then came an old woman to gather them all.

6   Old Roger rose up and gave her a bop!

7   It made the old woman go hippity hop.

8   If you want any more, then sing it yourself!

Perhaps your children sang and dramatized this song at an earlier grade. This time their task is to dramatize the song through the use of timbre and new melodies. Using the ideas from their sequence exploration, ask individuals to improvise melodies to 'comment' on each preceding verse. The bass accompaniment may be changed and unpitched instrument ostinatos may be added. For example, a drum may accompany the improvised melody for verse one, and fingers or brush scraping the drum head may describe verse four, and the vibra slap may be added to the improvisation following verse six. Of course, they can also act out this very old folk tale.

Examples of improvised phrases:

'Drill Ye Tarriers' was sung by the Irish immigrants of the late nineteenth century, and describes the hard, low-paying work required to blast out the railroad beds that contributed to the westward expansion across America. The verse–refrain form is outlined by two contrasting orchestrations. Teach the soprano xylophone descant and the unpitched percussion parts through notation.

Drill Ye Tarriers

Thomas Carey, 18XX

twen - ty tar - ri - ers a - work - ing at the rock.   And the

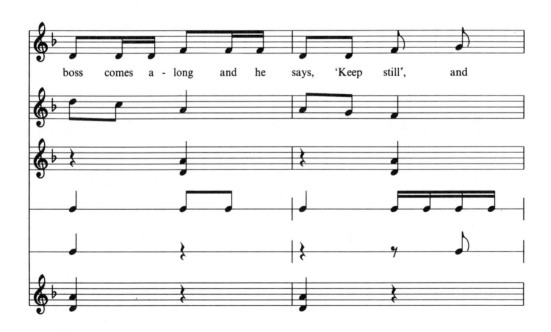

boss   comes a - long   and he   says,   'Keep   still',   and

come down hea - vy on the cast - ir - on drill, So

Refrain

V   drill ye tar - ri - ers, drill,   and   drill ye tar - ri - ers

SM

AM

BX

drill.   Oh, it's work all day for su - gar in you 'tay',

2 Our new foreman is Dan McCann,
   I'll tell you sure he's a blame mean man.
   Lask week a premature blast went off,
   And a mile in the air went Big Jim Goff. (Refrain)

3 Next time payday comes around,
   Jim Goff was short one buck, he found:
   'What for?' says he: then this reply,
   'You're docked for the time you were up in the sky,'

After the students have learned the song by rote, ask them to write down the melodic outline of the verse. They will discover the melody is Aeolian, and outlines the tonic chord, repeating the pattern once. The descant fills the outline of the chord as well.

To explore the Aeolian scale, consider the melodic model of the verse. Four of the beats moved from one chord note to another, while the last four beats remained on one note, ornamenting it with rhythm. Instead of repeating the phrase, as found in the verse, ask one student to improvise the first phrase and another to improvise the last phrase. Notice that to lead into the refrain, the composer Thomas Carey ended on the fifth, or *mi*. Your melodies could also avoid ending on the tonic, or you could use a typical question-and-answer form where phrase one avoids the tonic and the second phrase ends on it.

With this exploration of the Aeolian and Ionian scales over one chord the study of harmony is prepared.

Additional resources
Orff and Keetman *Music for Children*, adpt.
   Murray, Vol. IV
   'The Jolly Ploughboy' (p. 114)
   An Aeolian melody over a dominant
   drone.
Steen *Orff Activities*, Grade 6
   'Chicka-Hanka' (p. 32)

2   *Imitate, then write down from dictation two, three and four pitches in Ionian and Aeolian modalities.*

Rather than spending entire lessons on this objective, it is wise to give a short amount of time to it each lesson over a series of a few weeks. I like to include my evaluation of a student's ability to sing or play back my examples in the lesson warm-ups or introductions. Asking individuals to respond can be alternated with class echoes. My lesson plan then defines the dictation task and leaves space where I can write in the names of students who respond, with 'a' for accurate or 'i' for inaccurate. Some teachers carry a class list or record book to gather this information.

There are a number of ways to test their ability to hear and identify pitch motion, but each way demands specific skills. My list reflects my experience with children and my experiments with this task. I may begin at any level, but if I do not get good results, I can often find the reasons for the difficulty by finding the point where they are successful. My students will also perform at a higher level when the tasks center around *do* rather than when the tasks center around *la*.

1   Play an interval from *do* (either C, F or G) on an alto xylophone, which is in view of the class. The student responds by singing accurately, using syllables. You are just

testing their ability to identify syllables with the correct pitch. Later, play any interval from *sol* below *do* to *la* above *do*. (If recorder is an integrated part of your program, you may want to use it instead.) Repeat the exercise, but begin with *la*, (a, d or e).

2 Sing on a neutral syllable or play an interval, beginning on *do*. The student responds by imitating on a recorder or barred instrument, physically identifying the interval in relationship to tonal center. Singing a matching tone is not required. When you repeat this exercise from *la* you will find the children less secure. They will need lots of practice singing, playing and practicing before the results parallel those you heard when testing from *do*.

3 Establish the tonal center. Then point out an interval beginning with the tonal center on the syllable ladder. The student responds by playing accurately on a barred instrument or recorder.

4 Point out an interval on the staff. The student responds by playing accurately on a barred instrument or recorder.

5 Point out an interval on the syllable ladder. The student sings it accurately.

6 Point out an interval on the staff. The student sings it accurately with correct syllables.

7 Begin with step one, but give three pitches in your example. Continue adding pitches until they can accurately identify short phrases. For many children it may be just as easy to respond to short motives, especially because they have been taught in this way.

If you have large classes that prohibit individual testing, ask groups of three or four to respond. You can usually identify the accuracy of each child.

Written dictation is easier, for accurate singing and playing are not involved. The evaluation tools will continue to be the same as those used in earlier grades. Dictation is more difficult only because there are more notes to choose from. The following sample worksheet uses one example of each type of dictation suggested previously. You can select one type of dictation and give several examples during one lesson. Then, in a later lesson, use another type, dictating several examples.

Place the correct note head above each syllable.

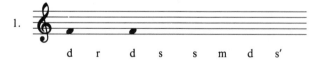

Place correct syllable below each note head.

Teacher sings
or plays:

Student places X below correct notation on test paper

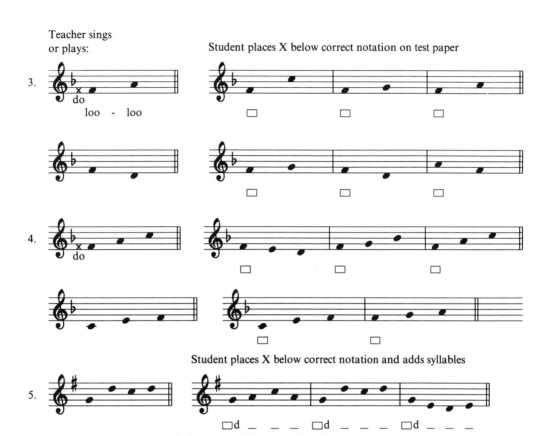

Student places X below correct notation and adds syllables

Teacher sings melodies in parentheses on neutral syllable.
Student adds missing pitches.

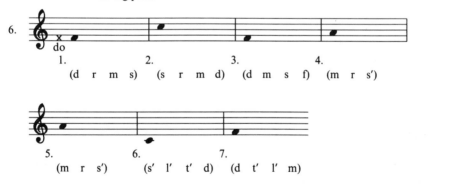

Teacher sings melodies in parentheses on neutral syllable.
Student adds syllables and pitches.

Consider the study of 'Harmony,' 1 through 4, before an analysis of Mixolydian and
Dorian modes.

3   *Perform to identify Mixolydian mode by its characteristic flatted seventh, or* ta *instead of* ti *(d r mf s lt d).*

Throughout our curriculum sequence we have presented new concepts using material containing familiar elements. Children sing many pentatonic and diatonic songs before they aurally and with symbols identify these pitch relationships, for the folk traditions of Western cultures abound with music that is Ionian or Aeolian (major or minor). There are not many Mixolydian or Dorian children's songs, and in my experience, even fewer Phrygian and Lydian songs. This fact could support an argument that it is not important to teach modes other than Ionian and Aeolian, for there is insufficient material. But it can also be argued that modern composers often do not think of tonality in 18th- and 19th-century terms, and we have an obligation to expose our children to the possibility of many types of scales. By calling the children's attention to new arrangments of whole and half steps they learn that there are many possible tonalities and harmonies.

Perhaps the most familiar Mixolydian American folk-song is 'Old Joe Clark.' You can find variants of it in most song collections, singing game anthologies and in several of the series. I introduce this song as part of our repertoire in kindergarten and first grade as 'Clap, Clap, Clap Your Hands' (see pp. 84, 130). Review the song, using one of your sources or one listed below, as preparation for this lesson and to enjoy the funny lyrics.

To introduce the Mixolydian mode to the children, begin with echo singing on a neutral syllable, using patterns similar to 'Swing A Lady.'

Then tell the students to listen for the mystery note, and have them learn the song by rote. Ask them to sing the song in their minds as you point to the first pitch of each measure on the syllable ladder. Some of the children will want to guess what the mystery pitch is. Next, place an alto xylophone before them and ask them how to prepare it to play in F. Beginning with the chorus, invite a student to echo each measure on the xylophone, beginning with the chorus. They will soon discover that you do not have the right bar to play the e flat. Change *ti* to *ta*, placing it close to *la* on the syllable ladder to show this new relationship. Write each measure on the staff, adding accidentals.

F Ionian   F Mixolydian

334

Swing a Lady

Kentucky dance song

there I spied a pret - ty lit - tle miss, and
if you don't mind, she'll jump out, so

there I spied a pret - ty lit - tle miss, and
if you don't mind, she'll jump out, so

there I spied my ho - ney.
fare you well my dar - ling.

there I spied my ho - ney.
fare you well my dar - ling.

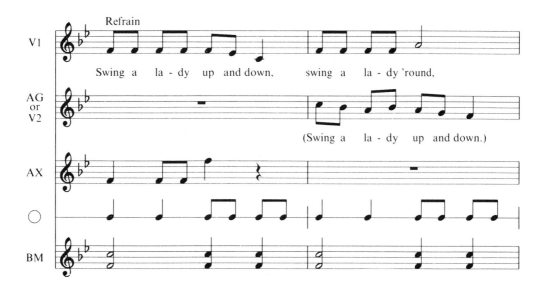

Add the orchestration, using a mixture of body percussion and reading preparation. The lyrics suggest movement, and a small group of students can work on this while others learn the orchestration.

This setting is in F because of the wide range of pitches in the melody. In another lesson challenge your students to play the chorus in C, adding b flat, and in G, adding f natural.

'Oh, Let Me Shine' is in G Mixolydian, or the G scale with no accidentals. Prepare for this lesson by reviewing 'Old Joe Clark' or 'Swing A Lady,' and asking them what was new or unique about each song. Then ask them to sing the scale in syallables, *do* up to *sol* and back. Play this as well. Then ask them to sing from low *sol* to *re*, being careful to use *ta* instead of *ti*. Point out the melodic outline of 'Oh, Let Me Shine' on the syllable ladder for the students to sing.

Our students will be able to follow the harmonic rhythm as they hear the song. They should also be able to write each phrase in staff notation.

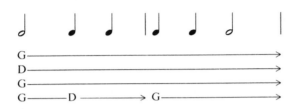

Oh, Let Me Shine!

American shout

Oh, let me shine.
Shine like Mat-thew, let me shine!
Shine like a morn-ing star!

Add the setting, using parts from the score mixed with ideas and suggestions concerning 'star music' from the class. Remember to maintain a good balance, use fewer instruments to accompany singing, and more instruments if the class chooses to play the melody on instruments.

A contrasting section can evolve from students' improvisations. It is helpful to use words, such as those from other folk songs to provide rhythmic phrasing. This is a paraphrase of a familiar spiritual.

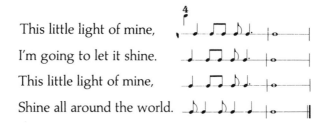

This little light of mine,

I'm going to let it shine.

This little light of mine,

Shine all around the world.

First chant and then practice the word rhythms in body percussion. If you choose to have the students improvise over a bordun, instruct them to begin and end each phrase on *do*, *mi* or *sol*, ending the last phrase on *do*. If you choose to ask them to improvise over the same harmonic rhythm, chant the words as you lead them from the same visual you used to present the song. Then place four barred instruments, preferably of the same range, before the children. Assign a student to improvise each phrase, using a pentachord from g for the first and third phrases, and from d for phrases two and four, the fourth resolving on g.

Our students now have materials to make a three-part form or a rondo. They can sing or play the melody to an accompaniment and they can improvise new melodies. Write out their outline and perform their composition. It may be fun to record this, for it is their first departure from our most familiar scales, Ionian and Aeolian.

Additional resources
Choskey and Brummet *120 Singing Games and*
    Dances
    'Old Joe Clark' (p. 120)
    A variant with singing game.
Goetze *Mary Goetze Series*
    'Old Joe Clark' (no. 6125)
    Three parts composed on an ostinato
    principle.
    'Hold the Wind' (no. 6124)
    Four parts.
Steen *Orff Activities*
    'Old Joe Clark' (Grade 7, p. 17; Grade 8, p. 2)
    Two variant settings.

4   *Perform to identify Dorian mode by its characteristic raised sixth degree, or* fi *instead of* fa *(l td r m fs l).*

As pointed out in our discussion about Mixolydian, we can introduce our children to the sounds of less familiar modes by using good examples in earlier grades. 'O Belinda' is an American singing game that is described by Richard Chase in his *Singing Games and Playparty Games* as a line dance to the familiar sea shanty 'What will we do with a drunken sailor?' Both the melody and line-dance appeal to fourth and fifth graders.[6]

I like to teach the song and singing game first, even in an earlier grade. The song and game can then be reintroduced for analysis of the mode. Begin by asking the children to identify the quality of the first phrase as outlining a major or minor chord. One of the students will be able to play the phrase on recorder or a barred instrument. Put the pitches used on a staff, beginning with the lowest, d, to begin an inventory or scale. Continue in the same manner with each phrase, adding to the inventory. Lead them to decide that d is the tonal center because of the final sound of the ending and the outline of the d minor chord in the first phrase. Ask them to compare this scale with an Aeolian scale from d, which requires a b flat, but shares the same lower five notes.

You may wish to use the setting to accompany singing and dancing of 'O Belinda,' adding an instrument with each verse, or you may wish to develop an instrumental piece, using the setting as an outline of possible accompaniments. After the children have analyzed the melody and watched classmates play each phrase they will be prepared to play the melody on recorders or barred instruments.

6   From Richard Chase, *Singing Games and Playparty Games*. New York: Dover, 1967, p. 32.

O Belinda

'Drunken Sailor' tune/AS

Bow, bow, bow Be-lin-da, bow, bow, bow Be-lin-da,

bow, bow, bow Be-lin-da, won't you be my part - ner?

2. Right hand 'round.
3. Left hand 'round.
4. Back to back (do si do).
5. Promenade 'round.
6. Through the tunnel.

341

Another familiar Dorian song which never fails to captivate my children is 'Scarborough Fair.' Present it to the children as a mystery song which they must read to identify. The use of b flat in the key signature and the appearance of b natural in the score will help signal them that this is a modal song. Lead them to identify which phrases fall in the lower, minor pentachord, and which center around the upper tetrachord with the raised sixth degree.

Scarborough Fair

The song is beautiful when sung a cappella. If you wish, a simple accompaniment can be added from student suggestions, using only the tonic or d. Be sure to keep the setting spare, below or on both sides of the vocal range.

Your students can now experiment with the different modes to which they have been exposed. Review 'Ah, Poor Bird,' which they learned in grade four introducing them to *ti* (see Chapter 7, 'Melody,' 2, p. 270). Use a syllable ladder, staff notation and barred instruments as you guide the students to rewrite the melody in Aeolian and then Dorian. There are several solutions to this problem. They may change pitches on the existing rhythm or they may add passing tones to the existing melody. Ask them to sing, play and write their variations. (There are *s placed above the beats where these alterations could be made.)

Ah, Poor Bird

342

Additional resources

Choskey and Brummet *120 Singing Games and Dances*
  'Oh, Belinda' (p. 145)
Ladendecker *Songs for Young Troubadours*
  'Georgian Lullaby' (p. 18)
  'Song of Spring' (p. 8)

Harmony

1   Review the tonic (I) and dominant (V) chords.

In grade four we introduced our students to harmony by showing them how a chord was built and accompanied the melody above it. Then we built two chords, tonic and dominant, and discovered they shared one common note while the roots moved to accommodate the melody. After we have reviewed these understandings, our objective is to practice several ways to build textures and experience several harmonic rhythms using these most functional chords.

Begin by playing a tonic chord and ask the class what it is. Then play the dominant and ask them to tell you what changed. Give them a 'hearing test' by asking them to pat the beat when you play the tonic, but stop when you change to dominant. As you did in grade four (p. 283–4), give them several patterns to analyze.

Your students can tell you what harmony changes are needed by singing chord roots. First practice by singing *do* when your right finger points the conducting beat, changing to *sol* when your hands open. As you sing or play 'Line Dance Tune,' have them sing chord roots, changing as the melody dictates. They can check their solution by looking for chord pitches in the melody. Take just a few minutes to listen to chord changes each lesson for this will help them to develop the ability to hear vertically as well as horizontally.

Line Dance Tune

American/English play party melody

They already know the bass xylophone part from singing chord roots: you have only to add the ostinato rhythm. I suggest an alto xylophone ostinato on the common tone. It was written by the players in my class, so your students may certainly change it as long as it contrasts rhythmically with the melody and bass xylophone. The hand drum part may also be composed by students. My class learned each of the parts, including the melody, in small groups. They also decided to perform this setting by addding parts, beginning with the chord roots and moving to the next highest instrument with each repetition, and then removing one part each time.

Frequently at this point I have introduced one of the polkas from Volume III of *Music for Children* (adpt. Murray). Both accompany the melody with triad accompaniment in the bass, which I sometimes divide with two players at one instrument. In the 'Polka from the Ennstal' the melody, or top line, can be taught first; then add the third below, preparing the students for our last harmonic objective.

Additional resources
Frazee *Orff Handbook for World of Music* – 4
   'Some Folks' (p. 10)
Frazee *Orff Handbook for World of Music* – 5
   'The Gypsy Rover' (p. 12)
Ladendecker *Holidays and Holy Days*, Vol. 2
   'Children, Sing Out' (p. 21)
   'What a Lovely Baby' (p. 24)
   'I'll Tell My Ma' (p. 42)
McRae *American Sampler*
   'The Old Ark' (p. 28)
Orff and Keetman *Music for Children*, adpt.
   Murray, Vol. III
   'Polka from the Ennstal' (p. 95)
   'Two Polkas' (pp. 96–7)
Staton et al. *Music and You*, Grade 4
   'Sheep Shearing' (p. 24)
   'Zumba, Zumba' (p. 31)
Staton et al. *Music and You*, Grade 5
   'Pay Me My Money Down' (p. 40)
   'Mango Walk' (p. 68)

Steen *Orff Activities*, Grade 5
  'There's a Hole in the Middle of the Sea'
  (p. 6)
  'Streets of Laredo' (p. 15)
  'Norwegian Mountain March' (p. 17)

2   Identify the sub-dominant or IV chord, and then identify I–IV and I–IV–V patterns.

'Street Song' from Volume III of *Music for Children* (adpt. Murray) is one of the most challenging and popular instrumental pieces for fifth graders. Play and F and C chords and have the children sing the syllables for each one. Ask your students to listen to the first statement on a recording, to hear if more than the tonic (F) and dominant (C) chords are used.[7] After they have discovered a third chord (B flat), invite several students to play each chord on the piano, and then on alto xylophones. Begin the recording again, this time asking the students to listen for harmonic patterns. They can show you what they hear by holding up the appropriate number of fingers, one, four or five. Guide them by writing the number of each chord as the pattern progresses. These are the results when you write one number for each measure:

I	I	IV	IV	I	I	V	V
I	I	IV	IV	I	V	I	I
IV	V	I	I	IV	V	I	I

They will have practice hearing the patterns, for the entire sequence repeats eight times, adding instruments and changing patterns each time.

The students always ask to move to this exciting music, and it gives them an opportunity to internalize the sound of changing chords. I usually divide the class into eight groups. Each group is to pantomine a street game or activity which has a beginning, middle and ending to coincide with the length of one theme. Then as they listen we add one group's movement with each repetition of the 24-measure pattern.

In the next lesson ask the students first to place the F scale on the staff and then identify the notes of the tonic, dominant and sub-dominant chords by circling the pitches of each. Then write the chord in its vertical position at the end of the scale. From this they can see that the dominant and sub-dominant chords each have one note in common with the tonic chord.

'Hill an' Gully Rider' can be harmonized two ways, with the bordun (tonic-chord outline), or with tonic and sub-dominant chords. The song has three motives which your students can place in order after they listen. This analysis will define the form which will help your students to learn the place for each ostinato. An outline of the song and the accompaniment looks like this:

	A		B
Refrain:	a b a b	Verse:	c b c b c b
	AM/BM		BX
	G/AX		SX

7   This piece and many other Orff ensembles classics are found on cassette ED 12380, recorded by Harmonia Mundi and published by Schott, London. 'Street Song' is on Cassette 2, side 1.

Hill an' Gully Rider

Jamaica

Hill an' gul-ly ri - der, hill an' gul - ly.

*May be improvised by students.

Fine

Hill an' gul-ly ri - der, hill an' gul - ly. Took my

horse and come down, hill an' gul-ly, but my horse done stum-ble down.

V

SX

BX

D.C.

Hill an' gul-ly, And the night time came a-tumb-lin' down, hill an' gul-ly.

Prepare each pitched part by singing it in syllables and comparing the pitches with those in the chords circled on the staff. The form may be expanded by asking the students to add an introduction and a coda.

The next step is to combine the tonic, sub-dominant and dominant chords in various patterns. You may begin your presentation of 'Old Dan Tucker' by asking them to sing *do* on each beat as you sing the song to hear whether the song can be accompanied with a bordun. They will hear that the verse needs no chord changes, but the refrain has two

347

phrases over a repeated harmonic rhythm. Both the alto xylophone part and the descant over the refrain are challenging. The alto xylophone is most easily prepared by stepping the bass line and clapping the off-beats. The descant may be prepared by singing it in syllables. One variation of the refrain can be achieved by singing the descant on 'loo' or whistling while others sing the melody.

Old Dan Tucker

Dan Emmett, 1893

Old Dan Tuck-er was a fine old man, he washed his face in a fry-ing pan. He

Student-composed ostinato – changes each verse

combed his hair with a wag-gon wheel, died with a tooth-ache in his heel. So

The 'Wabash Cannon Ball' was popular in the 1870s when it described an early train that traveled coast to coast. This is one of many versions that can be found describing the Wabash Cannon Ball. My students enjoyed making a four-measure bridge of ostinatos, experimenting with timbres to create the train sounds they imagined.

The Wabash Cannon Ball

Hobo ballad, 1870's and 1930's

From the shores of the At - lan - tic to the wild Pa - ci - fic shore, from the coast of Ca - li - for - nia to snow-bound La - bra-dor, there's a train of fan - cy lay - out, that's well-known to us all, it's a

ride the bars and the emp - ty cars,_ on the Wa - bash Can - non Ball.

Train Sounds

(choked)   Fifth Grade composed

Piccolo

*Run mallets over top for glissando effect.

Additional resources

Frazee *Orff Handbook for World of Music* — 4
  'Hey, Dum Diddeley Dum' (p. 5)
  'Open the Window, Noah' (p. 20)
Frazee *Orff Handbook for World of Music* — 5
  'There's a Meeting Here Tonight' (p. 13)
  'Blow the Wind Southerly' (p. 16)
  'This Little Light of Mine' (p. 20)

Frazee with Kreuter *Discovering Orff*
   'Wimoweh' (p. 201)
   'In Bahia Town' (p. 202)
Ladendecker *Tunes for Young Troubadours*
   'When That I Was' (p. 10)
Orff and Keetman *Music for Children*, adpt.
   Murray, Vol. III
   'Street Song' (p. 48)
   Festive Procession' (p. 70)
Staton et al. *Music and You*, Grade 5
   'Fifty-Ninth Street Bridge Song' (p. 45)
Steen *Orff Activities*, Grade 6
   'The City Blues' (p. 22)

3   Identify the dominant and tonic chords in half and full cadences.

The children are aware that songs always end on the tonic chord. They are also aware that many songs have two or four phrases. In the past, they could anticipate the end of a phrase because the rhythmic activity increased, or the melody moved away from the tonic. They also could anticipate the ending because the melody moved toward the tonic and rhythmic activity came to rest. Ask them to walk as they listen, stopping when the harmony changes. When the harmony changes to the tonic they may move again. Then ask the students to explain why the harmony changes in the song 'The Old Sow.' Lead them to define a cadence which signals the end of a musical phrase. It will help illustrate the point if you can accompany yourself with chord roots on a bass xylophone. Assign one group to listen to the words, a second group to rhythm, a third group to melodic pitch and a fourth group to chord roots. Their analysis will indicate that the song is made of two musical questions alternating with two answers, and no two phrases are identical. The change of chord roots should also help them identify the question and answer phrases.

The Old Sow

353

2. What will we do with the old sow's tail?
   Make as good whip as ever did sail,
   Coarse whip, fine whip, any such thing,
   The old sow died with the measles in the spring.

3. What will we do with the old sow's meat?
   Make as good bacon as ever did eat,
   Coarse bacon, fine bacon, any such thing,
   The old sow died with the measles in the spring.

4. What will we do with the old sow's feet?
   Make as good pickles as ever did eat,
   Coarse pickles, fine pickles any such thing,
   The old sow died with the measles in the spring.

After they have learned the melody assisted by notation, ask them to help you decide where chord changes are needed, marking each chord above the melody. When they discover the dominant chord on the fourth measure label it a half cadence, for the song has moved to a note of the dominant chord. Then ask them to predict how the next phrase will end, and label this a full cadence, for it ends on *do*, the tonic root. The other parts are simple, so that the chord root's relationship to the melody can be heard clearly.

Additional resources
Earley *Something Told the Wild Geese*
   'Cotton Needs Pickin'' (p. 8)
Staton et al. *Music and You*, Grade 4
   'Oh, Won't You Sit Down?' (p. 9)
Steen *Orff Activities*, Grade 4
   'Polly Wolly Doodle' (p. 23)
Steen *Orff Activities*, Grade 5
   'Turn the Glasses Over' (p. 4)
   'There's a Hole in the Middle of the Sea' (p. 6)
   'La Cucaracha' (p. 22)

4   *Improvise over tonic–dominant chord patterns.*

Improvising over one chord using the diatonic scale can be challenging for fifth graders, for they must remember to play on *sol, mi* or *do* on metric accents. When they improvise over two chords they must remember two chord structures, *do, mi* and *sol*, and *sol, ti, re* and *fa*. Return to 'Line Dance Tune' to model the first improvisation experience. In this model each phrase is over one chord, except for the ending.

1	I	I	I	I
2	V	V	V	V
3	I	I	I	I
4	V	V	I	I

Begin by asking some students to play a single tonic chord note for phrases 1 and 3, using a rhythm of their choosing. Another group will play a single dominant note over phrases 2 and 4, moving to the tonic notes in the last phrase, improvising rhythmically.

When you repeat the exercise they may play two chord pitches. Continue giving them more choices, as described in *Discovering Orff* (p. 200). When they can play over one chord, change assignments. By this time many students will want to improvise an entire melody. Let them choose to play phrases one and three, two and four, or all four phrases.

When your class has improvised successfully under guidance of group instruction they may be ready for this duet project. Give each pair one instrument with b flats and assign them one of the following harmonic outlines. A box represents a measure, or two beats. One of the partners is to play chord roots on the low f and c. The second partner is to improvise or compose a melody which fits the harmony. They are not required to write their compositions, but I find that many of my students want to use notation to help them remember their ideas. Place the chord outline on a large visual before they begin this project.

356

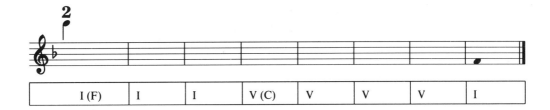

I (F)	I	I	V (C)	V	V	V	I

5   *Play and sing in parallel thirds or sixths with a melody.*

One way your students have already experienced singing in thirds is through canons. Purcell's 'Merry Minstrels' moves down the scale, repeating each step, so the students can hear the thirds clearly as they sing. When they have sung it successfully, write each line on top of one another on one staff, choosing a different color for each line. The thirds will be obvious visually as well as aurally.

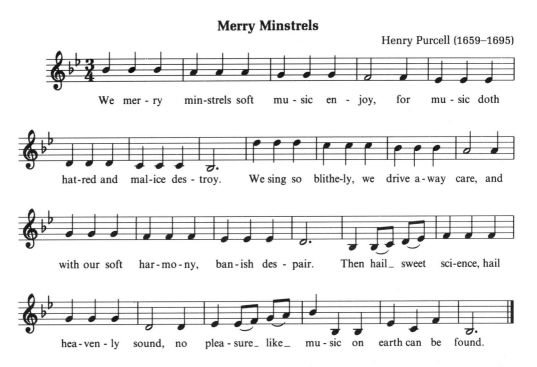

In 'La Cucaracha,' parallel thirds are achieved by staying on a melody note while others sing a third above or a third below. The two parts may also be played by two recorders or barred instruments. Begin by teaching the melody which outlines the tonic and dominant chords. Then, as the students sing, you can play or sing the harmony. Ask them to describe what they heard in relationship to what they sang. When you use notation to illustrate what they heard, consider writing the melody in one color and the harmony in another. I find that when I ask for volunteers to sing the harmony they are usually the strong leaders in the group so that when they sing the part is clear and the melody is also accurately sung. After practice encourage others to sing the harmony with these leaders.

La Cucaracha

Mexican folk song

If your class sings well in parallel harmony they may enjoy harmonizing a song. 'When I First Came to this Land' may be a good place to begin, for the first, second and last phrases are nearly alike. After they have learned the melody by sight-singing lines one and two, accompany them with chords. Then ask them to listen to you sing while they imagine singing in thirds below and then above the melody. Through trial and error they will soon come up with a solution similar to the one outlined on the score.

When I First Came to this Land

Pennsylvania Dutch

When I first came to this land, I was not a weal-thy man.

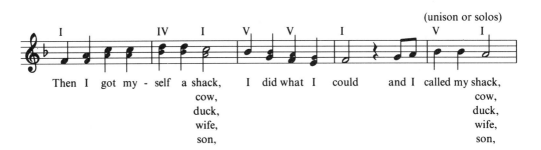

(unison or solos)

Then I got my-self a shack, I did what I could and I called my shack,
cow,   cow,
duck,   duck,
wife,   wife,
son,   son,

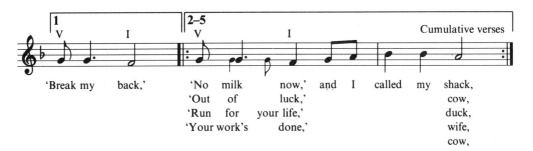

1
'Break my back,'

2–5 Cumulative verses
'No milk now,' and I called my shack,
'Out of luck,'   cow,
'Run for your life,'   duck,
'Your work's done,'   wife,
                                        cow,

Thirds

For the land was sweet and good. I did what I could.

Additional resources

Frazee *Orff Handbook for World of Music – 5*
    'De Colores' (p. 18)
Goetze *Simply Sung*
    'Shine Like a Star in the Morning' (p. 18)
Keetman *Stück für Flöte und Trommel*
    'Kleine Kanon' (p. 14, no. 1)
Ladendecker *Holidays and Holy Days*, Vol. 1
    'Christmas Song' (p. 13)
Orff *Music for Children*, American edn., Vol. 3
    'Janie Mama (p. 174)
Steen *Orff Activities*, Grade 6
    'When Johnny Comes Marching Home'
    (p. 16)

Timbre

1 Demonstrate an understanding of the characteristics of instrumental timbres when composing and improvising.

Throughout the year this objective has been met as students made choices when creating individual parts for assigned timbres and when selecting timbres to express their ideas. Each time our students have had these opportunities we will want to compliment them on good choices of timbre and question them in ways that help them evaluate when the timbre does not balance the ensemble or cannot produce the rhythm or melody accurately.

Texture

1 Perform alone or in pairs a single line in an ensemble

This is another objective that should be a part of every lesson. It is tempting to have all students play, but they and we become weary of the intense and often unmusical sound. When only one or two people play each part they feel especially responsible and they can hear themselves accurately. Each time a student plays or sings alone make it a point to recognize her and note the performance in your records. When individual performances are expected and frequent an atmosphere that encourages risk and acceptance of honest mistakes while learning is built. Our role is to prepare these opportunities so that success is assured.

2 Perform in canons of up to four voices.

I often introduce 'Jubilate Deo' early in the year, for singing it requires a light, well supported vocal quality. The children can sing it in two parts, then at a later time, in three parts. As the year progresses we test our ability to sing tunefully by adding another voice. By placing groups of children in separate spaces around the room they learn to listen to their own section while enjoying the antiphonal effect of other parts.

Jubilate Deo

Ju - bi - la - te de - o, ju - bi - la - te de - o. Al - le - lu - ia.

When presenting 'Laughing,' ask the students to consider dynamic contrasts and vocal articulations that will help us hear the melody even in a thicker texture. For instrance, should the canon begin softly and build with a crescendo toward the third measure? How can the eighth notes be sung in measures five and six in contrast to the proceeding measures? By giving our students the opportunity to determine how they will express the music they give more attention to the details that makes performance more exciting.

Laughing

Cesar Bresgen

Laugh-ing, laugh-ing, laugh-ing, laugh-ing, comes the sum-mer   o-ver the fields.

O - ver the fields comes the sum-mer, ha, ha, ha, laugh-ing o-ver the   fields.

Form

1   Analyze a theme and variation, and then compose a variation on a selected theme.

Throughout the year the fifth graders have been encouraged to learn about music themes by altering or playing with the characteristics of rhythm, melody, modality or expression. We can begin this summary of the year's experiences with basic movement. Divide your class into partners or trios. Tell them their task is to walk from point one to point two in any manner they choose. They may go backwards, slide sideways, stalk like a lion, etc. They must walk together as an ensemble. (This is most fun if you can clear a long pathway.) It will take only a few minutes to plan and practice their walks. Then establish an order and ask each group to begin their walk as soon as the preceding group has reached the end point. You can begin with the theme, playing a hand drum as you walk straight from point a to point b. Then, to highlight the differences, you may continue to accompany each group. When the last group finishes, ask them to describe each variation, writing key words on the board. With their assistance underline the words that describe your playing as well.

There are many examples of theme and variation form, for composers have frequently used it. Charles Ives's Theme and Variations on 'America,' for organ or as orchestrated for orchestra or band, holds the interest of students because they know the melody so well. Mozart's Variations on 'Ah, vous dirai-je, Maman' is another good choice, for children know the theme as 'Twinkle, Twinkle, Little Star,' or 'Baa, Baa, Black Sheep.' Another short, appealing composition is Igor Stravinsky's *Greeting Prelude*, on the theme of 'Happy Birthday'. When you listen consider giving the children a check list. As they listen they will write the number of the variation beside words that describes what they hear. This then becomes the basis of discussion. Your list may contain the following:

Adds pitches to the theme
Changes rhythm
Changes tempo: faster
                     slower

Changes dynamics: louder
                        softer
Changes accompaniment
Changes instrument, range
Adds instruments
Takes away instruments
Changes meter
Changes tonality

In order to make it easy for students to explore creating variations I choose a familiar melody, such as 'London Bridge.' After several students have played the melody, refer to the list and ask if they can think of a way to change or vary it. Several suggestions are given to demonstrate that the theme does not have to be changed much in order to become a variation. If your schedule and space allow, divide the class into groups and have each one compose a variation with accompaniment.

London Bridge (Theme and Variations)

Variation 1. Add eighth notes to fill longer notes

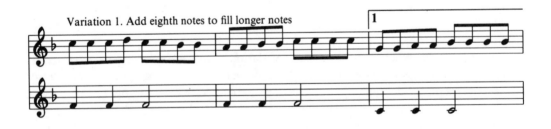

Variation 2. Change meter

Variation 3.
Change from major to minor

Additional resources

Frazee with Kreuter *Discovering Orff*
'Chaconne' from *Trois Leçons* by George
Frideric Handel (pp. 209–216)
Frazee and Kreuter *Sound Ideas*
'Variatons on "La ci darem" ' by Ludwig
van Beethoven, (pp. 18–21)
Orff *Music for Children*, American edn., Vol. 3
'Variations' by Bela Bartok (pp. 328–31)

The curriculum outlined for fifth grade is ambitious in content and demanding of our students' skills. There are certainly more objectives given than I have covered in any one year. But, because of student interest, abilities, and flow of the calendar year, I have, in different years, covered each of them. I make choices. These choices are determined by several conditions. First, each fifth grade year begins with a review of basic knowledge and skills. Whether they choose to perform in a choir or an instrumental ensemble in middle school, to continue general music studies, or to have no further music instruction, all children should have the opportunity to demonstrate their knowledge of music by performing, reading and writing basic rhythm patterns in common meters, and by singing and playing melodies in patterns and tonalities most often used in our musical heritage. When they have demonstrated musical independence in these areas I move to topics which broaden this base. My choices are determined by students' interest and abilities, the time needed to explore each topic and how that compares to the time available. A group that especially enjoys singing may be challenged by the exploration of modality and contemporary tonalities. We may explore harmony by discovering and then using a variety of chord combinations to accompany songs and improvisations. Or, to challenge a group who love to play instruments, we may explore unusual meters and rhythms through movement and instrumental ensembles. Rather than rushing through a challenging list, I choose each new objective carefully so that students end the year feeling successful and musically independent.

Certainly these and other topics in form, harmony, styles and timbre can be the subjects of future general music curriculums. The grid at the end of Chapter 1, Curriculum Planning, includes topics you can consider for a sixth grade music program.

The design of middle schools or junior high schools, based on the physical, social and intellectual growth patterns of adolescents continues to challenge school leaders. A recurring theme emerges, that basic knowledges explored in new and more demanding materials is the work of this age group. I hope that the suggested outline for fifth grade and the suggested topics in the curriculum grid for sixth grade may provide the first step in the design of your curriculum for the grades which follow.

Conclusion:
Artistry in the Classroom

The reason we give energy and time to issues of curriculum and lesson planning is our desire to teach music well. Yet we can become so trapped in the details of teaching that we fail to recognize beautiful music when it occurs, or our overly zealous process may prevent it from emerging. In recent years I have had the privilege of observing many music teachers through peer teaching and videotaping. I have seen lessons which have demonstrated artful teaching and expressive music-making. I have also seen competent teaching that is well crafted, but misses the point. All of us have had the experience of teaching about music, but the lesson ends without the essence of expressive music making with our children.

Our lesson plans are carefully ordered to assist our students in demonstrating what they know. It is harder to describe in our plans how learning is stimulated when our first graders describe the wonders of star light as they sing and play magically on triangles and cymbals. Responses such as curiosity and willingness to take risks are learned, just as skills and concepts are learned, by performing, by acting in response to music and to one another. Our students become musicians because they imitate the behavior of musicians. They acquire curiosity because they are encouraged to experiment as composers do. It is then impossible to escape the issue of artistry in our teaching because performing music demands that we too be expressive. By not asking children to behave as artists we assume that children cannot become artistic. But if we model and then expect artistic responses, we discover that children can perform in expressive, musical ways. Making beautiful music should be an important objective of every lesson. A perfect unison line sung by a squirming class can catch the breath of everyone in the room with its beauty. There is an electric feeling when everyone realizes they have just heard a lovely improvisation, sometimes only a few beats long. Making music without the satisfying feeling that the sounds are good is making music without aesthetic sensitivity.

How can we be sure that artistry in the classroom prevails so that students recognize it and then seek to attain it in their music making? Beautiful music certainly isn't present routinely, automatically or even accidentally without a nurturing, accepting environment. It begins with encouraging children to experiment, to make suggestions, to hear ideas and to make decisions about their performance goals. When the learning process is laced with humor and playfulness many students participate openly as they learn more easily. As the children learn that their responses and ideas are accepted they will understand that they share responsibility with the teacher for the quality of their performance.

Children who feel that music can be a means of self expression will value it. That expression requires skills which are appropriate for the children's age and experience. It is the teacher's responsibility to guide the students with confident skill through tasks that can be performed and hold potential for artistic outcomes.

Beginning at a comfortable level, events can be sequenced to challenge skill development while helping the children recognize that they are capable of giving pleasing responses. Planning lessons carefully and cultivating an openness to students' interaction with the lesson will contribute to artistic music-making. Skills and attitudes are equally important and inseparable contributors to beautiful classroom music.

Another factor which contributes to the quality of music is the model for music performance, the teacher. The teacher who plans carefully can contribute significantly to a child's musical growth, but a teacher who models musicality inspires. Dynamics, inflection of words, accuracy of pitch, subtlety of phrasing, even sincerity of delivery, are all unconsciously imitated by the students. The music teacher is a musician *first* when he or she teaches. Realizing this is a factor in artistic teaching implies that we, as well as our students, may need to practice in order to model accurate musical responses. It also implies that students will gain from our growth as practicing musicians.

Teachers are not the only possible models. Children will benefit from hearing and seeing the artistic performance of other musicians. These may include other students or teachers, video programs of performances, field trips to concerts, concerts in the school, and performances for one another. These occasions provide opportunities to guide students to recognize good models of artistic music-making. You do this by listening attentively, by openly complimenting good performances, and by reviewing performances with them in constructive ways. These seem like insignificant points until we realize that it is by emulating others that students learn responses to music. It is one of the ways they can develop the disposition to learn more about it themselves.

Performance is the normal and natural way to learn about music, and whenever we participate in music the potential for expressiveness is present. There are then three factors that contribute to the artistic quality of the music we create in each lesson. The first is an environment that encourages and respects the children's responses to tasks with potential for good sounds. Secondly, the Orff approach, with its recognition of imitation as the starting point, places importance on the musicality of the teacher. Finally, the possibilities for musical exploration and creativity are enhanced by the quality of the materials the teacher introduces. As Carl Orff stated, 'It is at the primary school age that the imagination must be stimulated; and opportunities for emotional development, which contain experience of that feeling, must also be provided.' Your challenge is to be conscious of each of these contributing factors as you plan and teach. Your reward will be to experience the children's pleasure as they make their own beautiful music.

Additional Resources

Andress, Barbara, Eunice Boardman Meske, Mary P. Pautz, Fred Willman and Arvida Steen, *Orff Activities*, Grades 1 and 2. New York: Holt, Rinehart and Winston, 1988

Andress, Barbara, Eunice Boardman Meske, Mary P. Pautz, Diane Cummings Persellin, Fred Willman and Arvida Steen, *Orff Activities*, Grade 3. New York: Holt, Rinehart and Winston, 1988

Boshkoff, Ruth, *All Around the Buttercup; a supplement to 'Music for Children'*. London: Schott, 1984

Boshkoff, Ruth, *Ring Around, Sing Around; a supplement to 'Music for Children'*. London: Schott, 1988

Bisgaard, Erling, with Tossi Aaron, *In Canon*. St. Louis: Magnamusic, 1978

Britten, Benjamin, *Friday Afternoons*, op. 7. London: Boosey & Hawkes, 1936

Carley, Isabel, *Recorders with Orff Ensemble*, Book 1. London: Schott, 1982

Chase, Richard, *Singing Games and Playparty Games*. New York: Dover, 1967

Choskey, Lois and David Brummet *120 Singing Games and Dances for Elementary School*. Englewood Cliffs, NJ: Prentice-Hall, 1987

Earley, Craig, *Something Told the Wild Geese; a supplement to 'Music for Children'*. London: Schott, 1988

Fowke, Edith, *Sally Go Round the Sun; 300 children's songs, rhymes and games*. Garden City, NY: Doubleday, 1969

Frazee, Jane, *Orff Handbook for World of Music*, 7 vols. [Grades K, 1–6]. Morristown: Silver Burdett & Ginn, 1988

Frazee, Jane, *Singing in the Season*. St. Louis: Magnamusic, 1983

Frazee, Jane, *Ten Folk Carols for Christmas from the United States*. London: Schott, 1977

Frazee, Jane, with Kent Kreuter, *Discovering Orff; a curriculum for music teachers*. New York: Schott, 1987

Frazee, Jane, with Kent Kreuter, *Sound Ideas*. Allison Park, PA: Musik Innovations, 1984

Frazee, Jane, and Arvida Steen, *A Baker's Dozen*. Minneapolis: Schmitt, Hall & McCreary, 1974

Fuoco-Lawson, Gloria, *Street Games*. London: Schott, 1989

Gill, Richard, *Have You Any Wool? Three Bags Full; 'Music for Children'*. New York: Schott, 1981

Goetze, Mary, *The Cat Came Back*. St. Louis: Magnamusic, 1984

Goetze, Mary, *Mary Goetze Series*. Boosey & Hawkes

Goetze, Mary, *Simply Sung; 'Music for Children'*. London: Schott, 1984

Goetze, Mary, *Sing We Noël*. St. Louis: Magnamusic, 1984

Hamm, Ruth Pollock, *Crocodile and Other Poems*. London: Schott, 1988

Johnson, Lynn W., *The Magic Forest; a supplement to 'Music for Children'*. London: Schott, 1988

Ladendecker, Dianne, *Holidays and Holy Days*, 2 vols. San Diego: Curtis, 1986–8

Ladendecker, Dianne, *Tunes for Young Troubadours; a supplement to 'Music for Children'*. London: Schott, 1988

McRae, Shirley W., *American Sampler*. Memphis: Memphis Musicraft, 1985

Orff, Carl, *Music for Children*, Orff-Schulwerk American edition, Vol. 1 (Preschool). New York: Schott, 1982

Orff, Carl, *Music for Children*, Orff-Schulwerk American edition, Vol. 2 (Primary). New York: Schott, 1977

Orff, Carl, *Music for Children*, Orff-Schulwerk American edition, Vol. 3 (Upper Elementary). New York: Schott, 1980

Orff, Carl, and Gunild Keetman, *Music for Children*, edited by Doreen Hall and Arnold Walter, 5 vols. Mainz: Schott, 1956–61

Orff, Carl, and Gunild Keetman, *Music for Children*, adapted by Margaret Murray, 5 vols. London: Schott, 1958–66

Staton, Barbara, Merrill Staton and others, *Music and You; orchestrations for Orff instruments*, 4 vols. [Grades 3–6]. New York: Macmillan, 1988

Warner, Brigitte, *Orff Schulwerk: applications for the classroom*. Englewood Cliffs, NJ:

Prentice-Hall, 1991

Wirth, Marian, Verna Stassevitch, Rita
Shotwell and Patricia Stemmler, *Musical
Games, Fingerplays and Rhythmic Activities for
Early Childhood*. West Nyack, NY: Parker,
1983

Index

Title	Grade—Page	Medium
Cindy Lee, Can't You See?	I—94	poem/chant
Clap, Clap, Clap Your Hands (G)	I—84, 130	song
The Cobbler Song (I)	K—59	song
Cotton-eyed Joe	K—75	song
Count 5	V—324	instruments
Crawdad Hole	II—147	song
Crossing Mallets	III—220	instruments
Diddle, Diddle Dumply	II—164	poem
Ding Dong Bell	I—112	song
Doctor Foster	I—128	chant
Don't Let the Wind	V—316	song/speech
Don't Let Your Watch Run Down (J)	V—303	song
Down Goes the Lamb	I—106	poem
Down in the Meadow (C1)	II—169	song
Down the River	IV—263	song
Drill Ye Terriers	V—327	song
Ducks in the Millpond (C1)	K—55	song
	II—139	song
Early in the Morning (H)	III—35	song
Echoes (bordun exploration)	II—172ff.	song
Engine, Engine, Number Nine	I—98, 129	chant
The Farmer in the Dell	K—68	song
Five Little Snowmen (C1)	K—54	song
	I—33	song
Flower Song	I—113	song
Fooba Wooba John	V—229	song
The Frogs	III—219	canon/song
The Ghost of Tom (M)	IV—271	song
Going Down to Cairo	III—230	song
Gonna Sing a Song (A)	II—150	song
Go Round the Mountain (B)	K—57	song
Go to Bed, Tom	II—164	poem
Grand Old Duke of York (K)	K—56	chant
	III—212	song
Grannie Caught a Flea	II—144	poem/chant
Grinding Corn (L)	III—201	song
Growing	III—184	poem
Hey, Ho, Anybody Home	IV—240	canon/song
Hickory Dickory Dock (C1)	K—55	song

Title	Grade–Page	Medium
Higglety Pigglety Pop	K–68	song
Hill an' Gully Rider	V–346	song
Hineh Ma Tov	V–319	song
Hop, Old Squirrel (G)	I–96	song
Hop Up and Jump Up	IV–246	song
Hop Up, My Ladies	III–217	song
How Many Miles to Babylon?	II–175	poem
How Long, Watchman? (B)	III–187	song
I Have a Little Sister	K–65	poem
	K–66	chant
I Heard the Angels Singing (B)	III–196	song
I Like Coffee	I–94	poem/chant
Icky, Bicky, Soda Cracker	I–100	chant
I'll Sing You a Song (B)	III–206	song
In and Out	K–59	poem/chant
	I–97	
It Rained a Mist (C1)	K–56	song
	IV–268	song
Jack and Jill	K–65	poem
Johnny Works with One Hammer (C1)	K–54	song
Juan Pirulero (B)	I–126	song
Jubilate Deo	V–360	canon/song
Jump or Jiggle	I–91	poem/chant
La Cucaracha (P)	V–358	song
Lady, Come Down	III–219	canon/song
Laughing	V–361	canon/song
Leaves	I–109	song
Line Dance Tune	V–343	instruments
Listen to the Drums	I–101	chant
Little Boy Blue	I–106	poem/chant
Little Drops of Water	K–46	poem
Little Wheel	K–61	song
London Bridge	V–362	instruments
Mama Paquita	IV–248	song
Mary Wore a Red Dress (C1)	K–54	song
Merry Minstrels	V–357	song
Mr. East Gave a Feast	II–164	poem
Mr. Rabbit	III–221	song
Monkey See, Monkey Do (Q)	K–45	song
Moon Magic	IV–280	song

Title	Grade–Page	Medium
Walk in the Parlor (B)	K–77	song
Walk Straight Ahead	V–323	poem/chant
Watch My Feet	K–52	chant
We Are Giants	K–53	chant
Weather	I–117	song
Weather Report	II–154	song
Wee Willie Winkie	K–61	song
We're Going on a Field Trip	K–70	song
What a Goodly Thing	III–219	canon/song
When I First Came to this Land (H)	V–359	song
White Sands	II–171	canon
Who Built The Ark? (G)	I–127	song
Who Has Seen the Wind?	I–89	poem
Willowbee (B)	II–162	song
The Wind Blew Low	I–106	poem
Winter, Goodbye	IV–267	song
Winter Song	IV–265	instruments
Yankee Doodle	K–51	chant
	I–99	song
Yoo Hoo	I–108	song
Zum Gali	IV–247	song

Sources

A   Susan Kenney, *Circle Round the Zero*. St. Louis: MMB Music, Inc., 1983. Used by permission. All rights reserved.

B   Louise Larkins Bradford, *Sing It Yourself*. Alfred Publishing Co. Inc., 1978. Used by permission of the Publisher.

C1   *Music for Children*, vol. 1. Schott Music Corporation.

C2   *Music for Children*, vol. 2. Schott Music Corporation.

C3   *Music for Children*, vol. 3. Schott Music Corporation.

D   Lois Choskey and David Brummet, *120 Singing Games and Dances for Elementary School*. Englewood Cliffs, NJ: Prentice-Hall, 1987.

E   Brian Brocklehurst, *2nd Pentatonic Songbook*. London: Schott & Co. Ltd.

F   *American Sailor Men*. New York: W. W. Norton & Co. Inc.

G   Ruth Crawford Seeger, *American Folk Songs for Children*. Garden City, NY: Doubleday Publishing, 1948.

H   Reprinted by permission of Boosey & Hawkes, Inc.

I   Marian Wirth, Verna Stassevitch, Rita Shotwell and Patricia Stemmler, *Musical Games, Fingerplays and Rhythmic Activities for Early Childhood*. West Nyack, NY: Parker Publishing (a division of Simon and Schuster), 1983. Reprinted by permission of the Publisher.

J   Carl Sandburg, *The American Songbag*. New York: Harcourt Brace Jovanovich, 1927. Copyright renewed 1955 by Carl Sandburg. Reprinted by permission of the Publisher.

K   Jane Frazee with Kent Kreuter, *Discovering Orff*. New York: Schott Music Corporation, 1987.

L   Millie Burnett, *Dance Down the Rain, Sing Up the Corn*. San Francisco, CA: R & E Research Associates, 1975. © Millie Burnett.

M   *This Is the Day*. Belwin Mills, Inc.

N   Leon and Lynn Daltin, *Heritage Songster*. Dubuque, IA: William C. Brown Publishing, 1966.

O   John and Sylvia Kolb, *A Treasury of Folk Songs*. New York: Bantam Books, Inc., 1955.

P   *1001 Folk Songs*. Hansen Music, 1976.

Q   Edith Fowke *Sally Go Round the Sun*. Garden City, NY: Doubleday Publishing, 1969.

R   Richard Chase, *Singing Games and Playparty Games*. New York: Dover Publications, Inc., 1967.

S   Iona and Peter Opie, *Singing Games*. Oxford: Oxford University Press, 1985.

T   Lois Choskey, *The Kodàly Method*. Englewood Cliffs, NJ: Prentice-Hall, 1974.

U   *Folk Songs of Jamaica*, edited and arranged by Tom Murray. Oxford: Oxford University Press, 1952.

V   James Mursell *Music in our Country*. Grade 5. English words by Ruth Martin © 1962 (renewed) by Silver Burdett Co. Used with permission.

W   *Eighty English Folk Songs*, collected by Cecil J. Sharp and Maud Karpeles. London: Faber Music Ltd, 1968.

X   Brian Brocklehurst, *Pentatonic Songbook*. London: Schott & Co. Ltd, 1968.

Y   *Folk Songs from the Southern Appalachians*, collected by Cecil Sharp, edited by Maud Karpeles, London: Oxford University Press, 1932.

Z   *Juilliard Repertory Library*. Canyon Press, 1966.